SVL. FEITA. POLO. COSMO
ANVEL. GODINHO. DE. EREDIA.
DE. 1602.

BIMA.

ENDE.

ende)

Samba.

Sales.

TIMOR.

Rajoan.

Sabo

P. cambin.

P. nsior.

LVCA. VEA.

Luca. vea. ou beach. Scaquilla
antigo Prouincia de ouro. recon
Scida pellos Pescadores d e Sabo.

ta Ilha de ouro, crauo,
hano. reconScida
Sc Por antigos chamada

OVRO.
crauo e Sandalo

IAP.

Iap. Scaquilla Ilha de ouro e
Maca e sandalo, reconScida p
(Sinas)

LVCA. ANTARA.
VEL.
IAVA. MINOR.

D1265480

Malaca. Scaquilla antiga
Ilha del ssaurier.

'*Luca Antara* is a book-lover's book, a graceful and mesmerizing blend of history, autobiography, travel and romance.'

JM Coetzee – Nobel Prize winner in Literature 2003

'Combining elements of a detective story with the laconic unwinding of a campfire yarn, *Luca Antara* is a thoroughly original, real and fantastical account of a continent that is, in the hands of Martin Edmond vividly discovered and discovered again…a book written under the spell of…several fascinating compulsions – to search, enquire, dream, and to travel.'

Roger McDonald – Miles Franklin Award winner 2006

Luca Antara will suit anyone with an interest in the early voyages of discovery to Australia and in contemporary life in our largest city.'

Bookseller and Publisher

'Graceful, uninhibited, eccentric and filled with humorous pathos *Luca Antara* is a rare book. Part memoir, travelogue, history and part detective story, Martin Edmond's latest book is filled with serendipitous moments in such places as an antiquarian bookshop. Bursting with quirky anecdotes *Luca Antara* is a browser's paradise as Edmond contemplates Australia with wry precision and luminous prose.'

Independent Weekly

'The search for the truth of a 17th-century voyage to a mythical Australia becomes a journey into the imagination.'

Sydney Morning Herald

'…a book rich in ideas, at once erudite and eclectic, and full of beautifully unexpected and evocative descriptions…This is back-packing for the mind, a trip full of remarkable sights.'

The Canberra Times

'… this is the best Australian novel of the last year.'

– Wet Ink magazine

'Martin Edmond quotes Mark Twain's well-worn `beautiful lies' remark about Australian history to suggest the way we should read his book, a long conversation about quests and origins, about the intersections of personal and social history, about literature and the nature of truth … Edmond's book evolves as an entertaining, erudite tale, with snippets of history and literary discussion as well as Edmond's somewhat salacious youthful affairs woven into the narrative of his developing love for the history of seafarers in the Pacific and the south.'

Weekend Australian

'Long before Australia was discovered by Europeans, it was imagined in the hearts and souls and minds of rulers, explorers and romantics on the other side of the world. Martin Edmond is a modern-day romantic who embarked on a journey to discover the mystery around Luca Antara, now known as Australia. This is not a standard historical text, nor strictly a memoir. Edmond has written a magical tale about himself and his obsession with the past.'

The Courier Mail

'This account of a sixteenth century Portuguese discovery of Australia takes what might be called a postmodernist approach to supplementing the limited documentary records, something to counterpose to the endless repetitions of the words of The Great God Cook about his experiences in Botany Bay. Martin Edmond's interweaving of personal memoir and historical documents of highly ambiguous provenance has to be considered creative non-fiction of the highest calibre.'

New Zealand Book Awards 2007 – Judges' Report

'I'm a huge fan of Martin Edmond. All of his books are about books. *Luca Antara* is rich and interesting and beautifully crafted. It's absolutely gripping, it's fabulous. It's a genre bending book!'

Radio NZ – Laura Kroetsch

'Martin Edmond is a genre-busting writer, too hard to pin down to any one category.'

Radio NZ

'Luca Antara is a compelling, involving read, a fluid mix of memoir, history, ideas and – presumably – invention all told in crisp and elegant prose. It feels like a book full of tricks, in the nicest possible way.'

New Zealand Listener

'The past is more mysterious than we presently know, and it's good to see the unconstrained intelligence, whatever eyebrows it may raise, channelled by such a compelling narrator.'

Dominion Post – NZ

'This is one of the more intriguing books to come out of Australia during the last year...The characters breathe new life into history's bones.'

The Press – New Zealand

Luca Antara achieves much, challenges on any number of levels, though first and foremost it's about the writing. Martin Edmond is an undeniably gifted wordsmith for whom words flow with rhythm and grace. Add to this a lack of rancour, an ability to probe below the surface for explanations and a gift for genuine engagement with his readership … he's a masterful story-teller.'

Ralph Wessman – Walleah Press

'Martin is an original, exacting, and measured writer and I found it very pleasurable to read his descriptions of Sydney, especially of buildings that no longer stand or are irrevocably altered … *Luca Antara* is a memoir but it is also an almost scholarly enquiry into some of the speculative tales and fables around the early seafaring discoverers of Australia. It is multi-faceted … There is a feeling of mystery, uncertainty and of the fantastic that backgrounds the entire book – What is real? What is dependable? – as his obsessions unfold in both intellectual and actual journeys to places that include the Marquesas Islands, Portugal, Paris, the straits of Malacca, Malaysia, Lombok and into encounters with possessors of old manuscripts like the weirdly mysterious Mr Henry Klang.'

Pam Brown – The Deletions – www.thedeletions.blogspot.com

Luca Antara

Passages in Search of Australia

Martin Edwards

OLDCASTLE BOOKS

This edition published in 2008 by Oldcastle Books,
P.O.Box 394, Harpenden, Herts, AL5 1XJ
www.oldcastlebooks.com

First published in Australia by East Street Publications 2006

A CIP catalogue record for this book is available from the British Library.

ISBN 978-1-84243-272-3 (hardcover)
ISBN 978-1-84243-289-1 (trade paperback)

2 4 6 8 10 9 7 5 3 1

Typeset by Avocet Typeset, Chilton, Aylesbury, Bucks
Printed and bound in Great Britain by Butler & Tanner, Frome, Somerset

Contents

Author's Note

This book was written, and should perhaps be read, in a spirit Mark Twain evokes in *Following the Equator* (1897): *Australian history is almost always picturesque; indeed, it is so curious and strange, that it is itself the chiefest novelty the country has to offer ... it does not read like history, but like the most beautiful lies. And all of a fresh new sort, not mouldy old stale ones. It is full of surprises, and adventures, and incongruities, and contradictions, and incredibilities ...* While I would not claim that everything that follows is in accord with Twain's next remark—*but they are all true, they all happened*—I do believe the clues necessary to resolve whatever incredibilities remain can all be found within the text. As always, readers must make up their own minds.

*In every art the first essential consists in the imitation of former masterpieces. So I follow
in the footsteps of the writers who described many things that were of pre-eminent
interest in their own times. But present day knowledge discloses errors in statements that
were insistently asserted to be true; not that the authors lacked erudition or ability, but
they were much too far away, in Europe and Egypt, to obtain accurate information.*

Manoel Godinho de Eredia

*Everything stated or expressed by man is a note in the margin of a completely erased
text. From what's in the note we can extract the gist of what must have been in the text,
but there's always a doubt, and the possible meanings are many.*

Fernando Pessoa

*I tell you
these things are real.
... Beyond is anything.*

Ern Malley

I

Castaway

Antiquarian Books was at the top of Botany Road, Redfern, one of half a dozen big old premises in a terrace built perhaps a hundred years before. The thin iron poles supporting the rolled-metal veranda stepped delicately down the asphalt from the head of the rise to the end of the terrace, where the contiguous next-door building began. It was always cool and dark under that veranda; even the incessant roar of traffic seemed to falter and dim. The bookstore was the second of the shops, next to a Greek coffee bar with blue and white floor tiles, a long grimy counter stretching the length of the room and, opposite, half a dozen rickety Formica-topped tables with uncomfortable folding chairs beneath a dusty mirror. Here the ancient, sad-faced owners, a man and wife, served coffee in orange glass mugs whose glazing, after years of use, had worn from the lips and handles, and delicious sweets—Turkish delight, *baklava*, crescent-shaped almond cakes in a thick coating of icing sugar—which they perhaps made themselves in the kitchen out the back, along with the usual range of greasy snacks from the heated metal trays at the front. They sold sandwiches too, and meals could be ordered off the dog-eared cardboard menus that lay on the tabletops, though no one ever seemed to do so.

I had a coffee and a *baklava* there after my first visit to the bookstore, feeling slightly dizzy from the encounter with such a vast and disparate accumulation, and needing somewhere to sit while I considered what I then thought would be the first of many purchases: *The Stars of the Southern Heavens* by James Nangle (Sydney, 1929). *Anyone with a telescope, a pair of field glasses even, holds a magic key to the universe of the infinitely great,* it said on the cover. The book, a hardback still in its dust jacket, was inscribed to a Miss Jean Mackaness by someone who called themselves, mysteriously, The Sender. It cost four dollars.

I discovered the bookstore on one of my early rambles through the neighbourhood after moving to live in Golden Grove, Sydney, in 1981. It was in every respect something out of the far past of the city: the glass-fronted door which set a bell tinkling when you opened it; the faded linoleum on the uneven floor which sighed gently as you walked across it; the rows of heavily varnished wooden shelves lining the walls; and the other, no less heavily varnished, free-standing bookcases down the middle of the room; the locked glass cases for rare and expensive volumes behind the wide bare counter at the back of the room; the owner himself, a small man in a too-big brown suit, white shirt, loosely knotted tie, glasses, with greying hair and skin that was liver-spotted and somehow shady from years of delving in murky rooms.

There was no one there but himself, sitting quietly behind the counter at the back, pricing books with a pencil. He looked up at me for a moment then returned to his task, inscribing the relevant amount in the top right-hand corner of the flyleaf in an elegant, decisive hand. I was to learn later that this man never engaged in conversation with casual browsers and was disinclined to make small talk even during the ritual exchanges of a purchase. He was as impenetrable and inscrutable as some of his more obscure wares. His shop was unusual in that he kept no contemporary books and therefore nothing, apart from the odd wartime novel and the stacks of old magazines, that was paper bound: all his stock belonged to the era of the hardback. This is what gave the shop its strange aura, as if to step into it was indeed to step back fifty or more years. I also note that, among those I still have of the books I bought from him, almost all have inscriptions, suggesting much of his collection was purchased from deceased estates. Perhaps that is what gave him a slightly mouldered feeling as if he too was foxed with age, mildewed at the edges, nibbled by silverfish, even dank, though in fact both the air in the shop and he himself seemed suffused by a dryness almost beyond report.

I sought out, as usual, the Pacific section and spent ten or fifteen minutes examining the titles. Although there was much there I would have liked to own and more I had not heard of, the section was disappointing: not in itself, but because, as I was to find in most second-hand bookshops in Sydney, the selection was skewed towards the literature and anthropology of Melanesia and especially New Guinea, whereas my obsession lay with the cultures of Eastern Polynesia. I moved on to look at the Australiana, which is where I found *The Stars of the Southern Heavens*.

Though it is a fine book and I am pleased to have it, I chose it primarily because I felt a need to buy something, as if thereby laying a claim to the shop. The bookseller—was his name Mr Durham?—tore a length of brown paper off the roll affixed to the back of his counter, wrapped the book and, with coarse brown string cut from a ball on a peg next to the roll of paper, tied the parcel up in a flamboyant bow. I gave him a pair of the now obsolescent green two-dollar notes with the Macarthurs' merinos upon them and made some remark about his interesting collection of books. He nodded but did not answer. Feeling slightly embarrassed I left, went next door, ordered my coffee and sweet, then found myself unable or unwilling to unwrap that splendidly anachronistic package. I waited instead until I was home.

I had arrived in Sydney a few weeks before with no money to speak of, and enrolled immediately at Combined Services Taxi Training Centre in Paddington. Here I sat hour after hour with a dozen others in a small windowless room above the vast internal garage where the cabs came and went, listening through headphones to the local version of the knowledge, studying maps and learning by rote the names of suburbs and the major routes between them. This intensive training, which always seemed somehow military, perhaps because the classes were taken by a stentorian naval seaman turned cab driver turned instructor, did not last much longer than a week; then we were off to a Ministry of Transport office in Cammeray to sit for our licences. I went by car with Gerry, a Neapolitan I'd become friendly with not so much through conversation, which was not allowed, but simply by eye contact and the mute expressions with which we accompanied it.

Gerry was older than me, with a wife and three children; he had the rubbery, melancholic face of a circus clown. Like me, he had not long been in Sydney and again like me was desperate for work. His problem was that he didn't have much English and what he did have he spoke with such a strong accent most people didn't understand him: he could not forget, it seemed, the open locutions of his native tongue, nor close his lips or throat to make the mizzle of languishing vowels and swallowed consonants Aust-English demands. We talked about this as he drove his battered Vauxhall Victor over the harbour bridge to the MoT office, I with a willing if hopeless desire somehow to help, he with a humorous self-deprecation which concealed, I knew, the desolate conviction that he would fail the test because he lacked the required language skills.

In the bare well-lighted room upstairs at the MoT we sat at big rectangular tables which each had space for four aspirants, two either side. Gerry, opposite me, laboured over his answers. I had already completed the numerous questions the written test consisted of, and was now required to sit in silence until the appointed time for our exam was over and the successful among us could go to book our Medicals. Gerry looked despairingly at me, then down at his paper. I shrugged, almost imperceptibly: what could I do? He glanced up at me again, meaningfully this time, while his hand lingered over the four options to one of his many unanswered multiple-choice questions. I watched as he moved his pencil slowly from A to B to C, at which point, with a thrill of guilty collusion, I gave the merest nod of my head. Gerry, his dark eyes suffused with an emotion he was not able to express, checked the square and moved on to the next question.

In this way, in silence and in stealth, without ever once alerting either the invigilator or the other candidates at our table—not that they would have cared, but they were too intent on their own papers to notice—Gerry and I completed the rest of the multiple-choice section in such a way that his remaining answers were a mirror of mine. Just as well: when all the marks for the different parts of his test were tallied, Gerry passed only by virtue of his score on that section. Our subterfuge, while a danger to our prospects, was otherwise of no great moment: in fact I knew as little as Gerry about how to get around

Sydney and we were both aware—the superannuated sailor had told us at training—that you learned to navigate the streets by driving, not studying; the study was just to pass the test.

We were laughing as we barrelled back over the bridge to the depot with our brand-new licences. On the way Gerry insisted on stopping at a coffee bar where he bought me an extravagant late morning tea—a cup of coffee and a huge sticky bun with pink icing—and promised that if ever I needed a favour of any kind all I had to do was ask. I was touched but did not know what I might want from him nor how to find him if I did. The next day, from different bases, we each went out on the road. I didn't see Gerry again.

Is there a better way to demystify a city than by becoming one of its taxi cab drivers? I don't think so. You lose all hope of a gradual unveiling or lingering seduction. There is no luxurious exploring of byways, no odd encounters with the unforeseen around stray corners. You cannot even arrive at an honest appraisal of its authentic charms. In the first few weeks of the job, in cab #126, a white Falcon saloon with a collapsed front seat whose cab filled up with exhaust fumes if you went over 45 km/h, I whizzed down every major road in the inner city and many of those in the outer. Sydney seemed made up of narrow traffic-clotted arteries running between dark ugly facades, behind which were endless suburbs inhabited by pinched working people who transformed at night into desperate pleasure-seekers forever unable to find whatever it was they wanted. I could not believe in the big town's beauty or terror. There were too many glimpses into too many humdrum lives, too much ritual disparagement and abuse by that proportion of fares who treat you as a despised servant, too many disappointed drunks complaining violently or sadly after their night out seeking—what? It was better not to ask.

In this context the bookstore in Redfern took on a perhaps exaggerated importance in my mind, as a place where a tiny part of the romance of the city endured. It was a shock then, the next time I went there, to find it closed. I peered through the glass door: not just closed, empty. That eccentric collection had disappeared along with the magnificent shelves which had held it. Nor was there any way of tracking it: so far as I recalled, the shop had no other name than that announced by the faded gilt *Antiquarian Books* arching across the plate glass at the front. If that sign had not still been written on the window I might have doubted it had ever been there at all.

I went next door to the coffee bar (of the six buildings in that terrace it was now the only functioning business, although there was one other full of dusty disconnected baths and basins and lavatory bowls), ordered a flat white and a *baklava* and, as he began to get them ready, asked the old man what had happened to the bookstore. He shrugged, holding his hands open before him.

He close, he said. *He can't pay rent.*

Has he moved, I asked. *Or gone out of business?*

He did not know. He spoke to his wife in Greek but she just shook her head. I sat down to wait for my coffee. After he'd brought the faded orange mug and the white saucer with its *baklava* leaking honey and nuts over a folded triangular paper napkin, the man lingered a moment.

Business very bad, he said, nodding with a kind of grim satisfaction. *Very bad.* Then, rubbing sticky hands on stained white apron, he returned behind the long counter.

But the shop's disappearance from my purview was only temporary. Not very long after, on one of my visits to check my postbox down on the booming thoroughfare leading from the City to Parramatta Road and the Great Western Highway, I noticed that one of the formerly empty premises opening off the bottom of the stairwell leading down from the footpath next to the Post Office was now occupied. I descended the dozen or so steps to look and was amazed to find … *Antiquarian Books.* The same name in the same typeface newly emblazoned on the window; the same collection within, although it was now housed in a quarter of the space of the old place. Even some of the furniture seemed to be the same—I couldn't be sure because it was evening and the shop was closed. I remember climbing back up the stairs and seeing across the road the empty golden claws on the twin towers of Grace Brothers' immense emporium outlined against the pale blue evening sky like a promise that the great cloudy spheres they were designed to hold would one day be restored—as indeed they now have been.

After that, I returned to Antiquarian Books again and again; every time I checked my mail during shop hours I would go down those dirty steps and in the glass door to breathe the same dusty air that had apparently been transported from Redfern along with the stock and the shelves. Mr Durham—if that was his name—never did more than nod a greeting or murmur a farewell, but I did find out a little more about him. He brought a cut lunch in a brown paper bag with him to work and ate it at his counter with a cup of tea he made in a little room out the back. Did he also make these sandwiches at home before setting out, or was there a Mrs Durham who did it for him? He had a couple of friends who visited regularly, one a stooped cadaverous man in a black beret, and the other short and round with muttonchop whiskers; I once saw these two going in together, like Jekyll and Hyde, to the nearby Broadway Hotel, and on several occasions thereafter noticed Mr Durham himself, after he had closed the shop at six o'clock, sitting alone at the window before his glass canoe, smoking a cigarette with his hat on.

Such conversations as he had with his friends were so quiet it was impossible to know what they were about; but other seemingly clandestine exchanges that sometimes went on between bookseller and customer made me wonder if he did not also traffic in erotica. Perhaps he did, but if so it was done in a manner so discreet it could have been a trade in holy relics or remote antiquities. I once saw him in conversation with a smartly dressed woman in her forties who seemed to know him well—a sister? a cousin? his wife?—but, again, what they talked of I could not say. And perhaps after all there was no mystery; perhaps he was just a bookseller. Even so, I am in his debt for some of the things he sold me.

My *Rubaiyat of Omar Khayyam* (New York, 1942), including all five of Edward Fitzgerald's authorised versions, full of calligraphic flourishes, and with a glossary and a concordance, was from him; as were Robert Louis Stevenson's *In the South Seas* (London, 1925), *Memories and Portraits* (Edinburgh, nd) and *Across the Plains* (London, 1903); also

Joseph Conrad's *A Set of Six* (London, 1920), plus three volumes of
the collected edition of his works—*Almeyer's Folly* & *Tales of Unrest, The
Mirror of the Sea* & *A Personal Record,* and *Victory* (London, 1947); and
what was perhaps, at least in terms of this inquiry, the most valuable
book of all, a hardback copy of Kenneth Gordon McIntyre's *The Secret
Discovery of Australia* (Adelaide, 1977). This was the book in which I
first encountered Luca Antara—without quite realising where it (and
I) was. I thought it was another legendary lost land like Lemuria or Mu
and hence somewhere out in the Pacific or perhaps even the Indian
Ocean.

Mr Durham also one day sold me, again for four dollars, James Joyce's
Ulysses (New York, 1934) with a foreword by Morris L. Ernst (*The new
deal in the world of letters is here ... *) and the *Monumental Decision of the United
States District Court rendered December 6, 1933, by Hon. John M. Woolsey
lifting the ban on 'Ulysses'. Emetic* not *aphrodisiac,* Woolsey famously said.
The book also includes a letter from Joyce to the publisher concerning
the legal and publishing difficulties this and others of his works had
met with.

The inscriptions in this *Ulysses* are interesting. It belonged to Max
Harris who bought it, presumably in Adelaide, in December 1942 and
sold it, perhaps before, perhaps after he moved to Melbourne early
in 1945: a J. Baker inscribed his or her own name on the flyleaf in
that year. Harris thus owned the book through the tumultuous years
when he was one of the editors of the magazine *Angry Penguins,* and
it was on his shelves when the Ern Malley hoax was perpetrated upon
him and the magazine in 1943–44. *Ulysses* was at that time banned in
Australia; originally proscribed in 1929, the ban was lifted in May 1937,
then re-imposed—over vociferous protests—in September 1941; it
remained illegal until 1953. The copy of the Modern Library edition
Harris owned might have been purchased second hand but it might
equally have been imported clandestinely by its owner who in those
days had editorial contacts in Europe and North America including,
for example, Herbert Read, Henry Treece and the New Apocalyptics

in England, and James Laughlin, founder of New Directions Press, in the USA.

I have always wondered why Harris sold *Ulysses*, which I have now owned for more than twenty years, only a few years after he bought it. Perhaps he was not fond of the book; perhaps he could not take his library with him when he moved to Melbourne; or was it something else, an impulse to divest himself of unlawful goods in the aftermath of his derisory conviction for publishing Ern Malley's 'obscene' poems, a resiling from *Ulysses*' triumphant authority in the light of the ludicrous events with which his own name is ineradicably associated? Was the irony of legal vindication for Joyce while his own enterprises fell foul of the law too rich to bear?

If, as Michael Heyward writes in his definitive book on the hoax (*The Ern Malley Affair*, St Lucia, 1993), Harris was in later years proud of his role as Malley's first publisher and spiritual godfather, it is still the case that his own potential as a writer was obscured forever under the dark ecliptic of that posthumous and counterfeit poet. How he felt about this blasted promise I do not know, but perhaps there is a clue in this confession made in the inaugural issue of *Ern Malley's Journal* (Melbourne, 1953): *For me Ern Malley embodies the true sorrow and pathos of our time. One had felt that somewhere in the streets of every city was an Ern Malley ... in Hamburg, Vienna, Rome, Cleveland, Bombay ... a living person, alone, outside literary cliques, outside print, dying, outside humanity but of it. And setting it down.* There is no culpability in the omission, but Lisbon should have been included in that list of cities—the Lisbon of Fernando Pessoa and his heteronyms, those other writers he contained within himself and yet allowed an independent existence.

There are some who doubt the alleged facts pertaining to the composition of Ern Malley's oeuvre. These doubters suggest that the writing of the 424 lines of which Ernest Lalor Malley's life's work consists could not have taken place over the ten or so hours James McAuley and Harold Stewart, his originators, said it did. In their version, the sixteen poems were written after lunch on a Saturday afternoon in the spring of 1943 in Melbourne's Victoria Barracks. With McAuley doing most of the actual writing, the poems were set down on an army-issue ruled quarto pad, each leaf being torn off as it was filled. Taking only one break in which to eat, the two poets went through until nine or ten at night. *They worked rapidly, buoyed by the wickedness of what they were up to, and spurring each other on,* Heyward writes. *It was a hard day's work,* McAuley remarked later.

Those who disbelieve that such ecstasies of composition are possible should perhaps consider the case of Fernando Pessoa in more detail. In a much-quoted passage from a letter to Adolfo Casais Monteiro written on 13 January 1935, Pessoa described the circumstances of the genesis of his three most compelling and fully realised heteronyms:

One day it occurred to me to play a joke on [fellow Portuguese poet Mario de] *Sa-Carniero—to invent a rather complicated bucolic poet whom I would present in some guise of reality that I've since forgotten. I spent a few days in vain trying to envision this poet. One day when I'd finally given up—it was March 8th, 1914—I walked over to a high chest of drawers, took a sheet of paper and began to write standing up, as I do whenever I can. And I wrote thirty-some poems at once, in a kind of ecstasy I'm unable to describe. It was the triumphal day in my life, and I can never have another one like it. I began with a title,* The Keeper of Sheep. *This was followed by the appearance in me of someone whom I instantly named Alberto Caeiro. Excuse the absurdity of this statement: my master had appeared in me. That was what immediately I felt, and so strong was the feeling that, as soon as those thirty-odd poems were written, I grabbed a fresh sheet of paper and wrote, again all at once, the six poems that constitute* Slanting Rain *by Fernando Pessoa. All at once and with total concentration ... it was the return of Fernando Pessoa as Alberto Caeiro to Fernando Pessoa himself. Or rather, it was the reaction of Fernando Pessoa against his non-existence as Alberto Caeiro.*

Once Alberto Caeiro appeared, I instinctively and subconsciously tried to find disciples for him. From Caeiro's false paganism I extracted the latent Ricardo Reis, at last discovering his name and adjusting him to his true self, for now I actually saw him. And then a new individual, quite the opposite of Ricardo Reis, suddenly and impetuously came to me. In an unbroken stream, without interruptions or corrections, the ode whose name is Triumphal Ode, by the man whose name is none other than Álvaro de Campos, issued from my typewriter.

And so I created a non-existent coterie …

Pessoa always maintained that heteronymic work was different in kind from that which is pseudonymous; the one involves the assumption of another identity, while the other is merely the same author writing under a different name. Where to situate Ern Malley in terms of this dichotomy? Is he the pseudonymous fabrication of two poets or the inadvertent creation of a heteronym? If he is the first, which is what McAuley and Stewart thought he was, why then has he outlived both of them, continuing to attract readers while their own verse languishes largely unread? If not, how to account for the inadvertence of his genesis? McAuley and Stewart were quite certain about what they were doing: constructing a hoax poet. Interestingly, Pessoa also began by attempting the creation of a hoax; and it was only when he abandoned this attempt that the real poet Alberto Caeiro appeared, trailing his avatars behind him. Everything about the Ern Malley affair suggests that McAuley and Stewart—involuntarily, perhaps even unconsciously—did the same thing: they created a real poet.

One thing we must be clear about: there is no hint of a desire to deceive in Pessoa's heteronyms, just as there is no forgery in their work. He himself always treated his heteronyms with the utmost respect, both when they argued among themselves and when they criticised his own work. He even allowed the incendiary ship's engineer, Álvaro de Campos, to intervene in his love affair with the evocatively named Ophelia Quieroz. And for the rest of his life Pessoa continued to add to the works of his three fellow poets, even though the innocent Caeiro died in 1915 and Reis, a Royalist and a doctor, left Portugal permanently for Brazil in 1919. Along with the semi-heteronym Bernardo Soares, Assistant Bookkeeper in the City of Lisbon and author of the incomparable *Book of Disquiet*, Caeiro, Reis and de Campos are the major voices among the seventy-two or more literary identities Pessoa assumed in his short life.

McAuley and Stewart, however, no sooner gave birth to their poetic son than they abandoned him. He was, of course, already dead (of Grave's disease, a usually non-fatal thyroid condition) by the time his sister Ethel sent his poems to Max Harris. There were, Malley explained in a brief introductory statement, *no scoriae*, no dross, evoking, perhaps knowingly, a remark of Carlyle's which Pessoa was fond of quoting: *Disjecta membra are all that we find of any Poet, or of any man*. Once the hoax was revealed it took on a life of its own, becoming for a short while front-page news throughout Australia, with reverberations felt, if not around the world, then at least in selected parts of it: both the London *Times* and *Time* magazine ran the story. Faced with the monstrous success of their deception, McAuley and Stewart ducked. Ern Malley was no sooner celebrated than he was disowned, and had to make his further way in the world as the bastard foster-child of the man whose literary career he had wrecked.

If the shadows of Fernando Pessoa and his heteronyms do not exactly fall across this imbroglio, they remain one of the means of understanding it: Ern Malley, though invented, is as real as Alberto Caeiro or Bernardo Soares; more real, somehow, than Max Harris himself. This is so despite the fact that Pessoa's heteronyms were a semi-conscious creation, born from equal parts elation and despair, while Ern Malley was made maliciously and, as it were, unconsciously: he exposes his creators' inhibitions as well as their alternative biographies as other kinds of poets. This is where McAuley and Stewart seem peculiarly twisted, their reflexive exhibitionism showing off to advantage something they would almost certainly have condemned in themselves.

Max Harris, the proto-modernist, was humiliated, even crushed, by the *faux* modernism of two conservative poets. Did he sell *Ulysses* as a result? It is impossible to know and perhaps does not matter. What is certain is that his periodical, *Angry Penguins*, didn't long survive the controversy and the trial (for publishing *indecent advertisements*) that followed. Sale of the periodical in South Australia was banned and the last three issues came out of Melbourne. Shortly afterwards the magazine, which was losing money, was wound up. When Harris returned to Adelaide after the war he became a bookseller. In 1952 he announced he was giving up poetry altogether because *he didn't have*

anything to say any more. Angry Penguins, he went on, *built up an astounding monolith of obscure cult-ridden subjectivism.* He further admitted to *excesses, absurdities and intolerable posturings* and declared that *the poetic output of the modernists was of nugatory value.*

This paroxysm of self-castigation seems as excessive as some of Harris's earlier ecstasies in support of the authors he published in *Angry Penguins*, including Dylan Thomas, James Dickey and, perhaps surprisingly, Gabriel Garcia Marquez who, in the first volume of his autobiography, had this to say about *Ulysses*: ... [it] *provided invaluable technical help to me in freeing language and in handling time and structure in my books.* In one of Harris's more regrettable flights of fancy he compared his role with respect to Ern Malley to Max Brod's custodianship of Franz Kafka's oeuvre. From Kafka, however, Marquez writes that he learned: *it was not necessary to demonstrate facts: it was enough for the author to have written something for it to be true, with no proofs other than the power of his talent and the authority of his voice.* This insight, at once graceful and audacious, would surely have been a comfort to Max Harris had he been able to arrive at it. As it is, it provides perhaps the best means of understanding the paradoxical power of the hoax poet's poems, as well as a way of penetrating the labyrinth that is Fernando Pessoa's life work.

Antiquarian Books was not my only haunt among the bookshops of Sydney Town; there were others, including one to which I went, at least for a time, as often as I did to Mr Durham's Broadway shop. Antipodean Books was a specialist offshoot of venerable Australian publishers and booksellers Angus & Robertson, selling books exclusively about or from Australia, New Zealand and the Pacific. It was upstairs from where Abbey's bookshop on York Street is now, opposite the southern end of Queen Victoria Building and just along from the Town Hall. You walked up some dark stairs into an only slightly less dark room where thin metal shelves set too close together held a huge collection of books from our part of the world. All the novels of Janet Frame and Ruth Park were there; all the works of Henry Lawson and William Satchell, among hundreds, perhaps thousands of other books, both fiction and nonfiction. Most of these were new, by which I mean they had never been sold, and most were covered in dust. The place felt more like a disused library than a shop. Clearly Antipodean Books was a worthy idea but not a commercial one. Hardly anyone went in there.

If you could ignore the distraction of those claustrophobically displayed volumes you walked up a slightly wider aisle to the front of the shop where big windows let in a glare of light which in my memory is always dove-grey, so unlike the blazing yellow and blue of a typical Sydney sky. Here, on the right, behind a counter, sat the proprietor of the shop, an Englishman by the name of Steven. Opposite him stood a rack upon which were displayed books pertaining exclusively to the Pacific. This was where I would go, leafing through this volume or that, trying, as always, to calibrate my desire for a book with my means to buy it. In those days the Australian National University was embarked upon an ambitious programme to republish scholarly versions of various nineteenth-century texts written in or about the Great Ocean of Kiwa. Although I did not realise it at the time, this project was already languishing for lack of funds and would soon cease (or had already ceased) altogether, leaving such gems as the Reverend William Pascoe Crook's book about the Marquesas in manuscript in the Mitchell Library. My first purchase from Antipodean Books was in fact a book about the Marquesas—*Islands and Beaches*, by Greg Dening (Honolulu, 1980). This work initiated an obsession that is still with me.

I do not believe I struck up an acquaintance straight away with Steven; it took several visits before we started to get to know one another. Because I spent so long leafing through the books on that particular stand, and because so few customers entered the store, I suppose it was inevitable that we would eventually begin to talk. Steven was tall, pale-skinned, balding, with a broad moon-face, blue eyes, and a large body which was somehow shambolic, as if it accompanied him unwillingly through the world, not protesting against so much as bewildered by the tasks it had to perform. He was clearly bored by the tedium of his days and stressed by the long-term implications of the lack of custom. However, although he probably wanted me to know what his situation was and was grateful when I made it clear that I did, it was not in his nature to complain or to seek any sympathy beyond that implied by the empathy between us. Instead, we talked about books.

Steven was more interested in literature in general than he was in antipodean writing as such, which he regarded with a mingling of bafflement and condescension. He read those writers who had escaped the local context into the larger world—Patrick White, whom he liked; Katherine Mansfield, whom he did not—but had never bothered to educate himself in the nuances or intricacies of that context. Probably he yearned to be elsewhere than Australia or, at the very least, elsewhere in Sydney where a more vibrant life might be going on: somewhere, perhaps, where London and its sophistications did not seem, as they were, 12 000 melancholy miles away. Again he did not complain; rather he expressed a wry appreciation of his predicament, an irony about his circumstances, his inhabitation of this upside-down world, which I found both attractive and amusing.

He showed some of the same mild scepticism toward my obsession with the Pacific which, after we got to know each other better, I did not try to hide from him. My first purchase from him, the Dening, is an unusual book: both scholarly and idiosyncratic, it is a lament for the largely extinct culture of the Marquesas, as well as a description of it and an account of the ways in which it was destroyed. I read it with fascination but at the same time found myself resisting its authorial voice and its plangent, somehow excessive, appropriation of Marquesan experience to fuel, I felt, Dening's own writerly ambitions. As soon as I finished the book I wanted to go beyond it to the source material used to construct it. Specifically, I wanted to find a copy of the beachcomber's book he, Dening, had previously edited for the aforementioned ANU series on the Pacific: *The Marquesan Journal of Edward Robarts* (Canberra, 1974).

Unfortunately it was not among the volumes on display in Steven's shop. Nor was he able to procure a copy for me. It was out of print, and it didn't seem likely that there would be another run. The ANU books were expensive hardbacks and they hadn't sold well—except, apparently, for this one. The series was probably being discontinued. There had been some talk of its being taken over by another company, the Pergamon Press, but no one seemed to know if this was anything more than a hopeful rumour. Perhaps I should write to ANU myself, Steven suggested, sympathetic to my predicament and faintly amused by it as well. That might work. Meanwhile I could try the library … he gestured languidly out the window towards the sandstone, copper-domed, ornate Romanesque monstrance across the road.

At that time the city branch of the Sydney Public Library was situated inside the largely derelict, mostly empty, Queen Victoria Building. You entered through an obscure dusty door on George Street, took an antiquated lift to the first floor, then went down dim corridors, past doors that never opened, to a small foyer where free-standing bulletin boards advertised incomprehensible and perhaps unworkable proposals for the redevelopment of the site or the building. Here was the entrance to the library itself, which was disposed in an interior without any windows to the outside world nor, indeed, any other indication as to where in the building it was. Once within you were contained by this abstract space, adrift, as it were, in a Tardis full of books. The vastness of the QVB itself, taking up one whole city block, seemed to press in upon you, while at the same time the fact that there was no other access to the rest of the building made those unseen interiors as mysterious, as vertiginous, as one of the architectural fantasies of Piranesi or Moreau.

The writer Ruth Park, who was among those who campaigned, successfully, to save the building, was also one of the few who managed to explore the QVB while it was derelict. She apparently entered via the Council Offices at the north of the building; her description of what she found is perhaps more reminiscent of a de Chirico or an Escher: beautiful tessellations glimpsed through floor rubbish, circular staircases climbing up to disappeared galleries, passageways and colonnades ending in blank walls, doors opening on nothing, in an alcove the yellowed bust of some forgotten dignitary wearing a pair of sunglasses, all accompanied by the smell of cockroaches and damp and illuminated intermittently by a wan light falling through grimy stained-glass domes above.

The Queen Victoria Building, built over the site of the first Sydney Markets, was originally conceived as a market building itself: a roofed and storeyed arcade with shops leading off on either side in which tailors, mercers, boot importers, hairdressers, chemists, tobacconists, florists and fruiterers plied their various trades. Designed by George McRae in 1893 and completed in 1898, the building's construction took place during a severe recession; the architecture was deliberately elaborate and grand so that many out-of-work craftsmen—stone-masons, plasterers, tilers, stained-glass window makers—could be employed. A concert hall seating five hundred, a Coffee Palace with fifty-seven rooms in which people could stay as in a hotel, a tearoom, offices, showrooms, warehouses as well as the wide variety of trades-people and merchants were accommodated. Soon, however, the character of the tenants changed: wine sellers, dance teachers, piano tuners, palmists and clairvoyants replacing shopkeepers and artisans. The Concert Hall was converted into the city library, the Coffee Palace to offices. Later, in the 1930s, the interior was drastically remodelled in art deco style. By this time the main occupant of the QVB was its owner, then and now: the Sydney City Council.

But many of the Victorian features remained, awaiting eventual restoration: the grand twenty metre diameter central dome, glass inside, copper sheathing without, along with its attendant twenty smaller copper-sheeted cupolas; the stained glass, the wood panelling, the intri-cately tiled floors, the circular staircases, the two groups of allegorical figures over the George and York Street entrances, the Royal Wishing Well and the statue of Queen Victoria outside at the south end. Up on the hanging clock was a series of large dioramas of British kings and queens, culminating in the beheading of Charles I. Elsewhere replicas of the British Crown Jewels, an oriental coach and a series of royal paintings were incorporated in the structure. There was even a Foucault pendulum. After its refurbishment by Ipoh Gardens Berhad of Malaysia, completed in 1986, Pierre Cardin called the Queen Victoria Building the *most beautiful shopping centre in the world*.

It would have been appropriate if there had been some kind of Borgesian universality to this paradoxically situated library, but it was in fact smaller and contained a tattier collection of books than might have been expected in a great metropolis such as Sydney. This may have reflected the peculiar structure of local politics, which has made the City itself no more than a tiny enclave with, in those pre-city apartment block days, hardly any permanent residents; or it may have been the result of a certain amount of decentralisation in the library service, which meant there were rather better-stocked branches in nearby locations like Kings Cross, Paddington, Woollahra, The Glebe and Leichhardt. Equally it may have had something to do with maladministration of the City branch or even a lack of morale among those who worked there, pale and harassed as they were in their curious limbo. The consequence for me was that I distrusted this library almost on principle. I came to expect that almost any book I wanted either wouldn't be in the catalogue or, if by some chance it was, would not be on the shelves, having been stolen or lost by some previous reader or researcher.

This was not, however, the case with *The Marquesan Journal of Edward Robarts*. A red hardback with a cover illustration showing a tattooed man glimpsed behind a torn paper veil, it was among half a dozen other books on those fabled islands leaning companionably together down the bottom of a metal shelf in the 919s. I quickly had it issued to me, then, I am ashamed to say, kept it for many months, perhaps years. The fact that no one else in the entire history of the book's sojourn in the library had ever borrowed it is no excuse; all I can say in my defence is that when the library billed me for the 'lost' volume I happily paid the five dollars they demanded and, much later, when at last I did find another copy for sale in a second-hand bookshop on the North Shore, immediately returned the purloined book to the library without any attempt to recover the nominal amount I had already paid for it.

Edward Robarts was a ship's cook off the *New Euphrates*, an English whaler, who deserted or was marooned at Vaitahu on the island of Tahuata in the Marquesas on Christmas Day 1798. He was nineteen years old and had already sailed in the African slave trade and visited St Petersburg. He was not the first white man ashore: in his *Journal* he records his wonder at finding in a hut at Vaitahu an Englishman's chest containing, among other things, a Bible. This belonged to the missionary William Crook, set ashore there with a companion by the London Missionary Society ship the *Duff* in 1797. Crook stayed on alone when his partner, spooked by the attention of Marquesan women, fled back to the ship after only one night ashore and departed with the *Duff* when she left. Crook went on to spend more than two years in the islands, first on Tahuata, later on Nuku Hiva. Upon his return to England in the company of a Marquesan man called Temouteitei, he sat down for some weeks with the London Missionary Society scholar Samuel Greatheed, who had already written an account of Tahiti and also collected from Peter Heyward of the *Bounty* a Tahitian vocabulary for the benefit of missionaries going into the field. The three men—Crook, Temouteitei, Greatheed—at Newport Pagnell together compiled the *Account of the Marquesas Islands*, the manuscript of which remains unpublished in the Mitchell Library in Sydney.

While Crook was earnest and particular in both his observations and his proselytising, Robarts is an early and pure example of the unreliable narrator, as we know both from the contradictions and obfuscations within his own text and from the indefatigable labours of scholars, especially Greg Dening, who uncovered numerous errors—if they are not straight-out lies—in the account which he has so meticulously edited. Robarts was also inclined to discuss affairs on the islands, especially sexual interactions, in language whose origin lies in chivalric romance. He wrote his book in Calcutta in the 1820s under the patronage of Sir Thomas Stamford Raffles, a Dr Leyden and a Mr T. Hare, the Scotsman who preserved the manuscript for posterity. These men encouraged him to set down the progress of his

long and singular career of an enterprising and unfortunate life and gave him
space and time—and perhaps pen, ink and paper as well—with which
to do so. As an account of the seven years he spent in those islands
it is remarkably detailed, even though reconstructed entirely from
memory. If Robarts were a painter we would call him a naive artist; as
an author, he is trustworthy once you know who it is you are reading.
In other words, when you have grasped his naivety, his duplicity, his
self-interest, you may learn to take him at his word. Occasionally, too,
his laborious use of what he conceives to be a literary style breaks
through into something more genuine: early in his *Journal*, speaking of
his intention to return to England, he remarks that there he will *resume
my tender tale to my favourite fair.*

   He never returned home. When tribal conflict fuelled by the
recurring famines El Niño periodically visits on the Marquesas, as
well as the malign influence of an increasing number of other beach-
combing Europeans, forced Robarts to flee, he, his Marquesan wife
Ena o te Ata, their daughter Ellen and dog Neptune moved to Tahiti.
Robarts went pearling in the Tuamotus, trading at Kororareka, New
Zealand, rum selling in Botany Bay; was for a time cook and butler
to Raffles' sister in Penang and finally, successively, a peace officer, a
gardener and a prison warder in Calcutta, where Ena, and a second
wife, and all of his five children save Ellen died of cholera. Ellen,
the only child born in the Marquesas, was his sole heir when Robarts
himself died in 1831 and she, part English, part Marquesan, defini-
tively dislocated, lived out the rest of her obscure life in the poor white
section of Calcutta.

   Robarts was a Crusoe, a loner who lived apart from his Marquesan
hosts, as self-sufficient as he knew how to be in his own hut with his
own garden, his own habits and ways. He seems to have conceived
of himself as a kind of civiliser as well as a representative ashore of
the European ships now entering the Pacific in large numbers. At
Taiohae on Nuku Hiva where, following Crook, he soon moved, he
surveyed the bay and set up markers for ships. When they arrived he
advised them on matters of trade and etiquette, offered his services as
pilot and translator, and solicited certificates of good character from
their captains. He did not marry or have himself tattooed until the

famine of 1803 forced him to do so: there were economic benefits to be had from marriage and from membership of the feasting societies that surrounded chiefs, of which a special tattoo on the chest was a marker.

Robarts' *Journal* is fascinating, but the somewhat obdurate and self-justifying personality of its author becomes tiresome in the end. You feel that an account filtered through the mind of such a man cannot help but be tainted by prejudice, ignorance, deliberate dissimulation. There is another character, far more enticing, to be glimpsed in its pages, rather in the way that the tattooed man on the cover is seen through veils of torn paper: Jean Baptiste Cabri. He was another deserter off another English whaling ship, the *London*, which called at Tahuata in 1799. He and Robarts took an immediate dislike to each other and remained enemies as long as both were in the islands. To Robarts, Cabri was that *stout boy*, *a bad person*, a troublemaker. Probably as a consequence of Robarts' antipathy, Cabri, on both Tahuata and Nuku Hiva, lived with the tribal enemies of those among whom Robarts had his hut, so that the two became severally identified in the endemic tribal warfare characteristic of the Marquesas. Cabri was no Crusoe; he became an enthusiastic participant in all aspects of Marquesan life, so much so that, when Krusenstern's Russian Touring Expedition inadvertently removed him from the islands in 1804, he was a fully acculturated Marquesan, having largely forgotten how to speak his native French.

Cabri also left an account—or rather several accounts—of his time in the Marquesas. But there were no copies of any of his pamphlets in the Sydney City Library, nor could Steven help me find one: printed in small runs in various cities and towns in France or Switzerland in the second and third decades of the nineteenth century, none has ever appeared in book form in English. When I dropped in to Antipodean Books to tell him I had found a copy of Robarts' *Journal* but was now consumed by the search for Jean Cabri, Steven nodded and smiled and again advised me to write to ANU. His was the weariness any bookseller must feel faced with a customer whose obsessions take him beyond the stock in trade. Perhaps, I thought, that was why he suggested I come round to his house for dinner—because he wanted to shift our relationship out of a commercial milieu into one where we were more equal. I was right about the shift in the nature of our friendship, wrong about the motive for it.

Steven and his German wife Mette had a small flat on the north-eastern fringes of Sydney University. Their place wasn't far from my own house in Golden Grove which, as I walked the few streets up towards Newtown in the late sun setting over the vast expanses of the western suburbs, lived up to its name: that incomparable buttery glow which wakes in grey or dun-coloured sandstone when it is bathed in direct light was all around me. There was gold, too, on the dome of St Michael's Melkite Church at the head of Abercrombie Street, where a man in a blue shirt was hosing down the forecourt behind the security fence. The seductive scent of frangipani lingered in the air and I picked up one of the fresh cream and yellow flowers to inhale as I went on my way.

Steven opened the door, took the bottle of wine I had brought, then showed me into the flat's sitting room, which was small and narrow, excessively tidy and, since it faced the west, also suffused with that same preternatural golden light. Mette was a slender, sad-faced woman with cropped dark hair, dressed entirely in black—slacks, slip-on shoes, a chiffon blouse. Her thin pale palm felt cool against mine as we shook hands, while the melancholy cast of her features lit up suddenly in an unexpectedly warm smile, before resuming their usual gravity. She and Steven were drinking white wine; he opened my bottle of red and put it on the table for later, then poured me a glass of the chardonnay. While Mette continued to prepare our meal in the kitchen, we sat drinking and talking together on the balcony at the western end of the lounge. The light turned from gold to red, and the great brown cloud of smaze over the western suburbs thickened as if the distant muted roar of the traffic had coalesced into solid form, sound made visible as exhaust.

What did we talk about? I no longer remember. My Pacific obsession? Steven's business worries? His own enthusiasm for the poetry of Philip Larkin? After a while Mette joined us with a plate of cheese and biscuits. We had more than books in common: all three of us were more or less recent arrivals in Sydney; we shared the skewed perspective of the outsider, alternately exasperated, charmed and bewildered by the insouciance of the locals, that peculiarly Australian chauvinism which truly does not believe there is any better way to live a life, nor any better place to live it, than how and where we do. Later, when it was dark outside and the first fruit bats were swooping past the balcony or screeching and squabbling in a nearby Port Jackson fig, we sat down at the little table inside to eat Hungarian goulash over white rice, with side dishes of sweet relish and a hot pepper salsa.

Mette was not a talkative woman. She seemed to defer to Steven in most things and periodically throughout the meal, as our desultory conversation faltered, she would look searchingly at him with her light brown eyes, as if seeking in his face some ultimate sanction for the life they were leading. For his part he was gentle and solicitous to a degree that seemed almost exaggerated, as if she were an invalid needing constant care or some kind of defenceless innocent in perpetual need of reassurance ... but even that is not quite right, because there was also a slight but distinct note of appeasement in his solicitation, as if a false move, a wrong word might bring some calamity down upon his head.

The red was soon gone, and in the pause after we had finished eating, as Mette silently cleared the plates away, Steven offered to go up to King Street for some more. Not wanting—why?—to be left alone with Mette, I said I'd come too.

Is that okay, dear? he asked.

Of course, she replied.

Are you sure?

You want me to say it again? How many times do I have to say it?

This was said with less asperity than the words on the page might suggest; she was half smiling, the merest trace of an accent in her voice: Mette spoke good idiomatic English which she had learned first at school and then later when she lived in London, where she and Steven had met.

Steven lit up one of the Rembrandts he smoked as we walked down

the stairs and out into the warm dark night. He puffed and blew up
the short sharp climb to the bottle shop, out of step, it seemed, with
his own body. We didn't say much until we'd bought the second bottle
of wine—Tyrrell's Long Flat Red with the plain bright yellow label,
a favourite in those days, since it was both cheap and more or less
drinkable—and were ambling more easily down the hill again.

What do you think of Mette? he asked.

I didn't know. We'd barely spoken, one to one.

She's nice. I like her.

The words sounded bland, insipid; but Steven seemed satisfied. We
walked on in silence for a while.

Does she seem … happy? he ventured. *To you?*

I don't know. I don't know her well enough. I thought for a minute,
wondering how far I could go. *When she's not talking, her face looks sad,* I
said. *But not when she smiles.*

She has a lovely smile, he agreed.

We had come to a corner where a road needed to be crossed. Steven
pulled out his cigarettes, took one and offered the pack to me. You
don't see Rembrandt cigarettes any more; they came in a green and
white packet with a picture of *The Laughing Cavalier* on the front. We
lit up. The lights changed but Steven made no move to cross. He was
working up to something.

*She—ah, she sometimes … sometimes she likes to see someone else. Apart
from me. If you know what I mean.*

In the half-light, in the roar of traffic that had resumed, Steven was
looking self-consciously away down the street.

I don't mind, he said. *I want her to be happy. If that's what it takes, it's fine
by me …*

Now he seemed agonised. His confession lay between us like
something untouchable.

It must be quite hard … I murmured. *Sometimes …*

He looked earnestly at me, suddenly encouraged.

It's hard at the moment, he agreed. *It's always hard when … when there isn't
somebody else. That's why …*

He gestured awkwardly in my direction. I didn't know what he
meant and then all at once I did. I looked at him, not so much aghast as

astonished. In truth, I felt excited as well. Steven smiled, part relieved, part ashamed. We both looked away, pulling simultaneously, hard, on our cigarettes. The lights changed again and, still not looking at each other, we crossed over and kept on walking. We were nearly back at the flat now.

So what do you think? he asked as we came up the path that led to the stairwell.

I don't know, I said. I really didn't. *What does she think?*

Oh, she likes you, he said. *Anyway, think about it. There's no hurry.*

He put his arm round my shoulder and ushered me through the door.

I know it sounds weird, he continued. *But, believe me, you'd be doing me a favour. And it wouldn't affect our friendship.*

Once we were upstairs again and the wine had been opened, Steven excused himself and left Mette and me opposite one another at the table. The silence was intense, unnerving. I couldn't meet her eyes or think of anything to say. I'd never been in such a peculiar situation. We sat staring down at our hands, playing with the stems of our wine glasses. Finally, after what seemed an age, she spoke.

Did Steven talk to you? she asked huskily, without looking up.

Yes, he did, I replied.

And? Now she did glance at me. Her eyes, brown before, looked hazel in the light of the standard lamp beside me. They were flecked with yellow and seemed both anxious and hopeful.

Ah ... I had seldom felt so ill at ease. *Of course, I would like to ...* I was going to say *get to know you better,* but before I could Mette slumped back into her chair with a laugh that was half a sigh.

Oh, that's so good, she said. *Thank you. What you must do is call me at work sometime ... here's the number ...*

As she was writing it down on a piece of paper I heard the toilet flush, the bathroom door open, and Steven rejoined us.

Now, what do you think about Bruce Chatwin? he said cheerfully, moving towards the bookshelves. *Have you read this one ... ?*

No more was said that evening about any possible assignation between Mette and myself; we passed the time in Patagonia, or was it Ouidah, or even on the Black Hill? It was only when I came to leave and we were standing at the door saying goodnight that Mette, with a quick grateful glance at Steven, embraced me lightly so that I felt the whole lithe length of her body against me, then brushed her dry lips across mine. Steven patted me on the shoulder, a faintly avuncular gesture, even though I thought he was younger than me.

See you in the shop sometime, he said. *Goodnight. And thanks.*

His face in the gloom looked twisted, poignant, self-mocking, as if he were simultaneously embracing and rejecting the fate that was his. I raised one hand and went away down the stairs with Mette's number folded into the top pocket of my shirt. Halfway down, the timer on the automatic light clicked off and I found myself in semi-darkness. Steven's ghostly voice floated down the stairwell after me:

Be careful . . .

Although I always knew I would ring Mette, it took me a while to do so. How long is a while? A week, maybe. At that time I did the night-shift at the Redfern Mail Exchange where, it was rumoured, someone from every nationality in the world had worked, including an Eskimo, and where, it was also said, a serial killer once stalked the floors of Green Valley, the aisle of metal slot boxes at which we sat sorting letters. I lived alone and wasn't seeing anyone else. I knew I was lonely. Nevertheless I found the proposition made separately and together by Steven and Mette deeply ambivalent. Why would Mette want to have an affair with someone she barely knew? Why was Steven complicit in the arrangement, if it could be called an arrangement? From the small amount of information I had, it seemed that Mette needed another lover to feel happy and that Steven needed Mette to be happy so he could be happy. There were still unanswered questions: did Steven want to be present while his wife made love to someone else? If he did I was quite certain I did not want any part of it. Or did he just want to hear about it afterwards? Or merely know it was happening?

While I was mulling over these questions, I continued my pursuit of the enigmatic Jean Cabri. Dening's edition of Robarts' *Journal* included an extensive bibliography, much of which could be found in the State

Library of NSW, including the journal publication of an English translation of one of Cabri's pamphlets. I spent long hours sitting at expansive wooden tables under the soft milky light falling from cloudy skylights above, working my way through obscure volumes for crumbs of information. Jean Cabri's life, it turned out, fell neatly into two halves: the first part, during which he was born, grew up, went to sea, was shipwrecked or deserted and became a Marquesan, was lived in complete obscurity. The second, initiated when the two converted English ships of the Russian Touring Expedition, the *Neva* and the *Nadeshda*, sailed over the horizon into Taiohae, conforms to the now familiar trope of celebrity, even though it was celebrity of a peculiar kind. Furthermore, we know about the first half only because the second half was lived in, as they say, the glare of publicity, raising the possibility that the version Cabri gave of his early life, if not exactly false, may have been exaggerated in certain respects. Not for nothing did one who knew him call him *a second Munchausen*. But that is all we have.

Jean Cabri was born sometime in the early 1780s in the great seaport of Bordeaux, the child, he said, of an unknown sailor and a woman of the streets whose name he never divulged. His own name, Cabri, was neither his father's nor his mother's but rather a nickname picked up when, as a young child, he danced for coins on the Dock of the Moon on the left bank of the Garonne. *Sauter comme un cabri* is or was a saying common in the south of France, meaning to dance like a young goat: Jean Baptiste was *the kid* from the very beginning. He was in fact a dancer all his life, and dance played a part in even his earliest recollections. One of the revenant images that came back to him once the Russians had him aboard was a view, perhaps through a window, of women and girls turning together in the beautiful light: *Beaucoup de chandelles, beaucoup de violons, beaucoup de musique, les madames, les mademoiselles!*—surely a memory of pre-revolutionary gaiety in some theatre or dance hall. He also recalled a funambulist balanced on a tight rope high above a pond in the Jardin Public while jugglers juggled, clowns clowned and an accordion played. Somewhere, too, he learned to wear the Phrygian Cap of Liberty and dance the Carmagnole around a Freedom Tree.

Jean Cabri went to sea as a young boy, not even ten, initially on
a fishing boat owned by a Captain Carnac working out of L'ile aux
Oiseaux off Archachon, west of Bordeaux. After the proclamation
of the *Inscription Maritime* in 1793, Year II in the new dispensation,
he was inducted into the Revolutionary Navy as an ordinary seaman
on the ship *Dumouriez*. In 1795, when he must still have been in his
early or mid-teens, the *Dumouriez* was one of the ships which fought
against the combined forces of an émigré army and the English navy
in the battle of Quiberon. Upon blood-coloured decks, under halos
of smoke, to the incessant noise of the ordnance, Cabri's job was to
bring water to cool the red-hot guns or drag away the bodies of the
dead and the maimed or fetch more powder—whatever in the crazy
heat of battle he was ordered to do.

The revolutionary forces won the battle, thereby preventing the
landing of the émigré army, but the *Dumouriez* was lost and Jean
Cabri made a prisoner of the English. He was held for an indeter-
minate period in the hulks at Southampton, where men lay spoon-like
together on bitter nights to protect themselves from the cold, there
were societies dedicated to cultivation and consumption of lice—they
would later compare their verminous hordes to the bees on Napoleon's
cloak—and the merchants who owned the right to feed the prisoners
served over and over again the same portions of meat so wormy it was
inedible and bread that could break your teeth. Cabri escaped over the
side one night, waded through stinking sewage-contaminated mud,
then swam across the dark water to a whaler moored on the other side
of the harbour. Here, in what Dening calls *an early example of his powers
of persuasion*, he talked the captain into signing him on as a common
sailor; and so sailed for the South Seas.

There are conflicting versions of how he came to be in the
Marquesas: that he deserted the *London* at Vaitahu is Dening's belief,
but Cabri himself in one of his pamphlets says he came off a ship
called the *Liberty* which was hit by a storm while the crew were cutting
up six whales they had caught north-west of Nuku Hiva. In this
account Cabri, the ship's cook and a cat are the only survivors, clinging
to wreckage and drifting ashore on the uninhabited northern coast of
the island. Two Marquesan men out fishing rescue the shipwrecked

sailors and take them, sometimes on their backs, over a precipitous mountain track and down into the verdant populous valleys of the south, where the whiteness of their skin causes a sensation and the women crowd around pinching their flesh and trying to look under their clothes. Three months later Jean Cabri, along with other young men of his generation, received his first tattoos. Then, since it was time for the annual voyage to trade loaves of turmeric perfume into the south-eastern group, he went with the canoes for the first time to the leeward islands. His Marquesan life had begun.

Robarts was a cook and perhaps Cabri's mention of him here (if it is him) is another and characteristic piece of mischief on his part. He was certainly mischievous. Some early accounts of life in the Marquesas in the late eighteenth and early nineteenth centuries speak of an *Italian Renegado* loose in the hills behind Vaitahu, marshalling the tribes against the Europeans, as if some of the revolutionary fervour of the times had reached that far-flung spot. This may or may not have been Cabri; however, it is incontrovertible that on later occasions he, in company with other Marquesans, attempted to cut off European ships. This was a popular and sometimes successful strategy used by Islanders all across the Pacific in the contact period. When his attempt to do this to one of the Russian ships failed, he shrugged insouciantly and pretended it was not an act of attempted piracy at all but an effort to avert the danger the ship was in.

As to the kind of life Cabri led in the five years he was on the islands, who can say? To me this was the heart of the matter, the reason for my obsession: I wanted to know what it was like to become wholly other. But how can you know that without doing it yourself? Through an act of imagination, I thought. With the character of Cabri as focus and filter, I wanted to reconstruct the pre-contact culture of the Marquesas, to resurrect in words a life that has gone forever. I was fascinated by aspects of the culture not found anywhere else in the Pacific, particularly the elaborate, intricate tattooing, which has never been equalled anywhere, and the no less flamboyant and bizarre sexual behaviour.

Marquesan girls were prepared for their sexual life from just a few weeks after birth by massage of the genitals and the application of various plant-based oils and astringents meant to improve muscle tone, olfactory quality and the consistency of vaginal secretions. Pre-adolescent boys underwent sub-incision of the penis to make it thicker and stronger. Both sexes were expected to practise sexual technique as soon as they were able. In boys, speed to ejaculation was admired; in adulthood, all sexes were adept at coming to orgasm quickly and often. It was customary for any man entering a house where women were sleeping to climb under the covers with one of them, though whether this automatically meant that lovemaking followed is not clear. On Robarts' first night ashore, when he refused the offer of the wife of the man in whose hut he was to stay, another young woman was found to share his mat. Evidently no man or woman was to sleep alone if it could be helped. It is further stated in one of the sources that any man and woman meeting alone on a forest path would certainly have sex with each other, although probably what was observed were planned assignations of proscribed lovers rather than random encounters.

Funerals of prominent individuals included day- and night-long dances before the corpse in which women exposed their genitals first to the body, then to the audience; when missionaries remonstrated with them about this abandoned behaviour, the Marquesans protested that not to do so would show a profound lack of respect for the deceased. The wilful mutilation of the genitalia of the dead before their consumption in cannibal feasts—observed in Fiji as well as the Marquesas—is perhaps part of the same complex, which seems to contrast the doomed fertility of the living with the perfect sterility of the dead.

The *pekio* complex is more interesting, institutionalising as it did a rare form of polyandry. Robarts remarks: *It is a custom for a woman to have two husbands. So in this case one is at home when the other is absent.* It wasn't quite as simple as that. The *pekio*, sometimes also called a fire-lighter, behaved in some respects like the women of the household: he might use *papa* juice to lighten the colour of his skin, as women did; he might eat with and in the manner of women; he might spend his time in and around the house doing women's work. On the other hand, the *pekio* was also the stand-in for the husband when the husband was away from home, making love as a man with the women of the household.

They were perhaps a kind of half man half woman, partaking of both roles; and in a society where there seem to have been more men than women, the institution provided an occupation for unattached men: some couples had as many as five *pekio*. Frequently they were younger than both the woman to whom they were pledged and the man who 'owned' them; sometimes they were exceptional for their beauty or strength. Mauhau, the *pekio* of Keatonui, principal chief at Taiohae on Nuku Hiva, when measured by the Russians proved to be a living replica of the Apollo Belvedere: *thirty-one and a half inches from skull to navel and ten and a half inches from navel to the division of his thighs.*

Was I being auditioned as Steven and Mette's fire-lighter? I wondered. Reading about this antique Marquesan custom made the invitation they had extended to me not just less bizarre but more enticing as well. I was tired from my job, tired of spending days reading in the abstract about old ways that will not come again. Hours spent bent over books in the unenthralled quiet of libraries began to drag. I decided to forget about Jean Cabri for a while and ring the number Mette had given me. One afternoon, leaving my books spread out all over the table, I went out into the foyer with its great tiled floor map of Abel Tasman's epochal voyage of discovery and down a corridor to a locker room where there was a red phone.

My call was answered on the second ring.

Hello? It was Mette's voice, light, hesitant, delicately accented.

Hello, this is Martin here, I said.

Hello, she said again, this time in a manner both scolding and coquettish. *I thought maybe you had forgotten all about me.*

No, I just … I've been busy …

Too busy to give me a call? That is very insulting you know …

I was finding her flirtatious tone difficult to deal with; she sounded absolutely unlike the cool, melancholy, somehow mysterious woman I had met at dinner.

Look, um, I just thought I'd ring and say … you know …

That you are coming to see me? Where are you?

Macquarie Street.
I am in Pitt, number 563, can you come now?
Alright ... alright, I will ...
Okay, good. It's a shop. Called Obelisk. See you soon.
She hung up.

Feeling that I had in some obscure way been hustled, I placed my books on reserve, collected my things and started walking slowly down towards Hyde Park's leafy avenues.

Obelisk turned out to be a small boutique set into the ground floor of the immense, empty mausoleum of the Anthony Hordern Building; it was one of the few shopfronts left on that stretch of Pitt Street. Like the Queen Victoria Building, Anthony Hordern & Sons' New Palace Emporium, built in 1905 on what was then called Brickfields Hill, took up a whole city block; also like the QVB, it had now fallen into disrepair and was mostly boarded up and abandoned preparatory to its impending demolition, which started not long after the time of which I write.

Hordern's began as a family business: Anne Hordern expanded her 1820s stay-making business into a millinery and drapery warehouse on King Street; her husband Anthony, who had a coach-building business round the back, joined his skills and labour with hers and together they opened a shop. The business grew and diversified until, by the 1880s, under the grandiloquent title of *Universal Provider*, Hordern Brothers Palace Emporium store in Haymarket *sold everything from needles to anchors.* Like many nineteenth-century emporia they operated by mail order as well as retail, advertising their goods in a comprehensive catalogue and selling across the colony. When the first Palace Emporium was destroyed by fire in 1901, the firm, renamed Anthony Hordern & Sons, built the larger and grander New Palace Emporium a short distance away, its decorative fittings and sophisticated window displays tempting customers with what *Australia* magazine described in 1907 as *a shimmering seductiveness.*

Hordern's reached its apogee in the 1930s when it had more than 3000 employees and a mail-order department occupying several floors of the building. Farmers in town for the annual Easter Show would stop off there to view and order the latest merchandise before returning to Central Station to take the train outback; their purchases would follow by rail. By 1980 the lower floor of the mostly derelict building had been converted to a car park. The other shops in the same stretch as Obelisk—record shops, head shops, shops selling second-hand clothes and bric-a-brac—clung to the fringes of that vast building, a tiny community of outsiders who would inevitably be sucked under in the coming gravitational collapse.

Obelisk: I say boutique but the word sits oddly with the studded collars and death's head belt buckles in the window, the punky clothes hanging up for sale inside, the great black rubber or leather boots, the heavy gothic jewellery, the roses, the swastikas, the skulls. There seemed to be nothing in that cluttered shop which was not either black, white or red, unless in the depths of one of the display cases there was a ring with a peridot or a sapphire in a silver setting. It was dim inside, quiet once the street door closed, and there was music playing, not loud as you might expect, and not the kind of music, either, that the goods for sale suggested: muted and repetitive, without lyrics or voice, some melancholy riff rolling over and over in the shadows.

Mette was like a shadow herself, standing behind a small counter towards the back of the store, her black clothes merging with those around her, her pale face lit from below by a light contained in the glass box beneath the counter top where more jewellery was displayed. With a shock of recognition I realised I had forgotten what she looked like: the phantom who had accompanied me since our last meeting bore only a passing resemblance to the woman with black lips and hooded eyes smiling somehow avidly at me as I walked towards her. I had conjured some kind of delicate sylph or sibyl, not this provocative white-faced ghost with small sharp teeth that in the dim light looked distinctly yellow.

Murmuring a greeting in a voice so low I could hardly hear it over the music, she came from behind the counter, eased past me so that I felt her thighs brush mine, and went to the front of the shop to lock the door and flip the *Open* sign to *Closed*.

Quick, she said, coming back towards me and taking my hand. *I can't stay shut for long.*

There was another room out the back of the shop, as dim but not so cluttered. This was where the tape deck was, the tapes, a sink and a tap, an electric jug for making tea and coffee, a small fridge. Here the ambience was more hippie than punk, with a beaded curtain closing off the way in from the shop, a Balinese cloth flung over the small table where the cups and jug sat, a *chaise longue* against the back wall covered in faded red plush. Mette pushed the tinkling curtain aside then, as I followed her through, turned to press her body against me. I felt her lips, so dry and impersonal that other time, now wet and full on mine. My trepidation vanished in an eruption of lust; without thinking we shed our clothes and made blind love on the *chaise longue*, and in all that expenditure of breath and fluid and desire not a single word was said between us.

Mette fucked with a kind of abstract intensity that seemed to have nothing to do with me as a person. How could it? She did not know me, nor I her. We were just bodies. Later I came to understand that I was literally a means to an end, a way of transcending whatever constituted ordinary reality for her and thereby gaining entry into some other place which I could not help thinking of as a void, or oblivion; but for the moment I was as carried away as she was, transported to that dimension where only sensation exists. Yet even in extremity, when I opened my eyes and looked at her, Mette seemed sad; or at least she did until towards the end of the act a change came over her: in her drive to orgasm she was overtaken by a sort of frenzy, she moaned and bucked as if seeking to leave her body or this earth behind.

Afterwards she fell back onto the *chaise longue* like someone from whom the soul had indeed departed, eyes closed, paler, if possible, than she usually was, and I wondered with a thrill of alarm if she had fallen into unconsciousness or something worse. This absence did not last very long, however, and when she did return to herself there was a moment I learned afterwards always to look for: a kind of panic when she first opened her eyes and saw the unrecognisable shapes of the familiar around her, followed by a quick glance in my direction, and then the slow, supernal loveliness of her smile. As I said, she hardly ever smiled but when she did her eyes became suffused with an other-worldly light and her face transformed into that of an innocent or a child.

But this post-coital moment of peace didn't last long either. As soon as she returned to herself she began to worry about the shop; she would dress, compose herself, then go out and open up again. This was not so much because Obelisk was inundated with customers—I hardly ever saw anyone in there; it was as quiet as Steven's bookshop—but because her friend Elaine, whose business it was, would be angry if she dropped by and found the shop closed. Furthermore, as I found out later, Elaine—naturally—had her own key and so might easily, if she did come by, open up and discover us *en flagrante delicto* out the back: though whether this actually constituted a risk for Mette or was in fact a provocation towards greater intensities of furtive desire I could never decide. As for me, I was, she said, welcome to stay and have a cup of coffee or tea, but then and subsequently I did not feel as if the invitation was genuine and so followed her lead, dressing, making myself presentable and going on my way. Our goodbyes, then, were those of strangers who share a not necessarily guilty secret, but one they cannot let anyone else in upon. Or no one else but one.

You will come and see me again? she said teasingly, but with a slight peremptory undertone, as if chastisement would be my fate if I did not.

I'll call first, I replied and, feeling unaccountably sad myself, half waved, half smiled, opened the now unlocked door and went out into the street, assailed, as always, by the roar of city traffic along Pitt Street. I walked in a kind of daze south through the fringes of Chinatown, past Central Station and on down Elizabeth Street to eat at one of the Middle Eastern restaurants clustered around the corner of Cleveland Street before going on to work at the Mail Exchange.

Those afternoons with Mette, which hardly varied, exist now in my memory not so much as erotic encounters in the shadowy room out the back of Obelisk as in the dreamy melancholy of those later walks through the grimy reaches of the lower town, as grit and rubbish blew in the streets, traffic snarled and the late sun slanted down the gaps between buildings like beams of liquid gold through dark murky water.

That day set the pattern for what became my routine at this time: I would work from eight in the evening until four-thirty or five the following morning, sorting mail in the fantastical, cacophonous Mail Exchange, then walk back home to Golden Grove to sleep as the sun rose. In the afternoons I went to the State Library to continue my research, cutting short my study once or twice a week to call Obelisk and make a tryst with Mette. Sometimes I did stay around the shop afterwards and chat with her for a while but these conversations, while not exactly inconsequential, were never intimate. We exchanged information or opinions, not confidences.

Craven as it may sound, in this period, which lasted some time— months rather than weeks—I never once dropped in to Antipodean Books to see Steven. I did not feel I could face him. What was it that prevented me? It wasn't simple: not shame, not guilt, not even remorse; I think I did not want to see in his eyes the knowledge of what we were doing, did not want to enter into any further complicity with him regarding the affair. Perhaps I was jealous of him: I suppose that somewhere in my head I assumed that my encounters with Mette, or rather hers with me, had some kind of vivifying effect on her relationship with Steven, that the plunges into oblivion which she accomplished with me left her free to engage in more loving congress with him. Or is this merely what I hoped was the case? The very oddness of our affair made it possible for me to ignore it most of the time, to treat it as an aberration and meanwhile get on with the rest of my life.

Just as there are contradictory versions as to how Jean Cabri came to be in the Marquesas, there is uncertainty as to how he left. At the end of their ten-day stay the two Russian ships spent a frustrating day negotiating inimical tides, winds and currents trying to sail out of Taiohae Bay which, as the submerged crater of an old volcano, makes an almost complete circle. It was during these manoeuvres that they saw Cabri on shore, evidently inciting his Marquesan friends to get ready to slaughter the Europeans and plunder their ships. Eluding this fate but concerned at the exhaustion of the sailors, who had been working since 4 am, Krusenstern decided to anchor for the night and make another attempt in the morning. Both Robarts and Cabri came on board to repeat their farewells but, while Robarts prudently went ashore after dinner, Cabri, who said he could swim to land whenever he liked, stayed on board. One suggestion is that he had too much to drink and fell asleep; another is that because of his rivalry with Robarts he was determined to be the later of the two to disembark.

Whatever the reason, when the Russians found, before dawn, a favourable wind blowing, they immediately set sail for sea; once they were outside the bay a squall blew up which made it impracticable for Cabri to be set ashore by boat and impossible for him to swim there safely as he had planned. They could not even spare the time to find him a plank to cling to, and so he had no choice but to accompany the Russians to Hawaii and beyond. Krusenstern wrote in his book that he *appeared rather to rejoice at, than regret, this circumstance, and I firmly believe he came on board with the intention of sailing with us.* But Cabri would later allege the Russians kidnapped him as a scientific curiosity, even stating on one occasion that he was lashed to a board like a common criminal. And for the rest of his life he would be prone to hysterical grief at the thought of his lost islands and particularly the family he left behind there.

There is no doubt that the Russians, and especially the German naturalist Georg Henry Langsdorff, found Cabri a fascinating subject of study. Langsdorff was particularly intrigued to observe the return of Cabri's native French, along with the fading of the Polynesian language in which he had seemed so fluent. Cabri also gave Langsdorff a wealth of ethnographic detail, as well as dancing Marquesan dances for him and demonstrating a form of sorcery which, however, failed in its object of killing a man because, Cabri thought, there was no proper place on board ship to bury the hair and nail clippings of the putative victim; perhaps, he suggested, he might have better success with rat poison if there were any aboard? Exploits like these led to Krusenstern calling him *our wild Frenchman;* elsewhere Langsdorff remarks that, although useful as a sailor, he was *but a mauvais-sujet, very ready in laying plans for stealing, lying and cheating, and not less adroit in the execution of them.*

He was not the only wild man aboard. There was, amongst the

retinue of Count Nikolai Rezanov, the Russian ambassador Krusenstern was taking to Japan, one Feodor Ivanovich Tolstoy, known as *the American*, an older cousin of the writer Leo Tolstoy who would later describe him as *an extraordinary personality, criminal and attractive*. Feodor was violent, extravagant, dangerous, courageous, mad. Entered at a young age into the St Petersburg Naval Academy but graduating into the crack Preobrazhensky Guards instead of the Imperial Navy, he was a superb shot and adept at fencing as well as with the sabre; the tales of his youth involve drinking, gambling, womanising and duelling, all indulged with an edge of genuine craziness. When the Russian American Company was gearing up for Krusenstern's expedition, Feodor Ivanovich's younger cousin, Feodor Petrovich Tolstoy, a talented artist who had also studied at the Naval Academy, was invited to join the retinue of Ambassador Rezanov, but declined. For reasons that remain unclear, Feodor Ivanovich took his place. Nikolai Tolstoy, the family historian from whom this information is derived (*The Tolstoys*, London, 1985) speculates that to Tsar Alexander I *one Tolstoy would do as well as another*; Tolstoys had served Russian Emperors since the fourteenth century.

Feodor, wearing the uniform of a lieutenant in the Preobrazhensky Guards, came aboard the *Nadeshda* in company with a pet ape of which he was *inordinately fond*. Another cousin described this ape as *an orang-utan, clever, agile and enterprising as a human*. Others claimed it was also his mistress. Feodor, who was addicted to practical joking, on one occasion took the ape into Krusenstern's cabin where he placed some of the Captain's writing materials and notebooks on a table, then proceeded to stain with ink, blot and screw up a blank sheet of paper. The ape was left in the cabin, where she duly imitated her master's actions with respect to Krusenstern's *valuable records*. Another time Feodor waxed the beard of a priest, Father Gideon, to the deck while he was sleeping off a drinking bout, then impressed the wax with the Captain's seal, showing the two-headed Imperial eagle. When Father Gideon awoke he faced an implacable choice: either lose his beard or commit an act of treason by breaking the seal. He cut off his beard.

Krusenstern seems to have been remarkably tolerant of these pranks, but when Feodor began fomenting mutiny among the crew he had no choice but to act. After several warnings, and a period spent under arrest on board ship, Feodor was told he would be put ashore unless he gave his word to cease preaching revolution to the sailors. He declined to do so and, when the ship's company landed on a deserted island off the Alaskan coast, Feodor, along with his ape and a supply of food, was left alone there. Clearly a resourceful character, he went to live with the Tlingit people, becoming as skilled with harpoon and bow as he was with foil and sabre. Eventually he attracted the attention of a passing ship and made his way south and east to the port of Petropavloskt on the Kamchatka peninsula; and from there, on horseback, by boat and on foot, across the whole of Siberia to Moscow. Tattooed (in the Marquesas), hairy, with bloodshot eyes, and still wearing the stained Preobrazhensky Guards uniform in which he had hunted walrus, he caused a sensation. As for the ape, it isn't clear what happened to her: sometimes Feodor claimed to have eaten her, at others he denied it. If it was indeed an orang-utan, it seems unlikely she would have long survived the sub-arctic cold.

Feodor Tolstoy got back home by land before Krusenstern returned by sea, and at least two other members of the expedition followed him across Siberia to Moscow: one was Langsdorff and the other Jean Cabri. A fourth whose history is also entangled with that of the Russian Exploring Expedition, and with the literary history of the nineteenth century, also made that epochal journey around this time—American ship's captain John De Wolf, an uncle of the writer Herman Melville. At least one authority (explorer and writer Tim Severin in his book *In Search of Moby Dick,* New York, 2000) has suggested that these three—Langsdorff, Cabri and De Wolf—made the journey together, but this seems unlikely. Langsdorff records that De Wolf set out four days before he himself departed Okhotsk; and although he caught up with his friend later in Irkutsk, they did not travel on together; and had Cabri been with him, Langsdorff would surely have said so in his very full account of his journey. Nor does De Wolf's own book (*A Voyage to the North Pacific and a Journey through Siberia more than Half a Century Ago,* Cambridge, 1861) make any mention of Jean Cabri.

✳

Perhaps, as another writer says, Cabri took his time going to Moscow, being handed from provincial governor to provincial governor as an entertaining diversion. Englishman Robert Ker Porter, brother of the novelist Jane Porter, saw him after he had arrived there and described how he danced Marquesan dances for the Tsar, how admiring observers compared his tattoos to damask, how he eloquently bewailed his fate as a castaway in Europe. Cabri took his place with other freaks at court: dwarves and giants; dancing bears; the remarkable horn music, a kind of organ in which each pipe was blown by an individual selected to conform in size to the scale of the pipe he played. Later Cabri made his way north to St Petersburg and, at the Naval Academy at Kronstadt, became a swimming instructor, teaching cadets heretofore unknown water skills.

He remained in Russia until the restoration of the French monarchy after the end of the Napoleonic Wars, then travelled across Europe to petition Louis XVIII to give him a ship to go back to his island; either before or after his return to his native land he also sought, for the same purpose, an audience with the King of Prussia. Neither monarch, nor indeed the Tsar, seems to have thought him more than a curiosity, and none gave him the ship or the money he wanted. His fate was to live out his days as a fairground attraction, perhaps the first ever illustrated man. He returned to his home town of Bordeaux and there exhibited himself in or at something called the *Cabinet des Illusions*—surely some kind of variety show, burlesque or circus. Either in company with other acts from the *Cabinet*—there is a story about his rage at being upstaged by a performing dog—or solo, he began to tour, styling himself *Judge of Nuku Hiva*. (The word he used for judge, *mehama*, is perhaps related to Marquesan *meama*, meaning judicious; Dening speculates that he meant to characterise himself as one who has the power of life and death over others.) Presumably his exhibition included the *haka* he had learned on Nuku Hiva, the practice of sorcery and also, perhaps, the hunt for human prey he demonstrated to the Russians. He had a pamphlet ghost-written which he then offered for sale; when stocks were exhausted, it was reprinted, with minor changes, in different cities along his way. One copy that has survived, from Geneva, has a note in it describing Cabri as well built, handsome, wearing a great feathered hat (probably made from roosters' tails), and able to answer with ease any question put to him.

This wandering, vaudevillian life came to an end in 1824 in the north-eastern French town of Valenciennes, where Jean Cabri was taken ill and died, probably of some kind of respiratory disease. I imagine him coughing in his caravan next to an empty tent while a pony tethered nearby stands head down in the rain; he is delirious and in his delirium thinks he is back in the islands, perhaps assisting in the birth of his daughter or making love to his Marquesan wife in a river pool immediately after the child is delivered, as custom demanded. Meanwhile the rest of the circus wends its way out of the fairground and on under the dripping linden trees to the next saint's day fair in Picardy.

His death did in fact enter the annals of the town, principally because of the interest of a young journalist named Aimé Leroy, who contributed an obituary to a local newspaper; it appears to have been based upon an actual meeting and interview. In it Leroy mentions that a dealer in curios had offered to purchase Cabri's tattoos off him before he died, intending to have him skinned post-mortem in such a way as to preserve these inscrutable markings. Whether or not Cabri assented to this gruesome bargain is unclear, although he may have; the municipal authorities certainly did not, for they made certain he was buried intact in a grave with two other men, perhaps paupers, one below and one above, to confuse any possible attempt to rob his grave and retrieve the precious skin. It was a melancholy end to an extraordinary life, one we should perhaps not too readily assume was of great unhappiness: Cabri may have been one of those extroverts who do not brood overmuch on their fate but rather look upon life as a series of opportunities in which to shine forth as the unique individuals they are.

While all tattoo motifs came out of a kind of pattern book carried in the memory of the tattooist and also anthologised on wood and stone carving, on *tapa* cloth, on the bodies of old men and women, in the

Marquesas individuality was nevertheless conferred by tattoo which was, in a precise sense, a narrative of events—war, peace, sacrifice, marriage, the learning of life skills—written on the body. Some of these life events could be located in the past in the sense that they marked occasions, rites of passage, during which a man or woman might be tattooed; other tattoos commemorated special occurrences like the killing of a man or the marrying of a woman. Still others seem to have been predictive, anticipating the fate of he or she who wore it. It is in this sense that we should perhaps interpret the untattooed skin Jean Cabri carried to his grave—as unlived life, or life unlived in his adoptive island home. At the same time the attempt to have him flayed after death has an eerie association with Marquesan custom, which required that a man's tattoos be scraped from his skin so that he could go back into the dark naked as he came into the world.

We know the extent of Cabri's tattoos because the Russian Touring Expedition left us a picture of him, drawn by a Mr Orloffsky and reproduced in Langsdorff's *Voyages and Travels in Various Parts of the World* (London, 1813). Using this illustration, and a variety of other sources, it is possible to decipher elements of this tattoo. Under his armpits were *mata hoata*, shining eyes, popularly thought of as lightning that flashed out as a blow was struck, the last thing seen by a man about to be killed. Round his left eye and extending up to the hairline was a dark rectangle called *mata epo*, shitty eye, a sign of a feasting society, a group of men who ate together. His other eye was surrounded by rays, making it into a sun: the insignia of a man who has killed or refrained from killing, and the ultimate origin, no doubt, of Cabri's fantasy of himself as a judge. Above that was a diagonal line crossing his forehead from the centre line to the corner of his right eye: it was called *pi'e'e*, diarrhoea. A dribble of shit down his face, for the Marquesans sometimes imagined themselves to be *the excrement of the gods* who were in every respect the opposite of humans, right down to the fact that they went untattooed.

On his arms and legs were concentric ovals representing at once shells, bathing pools, lagoons, bowls, vaginas and vulvas; and on his wrists were *honu*, turtles. The little men inscribed everywhere were called *enata*—rows and rows of *enata*, each one both representative and exclusive. The chevrons and cross-hatching on his right breast were another mark of a warrior, and below them on his belly, above two narrow lines marking the diaphragm crossed at an oblique angle by a broader stroke, was an image of his tobacco pipe. Finally, although we cannot see it in Orloffsky's drawing, on his back there would have been the *mata Komoe*, the face of Komoe, who was killed in war, and who protects a warrior's back in battle and teaches revenge; like the tiny *enata* which take up any other otherwise unadorned space, Komoe is a kind of doppeltiki.

Melville wrote in *Moby Dick* of the harpoonist Queequeg: *And this tattooing had been the work of a departed prophet and seer in his island, who, by those hieroglyphic marks, had written out on his body a complete theory of heavens and earth, and a mystical treatise on reading the truth; so that Queequeg in his own proper person was a riddle to unfold.* While these words might be held to apply to Jean Cabri, they do not encompass the full range of meanings of Marquesan tattoo. Tattoo, on completion called *pahutiki* or wrapped in images, was in fact a kind of armour against the sacred which, like the water surrounding a canoe, is always about to break into and destroy human life. The faces with which Marquesans adorned themselves were meant to stare down the gods; the *enata* they carried in ranks on their bodies were a defence against the supernatural. Tattooed skin was also called *crust, lid, skeleton*; it was analogous to crab or tortoise shell, protecting the soft parts within. After death, women with specially tattooed right hands would oil and rub the images from the skin and later, literally, consume them. The naked, skinned, untattooed body, made new again, could return to the realm of the untattooed gods; whereas the repatriated Jean Cabri wore his suit to the grave.

Usually when I rang Obelisk Mette told me to come down straight away, but there came a day when she was both cool and circumspect on the phone.

Hello, Obelisk, she said, formally, *can you hold the line a moment?*

There was a murmur of conversation in the shop, too faint for me to make out any words. It ceased. Her voice came back.

Can I help you?

It's me, I said. *I was going to come down.*

I see. Perhaps in half an hour's time? Three-thirty?

Alright. Is everything okay?

Fine. I'll see you then. Bye.

She hung up, leaving me none the wiser. The whole conversation, I realised, would have sounded to anyone else like an exchange with a customer or business associate.

I didn't feel like hanging around the library, so I packed up, went down into the park and spent some time watching the old men playing chess with giant pieces on the board near St James Station. I was annoyed by Mette's change of attitude, even though I was sure there was some good reason for it. The whole nature of our relationship was such that the least thing could make me feel uneasy. I was like some unpaid gigolo, and even though aspects of what we did were in some fantasy sense ideal—frequent, casual, ardent sex without any ties or obligations—I was beginning to tire of it. I wanted more than just a physical relationship. I wanted to get to know her better. Not to put too fine a point on it, I wanted our trysts to partake of the clichés of romantic love.

When I arrived at Obelisk more than half an hour later—deliberately, I wanted to make her wait—Mette closed up the shop but did not lead me out the back as she usually did. Standing beside the stand where the leather jackets hung, she touched the side of my face with her hand. It was cool. I was hot.

I'm sorry to make you wait, she said. *Elaine was here.*

So she finally came? I said, sounding unintentionally brusque.

What do you mean? Mette said, her eyes big in the dimness. *She often comes, only usually it is in the morning.*

It's just—you know—sometimes you seem worried ... about her ...

Do I? Well, not today. Today we have lots of time. I don't have to meet Steven until six o'clock.

The mention of Steven made me feel even more uncomfortable. I never wanted to think, let alone talk about him. But Mette obviously did. She asked me into the back room and offered me a cup of tea. When we were settled, I on the *chaise longue*, she on a small hard chair opposite, she returned to the subject.

Steven says you don't come and see him any more.

No.

Why not?

Why do you think?

Because of what we are doing? But he knows already. He is grateful to you. He would like to thank you.

Don't you think that's a bit weird?

Only if you think it is weird. If you don't, then it isn't. We are grown ups, we can do what we want.

I just feel odd about it sometimes.

But you like me.

Yes.

And we are good together, yes?

Yeah.

So—what?

I don't know. I was just thinking, on my way down, maybe if we got to know each other better ...

But I don't want to know you better. If I know you better, you will lose your mystery. I like mystery. If I get to know you, it is ... just normal. I don't like that.

So who do you think I am?

She shook her head.

You are anything I want, she said. *But if I tell you ... no mystery. Already, talking like this ...*

She shrugged, looked away, looking more than ever like the Lady of the Sorrowful Countenance, which is what I sometimes called her, though only to myself. The prospect of our making love again seemed suddenly a million miles away. Perhaps she was right ...

Maybe you're right ... I just ... I live alone at the moment, I don't have anyone. You have Steven.

If you don't want to come any more, that's alright.

I don't know.

Here we were having our first proper conversation and it was making us both unhappy. I felt like going.

Don't go just yet, she said, unexpectedly picking up on my thought. *There's something I want to show you. Come ...*

At the end of the wall upon which the *chaise longue* stood was a door. I had never seen it open and assumed it was no longer used. Now Mette unlocked it and pulled it ajar. I joined her there. It was dark beyond—as dark as anywhere I'd ever been.

Come, she said. *Your eyes will soon get used to it. Come …*

She was right: there was light at the end of the tunnel as she took my hand and led me through a corridor and up a flight of stairs onto a kind of boardwalk set above the car park which took up the whole ground floor of the vast building. It was only half full, the dim shapes of automobiles seen from above resembled dusty lozenges whose colours could only be glimpsed through the dirt adhering to them. Here were dull echoing noises rising as commuters slammed car doors or spoke to one another in faraway booming tones like voices calling down wells. About halfway along the boardwalk was another door, another staircase leading up to the next level; we took these stairs, which doubled back and then came out into an elaborately tiled foyer from which disused elevators had once come and gone: at the further end were double glass doors and beyond them a great wash of milky light falling.

We walked out these doors into an enormous room lit by high windows on three sides; the fourth side was of panelled wood, in which a line of offices was set. All across the dusty, debris-strewn, splintery timber floor of that room were set long wooden tables, bench height, clearly made for people to stand rather than sit at. Some of the windows were broken or had been left open, and through these generations of pigeons had come to sit and breed. There were hundreds of them perched in the higher reaches of the room, their soft throaty cooing somehow at odds with the stench of droppings piled in small hillocks on the floor below their habitual perches.

This was where they made up the mail orders, Mette said. *The things would be brought up from the stockrooms by boys and made into packages here.*

I walked over to one of the high windows and looked out. We were on George Street, which was, as usual on a weekday afternoon, a chaos of cars, trucks, buses, taxis; yet somehow, from above, and through the grimy window glass, it seemed muted, distant, almost abstract, like the future seen from the past. Mette, who had the ability to move silently, appeared at my side. I felt her cool hand touch mine.

There is a tower, she said. *Would you like to see?*

The tower, which may be seen in contemporary illustrations of the building, was midway down the south side of the building, facing onto Goulburn Street. It was square, squat, turreted, with a flag pole in the middle. We climbed three more staircases, walked down more dusty corridors full of junk, amongst which were many rodent droppings and from which I heard the occasional scrappling of what I assumed were rats. The air smelt of ammonia and damp. We came to another foyer, then went through another door and climbed another circular metal staircase into the heart of the tower. At the top was a trapdoor which Mette assured me I would be able to open; I went up first, shot back a bolt and pushed with my hands at the fitted slab, which would not give until I turned round, crouched precariously down, set my back against it and straightened my legs. Then, with a sudden muffled *crack!*, it did, showering dust over my hair and clothes and over Mette's pale upturned face below. I heard the sound of pigeons scattering.

We went out onto a roof enclosed on all sides by a waist-high balustrade and sheathed with some kind of heavy tarred material. The view was magnificent; but Mette had not come here to admire the view. As I looked south and west over the endless suburbs of the Cumberland Basin towards the ghostly line of the Blue Mountains on the horizon, with the strangely opaque sky behind arching over the whole continent, I felt her hands slip around my chest from behind, unbuttoning my shirt, then drifting down to fumble with my belt. I turned to face her, my back to the balustrade, and found she had already undressed, or at least as much as she needed to. I had only ever seen her half naked in the half dark of the dim back room of Obelisk; here, in the fuming afternoon light of the city, under the translucence of the sky, her pale body with its small breasts and slender thighs could almost have been that of a child, had it not been for the hair of her pubes; while beneath the ivory skin of her closed lids I could see a dark tracery of veins and at her temple a pulse exploding rhythmically. We kissed and then she wrapped her arms around my neck, her legs around my waist and clung to me as, with the unthreaded labyrinth of the city spread out all around us, we made love like forgetful gods, or gods who have been abandoned.

That was the last time I was with Mette. Afterwards as we wandered companionably through the smelly corridors of the dilapidated wreck of the Emporium, chatting idly about nothing in particular, then returned through the dark passages to Obelisk, she began to speak of Steven again, suggesting that I might like to come with her when she went to meet him after work at six o'clock. I did not want to, but could not say with any conviction why not; her insistence exasperated me, just as my intransigence irritated her. She was, despite her apparent passivity and malleability, an extremely stubborn person. In the end she said:

If you will not come, then you cannot see me any more.

Okay, fine, I said, *I won't see you any more.*

I remember looking at her then in the gloom of that shop full of dark relics with violent associations and seeing that her eyes were full of tears.

I'm sorry, I said, *I just can't do this any more. I'll end up wanting to take you off him.*

That you can never do, she said.

I know, I said, *so what's the point?*

The point is we had something good but now it's gone, she said, shrugging and turning away.

I felt like taking her slim shoulders and shaking her: an impulse I suppressed as soon as it arose. Instead I focused on something that had always bothered me in that shop: a small red badge carrying a black swastika on a white ground. It lay amongst the other jewellery in the light box below the counter where Mette sat when she was minding the shop.

I don't understand you, I said.

What don't you understand?

I pointed at the badge.

I don't understand that. You're an environmentalist, a socialist, a German. How can you offer something like that for sale?

What?

That Nazi badge.

She peered at it, then back at me. She shrugged her shoulders.

Have you seen Die Blechtrommel? *The Tin Drum?* she said.

The movie? Yes. What about it?

Do you remember at the end, when Matzerath tries to swallow his party badge?

Yes, I do. It chokes him, kills him. It was a badge just like that.

That's right. Well, for me, I would rather have that badge as a souvenir, for sale, than have him choke on it. Bastard Nazi though he is.

I still don't understand.

Don't you? It is quite simple. You can choke on the past or you can let it open out into the future.

But ... a swastika.

It's only a sign.

Yes, but of what?

Signs are not things.

Aren't they?

No, they are signs.

I can't forget the associations.

You don't forget them, you make new ones.

I can't do that—not with this.

Well, in that case, maybe it is better that we say goodbye.

She came close to me, went up on tiptoes and kissed me lightly on the lips. I felt my stomach turn over; suddenly I wanted her more than I had ever wanted anyone—not as a lover but as a companion, as someone to be with, all the time. I put my arms around her, drew her close and held her. She lay against me the way a wild bird lies passive in your hand when you have caught it; but, again like a wild bird, as soon as I relaxed my grip she moved away.

It is time for me to meet Steven now, she murmured. *You must go. Goodbye.*

✳

There is a coda to Jean Cabri's tale: not only did his life experience form a part of the rich background out of which Herman Melville made his books, particularly *Typee* and *Moby Dick*—John De Wolf, whose son, Melville's cousin and sometime playmate, was nicknamed 'Langs' after Georg Langsdorff, owned a copy of Langsdorff's book with Orloffsky's portrait of Cabri in it—but also, through the person of the young journalist, Leroy, intersected briefly with the literary avant-garde in his own country. This curious postscript, while merely coincidental and perhaps of no great moment, did not come to my attention until some years after the time of which I write; but I will tell it here.

Leroy lived out most of the rest of his life as a provincial journalist in Valenciennes. He married, raised a family and in all respects but one seems to have been an utterly conventional man. His one aberration, or indulgence, lay in his fascination with Pacific cultures and particularly those cultures on the islands administered by the French; out of all of these—Tahitian, Tuamotuan, Kanaky—it was of course the Marquesan that interested him most of all. He may also have inherited a desire from the illiterate sailor to go there himself: like the poet Stéphane Mallarmé to relocate to *the far Marquesas*. It was as if the riddle posed by Jean Cabri continued to tantalise him for the rest of his days, and in an attempt to solve it he assembled a formidable library of French writings on the Pacific as well as corresponding with a number of recognised authorities on the subject.

One of these authorities was a famous vaudeville artist of the Second Empire, a Monsieur Flan, who by 1870 had retired with his magnificent library to Neuilly just north of the Bois de Bologne in the western districts of Paris. Flan owned a number of books on the Marquesas, including the writings of their French discoverer, Etienne Marchand, Edouarde de Beaumont's *La civilisation aux iles Marquises* (Paris, 1843), Clément Vincendon-Dumoulin's *Iles Marquises* (Paris, 1843) and the three-volume *Voyage autour du monde sur la fregate la Vénus pendant les annees 1836–1839* (Paris, 1840) of Abel Dupetit-Thouars, the admiral who subsequently, in May 1842, annexed the islands to France. Flan also owned various other explorers' journals with less direct relevance to the Marquesas: Camille de Roquefeuil's, Dumont d'Urville's, Charles Pigeard's and others. Most significantly from Leroy's point of view, M. Flan possessed copies of all three books written after the Russian Touring Expedition: Krusenstern's, Lisiansky's (he captained *Nadeshda*'s sister ship, the *Neva*) and, most important of all, Langsdorff's. For in Langsdorff there was Orloffsky's portrait of Jean Cabri, the only one in existence apart from an inferior picture reproduced on the cover of Cabri's own pamphlet, a copy of which Leroy did own.

Quite what provoked Leroy, by this time an old man of more than seventy, to go to Paris when he did—the summer of 1870—isn't clear. In his *Diary* he merely says that, his wife having died and his children grown up and left home, it was time for him *to return to the future I left behind in the past*. Evidently he meant that he too felt he had lived the life of an exile and wished, before he died, to make some attempt at his own *Voyage to Cythera*. He could not have known that on 15 July, with no other pretext than the Prussian King Wilhelm's refusal to grant the French ambassador a further audience to ask for yet another guarantee against any recurrence of Bismarck's attempt to place a German prince on the Spanish throne, Emperor Louis-Napoleon would declare war. *France goes to war on a point of etiquette*, the *Illustrated London News* reported, thus initiating the military disaster of the Franco-Prussian War, the brief intoxications of the Commune and the civil disaster of its suppression.

Leroy was evidently already at the house of M. Flan, happily ensconced in the library, when war broke out. Within six weeks the armies of Louis-Napoleon had surrendered, the Emperor was in a German prison and there was revolution in Paris. As the nascent Commune set itself to the defence of the city, unavoidable losses occurred, both civic and personal: the beautiful trees in the Bois were felled to make barricades and provide fuel, and houses on the outskirts of Paris were appropriated and demolished to improve fields of fire for the artillery. One day the engineers arrived at M. Flan's house to tell him it would be razed that same evening.

But it will take at least a week to shift my library! Flan is reported to have said.

So much the worse for your bibliothèque, was the heartless reply, according to Alistair Horne (*The Fall of Paris*, Aldershot, 1967). Flan took a room that night in a nearby hotel, where he was found dead (of a broken heart, it was said) next morning. Leroy may have gone with him; or he may have begun his wanderings immediately. We next hear of him some weeks later, when the first entry in his *Diary* is made, at a hotel in Montmartre. The *Diary*, which remains unpublished in the Archives d'Outre-Mer de France, is of no great interest in itself. Much of it consists of an account of M. Leroy's daily activities—what he did, where he went, what he ate—and a fair proportion of the rest is more or less incoherent accounts of the ethnology of the Marquesas, apparently reconstructed from memories of his reading, if not entirely invented. (It is this second- or third-hand ethnology that led to the *Diary* being deposited where it is.) Clearly the shock of the events of September and subsequent developments unsettled the old man's mind and he rambled through his *Diary* as he rambled through the days. The most compelling pieces of writing are those passages in which he observes what is going on in the streets and notes it down. Then you can see a lifetime of work as a journalist re-asserting itself in precise description and compassionate understanding.

What is most significant about Leroy's *Diary* is the address of the hotel at which it was written: 7 Fauborg-Montmartre, which is also the last address of Montevidean-born French poet and writer Isidore Ducasse, the self-styled Comte de Lautréamont and author of *The Chants of Maldoror* and *Poésies*. Ducasse died at the hotel on the night of 23–24 November 1870, while Leroy was resident there. His death has remained a mystery ever since: the death certificate, signed by hotel proprietor J. F. Dupuis and a member of his staff, A. Milleret, gives no cause for it. Some have speculated he died of starvation: the last official distribution of fresh meat had taken place three days previously; already people were eating their pet dogs and cats, the animals in the zoo were going under the knife (all except the lions, tigers, monkeys and a solitary hippo perished) and rat hunting was becoming a favourite diversion of the National Guard. Breads were being made of wheat, rice and straw; 'milk' out of glucose, albumen and olive oil. *Osseine*, a bizarre concoction of bones and gelatine used as stock for soup, cost a franc a kilogram.

Others have suggested the young Montevidean (he was only twenty-four) was murdered by Louis-Napoleon's secret police. This seems as likely as any other possibility, since Ducasse was as radical a free thinker as was Rimbaud at this time, but with a far more sophisticated grasp of how power worked. Within the Commune there had been dissension between factions earlier in the month, and the police were keen to arrest the leaders of the Reds; but it is more likely that Ducasse, an obscure though inflammatory poet with no known political affiliations, had been marked down for execution under the old regime and killed now because, in the chaos of the time, no one would likely inquire too closely into the circumstances of his death. Suicide remains another possibility; yet, while Ducasse's writing, particularly *Maldoror*, is full of grotesqueries, not to say obscenities, he does not seem temperamentally to have been inclined towards despair. The later of his two works, *Poésies*, subtitled *préface à un livre futur*, has none of the gothic blood and thunder of *Maldoror*, rather it is an immensely ingenious rewriting of the maxims of French writers such as Pascal, Vauvernagues and De Rochefoucald, by turns luminous, cynical and strange. There is so much verve and élan in the work, it is so wildly ambitious, at once profane and yet sanctified too, and so deeply, gleefully insolent, it is difficult to imagine it as the preface to a suicide—unless self-slaughter is conceived as an act of absurdity, which of course it may be. The most original solution to the problem is that proposed by Antonin Artaud, who believed Isidore Ducasse was murdered by his alter-ego, the Comte de Lautréamont.

We may never know for sure, and Leroy's comment on the death, if that is indeed what his entry for 24 October refers to, is enigmatic: *The young man on the second floor was found dead in his rooms this morning, probably from poisoning. I saw him only last night on the stairs, when he passed me going out as I was returning from my evening walk. As usual, he greeted me ironically, asking when my ship to the South Seas was sailing. I replied 'Not yet,' then asked a question of my own: 'How is Monsieur's book proceeding?' 'Like a horse to the knacker's yard,' he replied. 'Now I must go, I have been invited to eat with my publisher. We are having cat. Such an opportunity is not to be missed!' Then he laughed and clattered away. I will miss his piano playing in the evenings, wild and discordant though it was.*

In *Maldoror*, the Comte had written: *Mervyn is in his room; he has received a missive. Whoever is writing him letters? His agitation has prevented him from thanking the postman. The envelope has black edges and the words are traced in a hasty hand. Is he going to take this letter to his father? What if the signatory expressly forbids him to do so? Filled with distress, he opens his window to breathe the scents of the air; the sunbeams reflect their prismatic irradiations from the Venetian mirrors and damask curtains. He tosses the letter aside among the gilt-edged books and albums with mother-of-pearl covers strewn on the embossed leather overlaying the top of his schoolboy's desk. He opens his piano and runs his tapering fingers over the ivory keys. The brass wires did not twang. This indirect warning urges him to pick up the wove paper again: but the latter curled back as if it had been offended by the hesitation of the recipient. Caught in the trap, Mervyn's curiosity increases and he opens the ready scrap of paper. Until this moment he had seen no handwriting but his own. 'Young man, I am interested in you; I want to make you happy. I will take you as a companion and we will compass long travels in the South Sea Islands …'*

Whatever summons Isidore Ducasse received on the night of the 23rd, it cannot have been to the South Seas. He was to lose himself in another empyrean, the one that arches above the strange house of Europe, full of whispers and echoes, where the destinies of nations were decided. The signatory, a mysterious Englishman who ended his letter with three stars and a bloodstain, is a *non sequitur*; the recipient was going elsewhere, but the glimpse, if that is what it is, into the Montevidean's room is unforgettable. And perhaps after all the tattooed shade of Jean Cabri, held in trust for fifty years by the faithful Leroy, did go with the disincarnate Comte on his last journey.

On the evening of the day of Ducasse's death there occurred what Alistair Horne calls *probably the most extraordinary mishap of the entire war.* For some time the Communards had been planning the Great Sortie, an attempt to break through the Prussian blockade of Paris and link up with revolutionary French forces in the provinces beyond. This attempt was initially planned to take place to the north west, where the German forces were weakest, but news of Gambetta's success in

Orleans decided Trochu, the Parisian commander, to change plans and attempt to break out in the south-east, before looping around to link up with Gambetta in the south-west. This change of plan took place only a few days before the planned sortie, necessitating a vast rearrangement of forces—400 guns, 54 pontoons and 80 000 men with their equipment and supplies—from one side of the city to the other. It was also necessary to inform Gambetta of the change of plan and the date of the new sortie. This was to be done by balloon.

The appropriately named *Ville d'Orleans* was the thirty-third balloon to leave Paris during the siege. It carried a crew of two—Rolier, pilot, and Beziers, navigator—and took off in darkness shortly before midnight from the Gare du Nord in a moderate south-south-east breeze. The two men aboard assumed they were heading towards unoccupied north-west France, even when, at dawn, they could see nothing below them but fog. As the fog finally rolled away, the men realised to their dismay that the rumbling noise below them, which they thought had been made by trains, was in fact the sound of waves. They were flying over the sea.

They saw ships below and let out a guide rope, hoping someone aboard might be able to grab it, but no one appeared even to notice their presence. Then they decided to seek safety in height and jettisoned ballast in order to rise: amongst it was the 60-kilogram bag of dispatches containing the message upon which the fate of Paris depended. It became so cold the men's moustaches froze; Beziers gallantly took off his mantle to warm the carrier pigeons also aboard. On the afternoon of the 25th the balloon began to descend rapidly, and suddenly out of the clouds the top of a pine tree appeared. Both men, without hesitation, leapt from the basket, falling twenty metres into deep soft snow. The *Ville d'Orleans*, relieved of their weight but still carrying their clothes and supplies, as well as the unhappy pigeons, soared aloft.

The aeronauts struggled down a mountain through thick snow for hours before finding a deserted cabin to shelter in for the night; they had no idea where they were until, struggling on next day, they came across another cabin, this time clearly tenanted. When its occupants, two peasants dressed in furs, turned up, speaking a strange language, and one of them lit a fire with a box of matches marked *Christiania*, Rolier and Beziers realised they had flown all the way to Norway, travelling 900 miles in fifteen hours. Remarkably, not only were they repatriated home but their balloon with its pigeons was also recovered, and later even the bag of dispatches was pulled from the sea by a fishing boat: unfortunately it reached Tours too late for Gambetta to do anything about coordinating his forces with Trochu's planned break-out, which was a débâcle.

This absurd episode is like something Lautréamont might have dreamed up for *The Chants of Maldoror*. It is impossible, for me at least, not to think of the Montevidean's dubious soul, with a train of attendant phantoms, as an unseen passenger on the *Ville d'Orleans*, voyaging north to trouble the lugubrious young Eduard Munch or to haunt the imagination of the ageing Henrik Ibsen. Or perhaps it dispersed into the ether as a principle of airy chaos, broadcasting across Europe the ability to revalue all values, recall lost time, or provoke the eternal recurrence of all things.

Leroy's own fate is better attested than Ducasse's, though just as strange in its way. His inconsequential, incoherent *Diary* continues intermittently right up until the last week of May 1871, the infamous Week of Blood, when French Government troops from Versailles slaughtered perhaps 30 000 Parisians for their actual or assumed part in the Commune. The most trivial of signs could lead to summary execution: a discolouration of the right shoulder, caused perhaps by a recoiling rifle butt, or the wearing of a pair of army boots. Then there was the hand test: anyone with blackened hands was assumed to have been involved either in incendiary operations or of firing a *tabatiere* rifle, which left tell-tale powder stains. One well-known French writer told how the sweep his grandmother employed to do her chimneys was apprehended by Versailles troops as he left her house after celebrating the end of the war, found to have blackened hands, put up against a wall and shot.

This too seems to have been the fate of Leroy, although in his case it was the ink-stains on his hands that caused his sudden death; or so it is related in a note in the front of his *Diary* by the same J. F. Dupuis who signed Ducasse's death certificate. It isn't clear exactly how the *Diary* came to be in the repository which now holds it; perhaps M. Dupuis was rather more careful with Leroy's writings than he was with Ducasse's literary papers, all of which disappeared, thereby fulfilling the poet's own prophecy: *Je ne laisserai pas des Mémoires.* This of course recalls the opening words of Ern Malley's Preface and Statement: *These poems are complete. There are no scoriae or unfulfilled intentions ... there is no biographical data.* If Malley is a fictional poet who seems real, Ducasse is the opposite: a real poet who seems like a fiction.

I did go to see Steven once more, some weeks after the last time I saw Mette. It was a melancholy occasion. Antipodean Books was closing down; the owners had pulled the plug on the enterprise because it wasn't making enough money to justify its existence. Steven was rueful but not surprised. Clearly he'd known for a long time that, despite his best efforts, this was going to happen. He was stacking books in what I always thought of as the library section when I came in. He seemed pleased to see me, if only because it gave him an excuse to stop what he was doing and relax for a while. We went and sat up the front under the big windows. There was a funny pause then, as we both wondered what to say next.

So, he said, *how's the work going?*

That was always an awkward question for me in those days because, self-styled writer that I was, I didn't actually do much writing. I just hung around libraries or stayed home doing background reading for the writing I was going to be doing at some later date.

Not too bad, I said. *I'm mostly just researching at the moment. Spending a lot of time at the State Library. You know.*

Half your luck, he said, looking gloomily around the store with its books piled everywhere.

I was relieved to have got past that one relatively unscathed.

What'll happen to them all?

The books? They'll go back to the warehouse and sit there doing nothing, instead of doing nothing here.

Could it have been different?

He looked hard at me then, as if it was a real question with implications beyond its ostensible intent.

I imagine it could always have been different, don't you?

He shrugged, eyebrows raised, as if we shared more than the equivocal status of our separate occupations. There was another silence.

How is Mette? I said, as if we had been talking about her all along, which in a way we had.

Ah ... she's depressed. She's lost her job too. Obelisk closed last week.

Oh dear.

Yeah, bit of a triple whammy, isn't it? Things were going quite nicely there for a while, then ... bang. Mind you, I always knew my days here were numbered. Speciality bookshops ...

I was mulling over the implications of that 'triple'. It seemed bizarre indeed that I should be feeling guilty over the breaking off of my affair with Mette, but that's how it was.

I was getting too fond of her, I said. *I wanted more.*

I know, Steven said. *I'm not blaming you. It's happened before. It's like asking for the impossible. You want things just so, and sometimes you get them just so, but it never lasts.*

He was being incredibly decent about it all, I thought; too decent probably. I would rather he'd got angry or upset. His calm resignation felt almost like an affront.

She's a fascinating woman, I said, inanely.

Do you think so? he replied, apparently genuinely interested in the comment. *I guess I know her so well I hardly think about who she is any more. I'm just trying to keep her happy. You know ...*

He looked as if he was going to say more but he didn't. Yet I knew what it was he didn't say, the way you sometimes do. He meant she was a potential suicide; but there didn't seem to be anything I could usefully say about it.

What will you do?

We might go back to the Old Dart for a while. A holiday, but check it out as well. I know people in the trade in London.

And Mette?

I don't know. Hopefully she'll pick herself up again. She's done it before.

What about you?

What about me?

His eyes were blue, wide open, empty as the sky. He seemed like one without illusions, lacking even the necessary fictions we use to keep us going.

I'll be fine, he said with finality, standing up and going over to the rack where the books on the Pacific were kept. *I'd better get back to work though. I've only got to the end of the week.*

He gathered up an armload of books, selected seemingly at random.

Here, he said, *you have these. I've got no use for them any more.*

But ...

Doesn't matter, they'll never miss them. Go on, take them. They're yours.

I took the books. H. E. Maude's *Slavers in Paradise: The Peruvian Slave trade in Polynesia, 1862–1864* (Canberra, 1981); the first volume of O. H. K. Spate's majestic trilogy, *The Spanish Lake: The Pacific since Magellan* (Canberra, 1979); *We, the Navigators* (Canberra, 1972), David Lewis's classic study of ocean voyaging in Micronesia and Polynesia; and Robert C. Suggs' *Marquesan Sexual Behaviour* (London, 1966), an anthropological and historical study of sexual practices in the islands.

Thanks, Steven, I said. *Thanks very much.*

That's alright, he said, giving me that cold blue look again. *Hope you make good use of them. Now ...*

I took the hint. We shook hands and I went to go.

I'd say come up and see us sometime, said Steven with a crooked smile, *except I know you won't.*

I might, I said. *See you then ...*

See you.

The next time I walked past the Anthony Hordern Building it was a roar of dust and noise. Demolition had begun. Most of it was timber, and while the more substantial pieces were sold off and reused in other buildings in Sydney or in country New South Wales, the bulk of it was trashed. Some of the window fittings and window displays were saved and are now in the Powerhouse Museum. The site itself, given over to a building, or group of buildings, modestly called World Square, was abandoned after the crash of '87 with only the foundations and a part of the core built. For twenty years a great oblong monolith stood erect like an unkempt obelisk in a waste of rusty iron reinforcing and bare concrete, an enormous crane hanging proprietorial over it, but now building has resumed. I never saw Steven or Mette again.

II

salvation

A little more than two years after *The Keeper of Sheep* by Alberto Caeiro was written, three small shepherd children in the *serra* north and east of Lisbon saw the Angel of Portugal appear above an olive grove belonging to one of their godfathers. Lucia de Jesus Santos and her cousins Francisco and Jacinta Marta used to take their sheep to graze on small plots of land owned by their parents in different parts of the *serra*, the mountainous plateau on which stood the villages of Fátima, where the parish church was, and Aljustrel, where the three *pastorinhos* actually lived. Two favourite grazing areas were the hillside facing Aljustrel, near an outcrop called Loca do Cabeco (Place of the Head), and the Cova da Iria (Cove of Irene) at some distance beyond Fátima. On this occasion they had gone to a plot at the bottom of the Cabeco, facing east, called Chousa Velha.

About the middle of the morning it began to drizzle so, followed by their sheep, they climbed up the hill in search of a rock to shelter behind. They found it in the olive grove that extended as far as the villages the children could see in the valley below them. The rain stopped and the sun began shining from a clear sky but they stayed where they were, eating lunch and playing a game with pebbles; Francisco was blowing his reed flute when a strong wind began to shake the trees. In the distance above the olives trees in the east they saw a light whiter than snow in the form of a young man, transparent and brilliant as crystal in the rays of the sun. They were astonished and said nothing to one another. The angel came nearer and told them to pray, and knelt down himself, bending his forehead to the ground. The children prayed with him, repeating after him three times the words he said. Then the angel rose, told them their prayers would be heard, and disappeared, leaving the children *in an atmosphere of the supernatural that was so intense we were for a long time unaware of our own existence.*

Some time during the summer of 1916 the three cousins were playing in the heat of the day in the garden near a well behind the Santos home in Aljustrel when the angel came again, this time to chastise them for their *lack of spiritual seriousness.* Why spiritual seriousness should have been demanded of such young children is a moot point. There was another apparition later that summer, at Cabeco; this time the angel appeared with a chalice in his left hand and, held over it in his other hand, a host which dripped blood into the cup. This was given to Francisco and Jacinta to drink, while the host itself was given to Lucia. Then, on 13 May in the following year, 1917, at the Cova da Iria, the Virgin Mary appeared to the children.

This was the first of six apparitions over the next six months, all on the thirteenth apart from the August event which was delayed because the Mayor had taken the children into custody. Again, all but one of the apparitions occurred at the Cova, above a Holm oak tree which still stands there. The Virgin came cowled and dressed in a white robe with gold threads, and spoke to the two girls; Francisco, the boy, saw but did not hear her. The girls would tell him later what she said. Her message seems, from this vantage, somewhat repetitive: pray; suffer; you will go to heaven; return here on the thirteenth of each month; in October I will accomplish a miracle.

The children tried to keep the apparition secret, as instructed, but Jacinta, aged only seven, was unable to stop herself telling her mother, and the news soon spread around the village and beyond. Lucia's mother did not believe her daughter and tried to make her withdraw her testimony, which she thought fraudulent if not actually blasphemous; when Lucia would not recant, her mother hauled her before the village priest. Soon local communities were divided between those who believed a miracle had occurred and those who thought the apparitions a fraud or a nonsense. This mirrored political divisions between the Catholic devout and atheistic Freemasons—for which read Republicans. Even the clergy at this early stage were not sure: perhaps the visions were of demonic origin?

In Portugal 13 June is the feast of St Anthony of Lisbon, known to most Catholics as St Anthony of Padua. It was and is the children's feast, so Lucia's parents thought that the festivities at the parish church in Fátima might distract her from the appointment at the Cova. However, Lucia and the Marto children proceeded undismayed to the site to keep their noonday rendezvous. When they arrived they found a small crowd awaiting them. The Virgin appeared as before, making the same exhortations but this time adding the advice that the children should learn to read and write. None of those who gathered saw what the children did, but some claimed to see the lightning which always preceded an apparition, some a dimming of the sun, others a little grey cloud that came and went as the apparition did.

The third apparition, on 13 July, was the most controversial, principally because it was during this event that the famous—or notorious—three secrets of Fátima were imparted to the children. In the month leading up to the July rendezvous Lucia experienced such tension and fear that she decided not to go—only to change her mind when the day itself came. The first secret was a vision of hell: *Our Lady showed us a great sea of fire which seemed to be under the earth. Plunged in this fire were demons and souls in human form, like transparent burning embers, all blackened or burnished bronze, floating about in the conflagration, now raised into the air by the flames that issued from within themselves together with great clouds of smoke, now falling back on every side like sparks in a huge fire, without weight or equilibrium, and amid shrieks and groans of pain and despair, which horrified us and made us tremble with fear. The demons could be distinguished by their terrifying and repulsive likeness to frightful and unknown animals, all black and transparent. This vision lasted but an instant ... Otherwise, I think we would have died of fear and terror.*

The second secret was a prophecy—the war will end, but if people do not mend their ways, a worse one will succeed it: *When you see a night illumined by an unknown light, know that this is the great sign given you by God that he is about to punish the world for its crimes, by means of war, famine, and persecutions of the Church and of the Holy Father. To prevent this, I shall come to ask for the consecration of Russia to my Immaculate Heart ...* The consecration of Russia, the Virgin says, will come; but if it comes later rather than sooner, Russia will spread her errors abroad and there will be martyrdom and the annihilation of nations.

The third secret told to Lucia and Jacinta was not to be revealed to anyone but Francisco—and for the time being it was not; but the possession of the secret was a great trial for the children. Family, neighbours, followers of the apparitions, even the clergy tried unsuccessfully to get them to reveal it. Finally, as 13 August approached, the local civil government, which was secular and anti-clerical and alarmed by the number of people taking an interest in the Fátima events, attempted to force the secret from the children and in the process expose the Church as a collaborator in a fraud.

Under the pretext of providing his personal automobile so that the children could travel safely to the Cova through the crowds pressing around their homes, the Mayor of the district, Artur Santos, *an apostate Catholic and high Mason*, arrived in Aljustrel on the morning of 13 August. He offered to take the three children and their parents to see the parish priest and then on to the Cova. At the parish house he abandoned this plan, and the parents too, taking the children alone from there to the district headquarters in Vila Nova de Ourem some nine miles away. Here, it is alleged, he offered bribes, made threats and locked the children in a cell with other criminals in order to get them to recant—to no avail. Meanwhile in the Cova there was no apparition, but the characteristic external signs appeared for the benefit of the crowd, the largest assembled to that time. The children were soon released.

In September 30 000 people gathered at the site, and for the sixth and final visitation there were more than twice that number. What followed became known as The Miracle of the Sun, reported in these words by the Lisbon daily *O Dia* (17 October 1917): *At one o'clock in the afternoon, midday by the sun, the rain stopped. The sky, pearly grey in colour, illuminated the vast arid landscape with a strange light. The sun had a transparent gauzy veil so that the eyes could easily be fixed upon it. The grey mother-of-pearl tone turned into a sheet of silver which broke up as the clouds were torn apart and the silver sun, enveloped in the same gauzy grey light, was seen to whirl and turn in the circle of broken clouds. A cry went up from every mouth and people fell on their knees on the muddy ground ... The light turned a beautiful blue, as if it had come through the stained-glass windows of a cathedral, and spread itself over the people who knelt with outstretched hands. The blue faded slowly, and then the light seemed to pass through yellow glass. Yellow stains fell against white handkerchiefs, against the dark skirts of the women. They were repeated on the trees, on the stones and on the serra. People wept and prayed with uncovered heads, in the presence of a miracle they had awaited. The seconds seemed like hours, so vivid were they.*

There was one further apparition three years later, when the Virgin appeared for the last time to Lucia alone—Francisco and Jacinta had both died in the aftermath of the influenza epidemic which followed World War One. Lucia became a discalced (that is, sandal-less) Carmelite nun, and, during World War Two, in August 1941, wrote down the first two secrets; later, at the behest of the Bishop of Leiria, in January 1944 she committed the third secret to writing. The text was sealed and given into the care of the Vatican in 1957; it was read by each new Pope on his accession and then returned to the archives. The contents, it was believed, were so incendiary they could not be revealed; most people thought they referred to trouble and strife within the Catholic Church itself and perhaps amplified upon the apocalyptic Revelations of St John the Divine.

I was researching the Cova da Iria apparitions because a friend of mine, Johnny Bear, was writing a screenplay called *The Third Secret of Fátima* and I'd said I'd help by talking things over with him and typing up his longhand draft. Johnny had been raised and educated a Catholic and carried the scars of it still—among other things, he had been sexually abused by a priest as a young child. Now he was writing his revenge. It was not, however, a bitter tract or tragic melodrama; it was a comedy structured as a road movie. I couldn't help laughing at some of Johnny's innovations. The hero of the movie is called Hero, a down-and-out courier who drives a battered Holden ute with only one headlight and a model of the Sydney Opera House and the Harbour Bridge permanently affixed to the tray. The model was made as a prop for a commercial but never paid for, so Hero kept it. He is under extreme pressure from the law because of unpaid traffic fines, and lives a fugitive life racing around the streets of the city trying, mostly unsuccessfully, to elude the parking police.

The heroine of the film, a beautiful, sexy, thirty-something advertising agency rep and, like Hero, a lapsed Catholic, is called Sheila. She is, despite herself, oddly attracted to the disreputable Hero, though to all appearances right out of his league. Once she realises he is a good soul on a divine mission she can't help but join him. The third main character, Bullbar, is an Aboriginal man who grew up on a Catholic mission station somewhere outback; he wields in equal measure the magic of his own people and that of the nuns who raised him. The film is not irreligious; instead, it is about a clash of good magic with bad, white with black. The villains of the piece are the Felicitae Society, the Vatican's secret police. They are in Australia because Lucia—Sister Lucy—has fled Europe in order to escape the oppressive scrutiny of the Papacy and to reveal at last to the world the Third Secret. Hero starts receiving messages from her via envelopes that appear, like parking tickets, tucked under the windscreen wipers of the ute. Or are they from the sinister Felicitae Society?

Hero, Sheila and Bullbar set out from Sydney for Darwin in the Northern Territory, braving the worst the Felicitae goons can throw at them, as well as a variety of bizarre characters they meet on the road, in a race to reach Sister Lucy before she dies or is recaptured. She has chosen Darwin because there is a branch of the Fátima cult there. Processions, which sometimes include flagellants, are held on significant feast days. The Fátima worshippers are displaced Portuguese-speaking Timorese who emigrated to Australia after the events of 1975, when the Indonesian military moved in and took over a few months after Portugal allowed East Timor its independence. In the film these errant Timorese are not exactly anti-Papal but nor are they quite orthodox either. The infallibility of the Pope is of less interest to them than the possibility of the direct intervention of the Virgin in their lives. Many of them live from the sea and Marianism in its various forms has always been popular with fisher folk. Now they are looking after Sister Lucy and, like everyone else, desperate to find out what the Third Secret is.

It is a perhaps curious coincidence that on 24 June 1916, at the exact same time as the first visitation of the angel to the *pastorinhos*, Fernando Pessoa wrote to his Aunt Anica that he had begun *to become a medium. Imagine! Me ... who was always a backward member in the semi-spiritualist séances we used to have ...* Pessoa's mediumship included periods of automatic writing during which he would take down drawings and diagrams; the intermittent ability to see auras, even through a person's clothes and skin; spirit possession; and the faculty to intuit events from afar, as when, also in 1916, he fell into a sudden depression *from outside* when his friend Sa-Carniero in Paris was going through the great mental crisis which led to his suicide. His spirits, rather in the way the angel exhorted the three *pastorinhos* to learn reading and writing, insisted that he make an effort to lose his virginity, perhaps thereby initiating the doomed affair with Ophelia Quieroz.

Pessoa only once in his writings so far as I know refers to the events at Fátima, and then it is simply to make it clear he thinks they are nonsense. With his longstanding interest in Freemasonry, the Rosy Cross, the Knights Templar, the Knights of Malta, Gnostic heresies, astrology and the personal relationship he had with Aleister Crowley, the Great Beast, he was hardly likely to go along with a mass delusion orchestrated and perpetuated by the Catholic Church, which clearly coached the children from early on and continued to watch over Lucia for the rest of her life. It is inconceivable, however, that Pessoa did not understand the part the Fátima events later played in consolidating the Salazar dictatorship, and it is probably also for this reason that there is in José Saramago's *The Year of the Death of Ricardo Reis*—the book which first made the name of Fernando Pessoa known to me—a description of the annual pilgrimage to Fátima, this from the year 1936.

Saramago's elegant fiction begins with the arrival of the heteronym Ricardo Reis in Lisbon. Upon hearing the news of Fernando Pessoa's death (in 1935, of liver failure after a lifetime of heavy drinking), Reis has decided to return from Brazil to his home country. He books into a hotel and embarks upon a new life which, progressively and eerily, decays into a half-life and then no life at all. He reads newspapers; begins an affair with Lydia, a chambermaid in the hotel; falls in love with another young woman, Marcenda, who has a paralysed hand;

has inconsequential encounters with various casually met people; is summoned and investigated by the police; becomes a locum for a heart doctor; and in and amongst all these events and non-events receives visits from his friend and author. Pessoa makes no bones about his status: he's dead, but the dead are able to persist in the world for a little while before their final departure from it. (He is in the same tomb as the Aunt Anica to whom he confessed his burgeoning mediumship and she is driving him crazy with her questions.) He also makes sly jokes about Reis' dependency upon him, as when he suggests the other has never had a thought without he, Fernando, having had it first.

The poignancy of the novel arises from the fact that Reis does not realise he is a fiction; he assumes, as we all do, that he exists and has some reality in the world. Over the course of the book the knowledge that this is not so is gradually borne upon him and he begins to fade. Meanwhile he continues to read the newspapers: a masterful strain in the novel is its understated yet devastating account of the rise of Fascism in Europe through journalistic accounts of the Italian adventure in Abyssinia, the genesis of civil war in Spain, the implacable tightening of António de Oliveira Salazar's grip on power in Portugal; with the awful shadow of events in Germany a grim cloud on the horizon.

The ironies of the novel are manifold and too complex to rehearse here. One which may be is that Ricardo Reis goes on a pilgrimage to Fátima on 13 May without telling Fernando Pessoa. Nor does he inform him afterwards that he has been there: the heteronym proves in this instance able to act without the fore- or post-knowledge of his creator—to go behind his back, as it were. He goes to Fátima not because he believes (Reis is a pagan) but in the hope of seeing Marcenda there. She does not believe either, but her father is devout and has convinced her that her afflicted hand, which she has not been able to use since the death of her mother some years before, might be healed through the intercession of the Virgin.

Over 200 000 people gathered *like a great black swarm of bees in pursuit of divine honey* at Fátima in 1936. As if observing the detail of a medieval pageant, Ricardo Reis inspects the hospital, the tents, the *bustling esplanade*, the open-air markets where scapulars, trinkets and baubles are sold; he distinguishes the false beggars from the true and watches the procession of the statue of the Virgin as it is brought out from the Chapel of the Apparitions, carried around, then taken back in. Saramago comments: *The blind still could not see, the dumb still could not speak, the paralysed were still paralysed, missing limbs did not grow back, and the pains of the afflicted were not diminished. Weeping bitter tears, they accused and blamed themselves* ... In the end there is no miracle and the usually impeccably turned out Reis, after spending a night sleeping rough and without finding any trace of Marcenda or her father, returns bedraggled and somehow disillusioned (but what illusions did he have?) to Lisbon, there to continue his inexorable progress towards unreality.

I found a copy of Giovanni Pontiero's excellent translation of *O No da More de Ricardo Reis* (Lisbon, 1984) in the Kings Cross library not long after I moved to live in Womerah Lane, Darlinghurst, at the end of the 1980s. Next to it on the shelf was Margaret Jull Costa's English version of *Livro do desassossego por Bernardo Soares*, which I read next—although to say that suggests a degree of finality which it is not possible to achieve with respect to the writings of Fernando Pessoa. There are multiple editions in both English and Portuguese as well as other languages of *The Book of Disquiet* but none include all of the pieces Pessoa intended to go into it, for the simple reason that none but he knew which they were and even he frequently changed his mind about what belonged in it and what didn't. Most of them were written on single sheets of paper and were among the more than 27 543 separate items found in Fernando Pessoa's trunk after he died; but the order in which he had placed them was soon irretrievably lost. *The Book of Disquiet* is in fact an infinite book, a labyrinth within the labyrinth of Pessoa's other writings in his own name or in the names of his seventy-two heteronyms. Anyone who engages with this oeuvre enters the maze without hope or perhaps desire of ever exiting; and, if they write as well, cannot avoid adding paths, with their inevitable false leads, non sequiturs and dead endings, to that maze.

For the moment, though, *The Book of Disquiet* was a perfect accompaniment to the life I was leading in my new flat, which I had inherited from a friend who had moved in with her boyfriend in Erskineville. I could sit in the window up one end, looking out into the leafy branches of the false cherries that grew there, with Barcom Avenue's traffic rumbling below and the vastness of St Vincent's hospital beyond, and imagine myself in some Lisbon of the mind. The flat was spacious and run down, the top storey of a crumbling terrace house in a row of crumbling terraces which you approached from a laneway, through a rickety wooden gate, a dusty garden and a set of stairs leading to a catwalk that terminated at the back, the kitchen, the only door.

It resembled a tram, I thought, with five rooms in a line. First the kitchen with its red plastic floor, its outré external plumbing, its false pinewood wall, its derisory facilities for cooking and washing: hot water had to be got from the caliphont in the tiny bathroom next door, beyond which was the only bedroom with its single window perched above a deep well leading to the entrance of the downstairs flat where another tenant lived. There was a curious revolving door above the bed, through which you could pass plates of food or cups of coffee into the double sitting room with its end wall made up entirely of windows that could be slid and left open—at least until a cat burglar one night contrived to hoist him or herself up the almost sheer wall and over the sill to steal the contents of my wallet. This sitting room was large enough to include dining table and chairs, a sofa down one end and a divan bed at the other, as well as my desk and bookshelves, without seeming in the least cluttered. The walls had been painted pale grey; the white ceiling with its complex geography of watermarks peeled and flaked gently above; and the floor was covered in green felt that made it look like a vast billiard table. This felt, unfortunately, was made with nylon and loathsome to touch; I covered it with cheap woven mats which inspired my landlord, a miserly Greek named Nick Marinakos, to call me a *pasha*.

Nick lived across the lane in Womerah Street with his aged sister Mary. They were from a small Egyptian town on the Red Sea. Nick had worked during World War Two in some capacity—stores, perhaps—for the RAF. After the war he and, later, Mary emigrated; Nick worked first in the Aeroplane Jelly factory, then in a commercial warehouse of some kind and finally, and for the rest of his employed life, at the Land and Deeds Office. He was now retired and stayed at home, where Mary had always been, looking after him: she had, it seems, come out to Australia for that very reason when their parents, whom she cared for previously, died.

To step into their house, as I did every fortnight when I paid the rent, was to step back in time to the 1950s. The front room, which gave onto the street, was draped and dim, with dark shapeless furniture ranged around the walls and a space in the centre for a small low table with small low seats on either side. Up the front and to one side was a tiny galley kitchen where Mary prepared their food. Every flat surface was covered in layers of a variety of lace, cotton or plastic sheeting without colour or definition; all cupboards were curtained with faded fifties clothes. It was dank in there and smelled of cooking and aged bodies and some indefinable other thing that probably had to do with the fact that the room was never aired. Here Mary would serve me the inevitable sweet cake which accompanied the handing over of the modest amount I paid them for the flat; and here for twenty minutes or so we would exchange remarks that hardly varied either.

Nick was a small man, upright, grey-haired, with brownish-grey skin; Mary was smaller, slighter, also grey, and stooped; her skin seemed not to have felt the sun for many a long year and was, in contradistinction to Nick's, greyish-brown. I never once saw her in the street, although she could sometimes be glimpsed in their concreted backyard, putting out or bringing in the washing; her life must have been one of scarcely believable circumscription and repetition. She washed, cooked, ironed, cleaned and mended her own clothes and Nick's, staying home alone on those days when he put on his suit and went out to the Greek Club to play cards with his friends and, perhaps, visit a brothel afterwards.

Whatever furtive pleasures Nick might have had, Mary had none; she was not even allowed elementary comforts like a heater in winter—because electricity cost money. My friend who preceded me in the flat tells a story about how Mary, one July or August, put out her hands so my friend could feel them: they were cold as ice. Nick can't have lacked money; he was just incapable of spending it. He would wait, for instance, until Iris, the Cypriot woman who ran the corner store, discounted the black bananas and the other fruit gone soft or bad before buying any. His miserliness took other, weirder forms: he would scour the lane for rubbish before the Council's weekly collection because as a ratepayer he wanted to take maximum advantage of the service by making sure his own bin was always full. To this end he would also gather up the leaves from the avocado and the frangipani trees overlooking my yard, then carefully carry them away too.

Nick had a small store of conversational gambits he liked to bring out like coins from his pocket. One of his favourites was: *Do we eat to live or live to eat?* He would say this and laugh and shake his head at the incommensurability of things. On one occasion Mary got out her schoolbooks to show me, ancient flat exercise books half full of faded pencilled writing: she had, long ago, a yen for languages, and these books represented her efforts to learn French and Italian to go with her native Greek and her English. More often, though, conversation with Nick and Mary led to a wordless lament at the way the world was going, a literal wringing of the hands accompanied by a shaking of the head and a low, throaty *ooh, pah-pah-pah-pah-pah*. I sometimes felt they talked at all only to arrive at an opportunity to make this lamentation, which they would indulge in chorus like two old peasants faced with the implacable enmity of fate.

Nick didn't only come over to sweep up the leaves; there was also the ritual of *collecting the pennies*. The gas caliphont that was the only source of hot water in the flat took not pennies but shillings, or rather ten-cent pieces; the only sensible way to operate was to keep every one you got and feed them en masse into the meter so it was always in credit and you never had the inconvenience of the shower going cold halfway through or there not being enough hot water to do the dishes. Nick paid the gas bill himself, and his weekly or fortnightly pilgrimage to *get the pennies* was always accompanied by the melancholy information that there was a shortfall between what he collected from me and what he paid the gas company. Clearly there needed to be either an upgrading of the meter so it took, say, twenty-cent pieces, or else some re-calibration so that my ten cents bought me less gas; but Nick was constitutionally unable, it seemed, to undertake any capital expense, even one that would save him money in the long run. Instead he would complain, perhaps resent, and lament ... *ooh, pah-pah-pah-pah* ...

Nick, I found out later, made other, unscheduled visits. On one occasion, a Saturday, when I had gone out early and left a friend sleeping in the bed, Elle was woken by the kitchen door opening, then heard the shuffle of Nick's slippered feet up the hallway and on into the sitting room. Next, the unmistakable rustle of a newspaper being opened. For the following half or three-quarters of an hour Elle lay quiet in the bed while Nick, at his leisure, a *pasha* himself for the moment, read the *Sydney Morning Herald*. When he finished he folded the newspaper and shuffled out again. I never said anything to him about this visit, which could not have been the only one: he was obsessive about security, and he and Mary watched the flat through their back windows at all hours; presumably he came over and read the paper in my sitting room whenever the opportunity presented itself.

Nick also visited the flat of Jimmy Bonus, the downstairs tenant, when he wasn't there. It was his rite of possession, I guess. Jimmy, a Filipino cook in the merchant marine, came and went, working six weeks on, six weeks off. When he was ashore his presence down below was olfactory before all else: he was fond of cooking up stews that were somehow pungent and rancid at once, so much so that I used to joke he was cooking up human flesh à la Jeffrey Dalmer. It was a sick joke that subsequent events made even sicker. Jimmy was a heavy smoker, so his tobacco residues also drifted through the floorboards and up the blocked-off stairwell, as did the startlingly aromatic cheap perfume he used to douse himself with before he went up to Kings Cross looking for action. When in a very good mood he would augment this odoriferous cocktail with a musical accompaniment, playing unidentifiable tunes on a tinny organ and singing moaningly along with himself. For all that, Jimmy was a good neighbour: pleasantly spoken, mostly unobtrusive, often away. Or so it seemed.

By the time I became a subject of Nick's little empire, Johnny Bear was so ill it was clear he would never finish writing *The Third Secret*

of Fátima. He had AIDS, contracted, he said, on an occasion which he and others who were present remembered: something weird went around the circle as one by one they shot up and passed the needle on. It could only have been the incursion of the virus, the alien breaching the boundaries of the body, the beginning of replication, the copy of a copy of a death.

What to do? It wasn't, strictly speaking, a collaboration in any usual sense; I was Johnny's scribe, his amanuensis, not his co-writer. I'd contributed various research and writing skills to the project but there was never any question that it was Johnny's story and he had to tell it. His comic touch with dialogue and action was something I couldn't match. Without ever really talking about it, we came to the realisation that there was nothing to be done. We had to leave Hero, Sheila and Bullbar stranded somewhere on the north coast of NSW, in a truck stop far from home and further from Darwin, with the goons from the Felicitae Society in their sinister long black limo closing fast. There was no revelation of any secret; as Ricardo Reis found at the Cove of Irene: *There was no miracle after all.*

Some years later, on 26 June 2000, the Vatican did release the text of the Third Secret, thereby bringing, the official press release said, *to an end a period of history marked by tragic human lust for power and evil.* The incumbent Pope, who believed he survived the assassination attempt on 13 May 1981 only through the intercession of Our Lady of Fátima, and who visited the Cova da Iria three times during his protracted Papacy, decided to clear the slate as the new millennium began. The disclosure of the secret was preceded by the beatification of Francisco and Jacinta Marto and by a conversation between the Pope and Sister Lucia, by then an immensely old nun in the Carmelite Convent of St Teresa at Coimbra, Portugal, after which the attempted assassin's bullet was placed, grotesquely, in the crown of the statue of the Virgin at Fátima.

Lucia's text reads: *After the two parts which I have already explained, at the left of Our Lady and a little above, we saw an Angel with a flaming sword in his left hand; flashing, it gave out flames that looked as though they would set the world on fire; but they died out in contact with the splendor that Our Lady radiated towards him from her right hand: pointing to the earth with his right hand, the*

Angel cried out in a loud voice: Penance, Penance, Penance! And we saw in an immense light that is God—something similar to how people appear in a mirror when they pass in front of it—a Bishop dressed in White, who was the Holy Father. Other Bishops, Priests, religious men and women were going up a steep mountain, at the top of which there was a big Cross of rough-hewn trunks as of a cork-tree with the bark; before reaching there the Holy Father passed through a big city half in ruins, and half trembling with halting step, afflicted with pain and sorrow, he prayed for the souls of the corpses he met on his way; having reached the top of the mountain, on his knees at the foot of the big Cross he was killed by a group of soldiers who fired bullets and arrows at him, and in the same way there died one after another the other Bishops, Priests, men and women Religious, and various lay people of different ranks and positions. Beneath the two arms of the Cross there were two Angels each with a crystal aspersorium in his hand, in which they gathered up the blood of the Martyrs and with it sprinkled the souls that were making their way to God.

I wish Johnny had lived to tell the tale; I wish, too, he was here to mull over with me what this secret really means and why it was concealed for so long. Upon its release the Vatican published a detailed interpretation of the meaning of the vision that is, at least to me, more or less unreadable. The general drift seems to be that we are still, as in 1917, involved in a war between atheism and the Faith, and unless humanity repents and does penance extermination will be our lot. From a lay point of view it looks as if the prophecy of the killing of the Pope along with all of his retinue might have had something to do with the long suppression of the secret; and the image of him passing through the ruined city *half trembling with halting step, afflicted* was of course strangely accurate to the aged John Paul II's Parkinsonian state.

Discalced Carmelites take a vow of silence, but after the April 2000 meeting with the Pope, Sister Lucia was given permission to write and publish a book on the apparitions. On 13 February 2005, at the age of ninety-seven, she died and was buried in the convent that had been her home since 1948. She had asked to be laid to rest alongside the two other *pastorinhos*; and so, on 19 February 2006, before 100 000 people and in persistent rain, her body was reburied in the shrine at Fátima. It is impossible to know what other secrets she may have taken with her to the grave.

Elle and I had been seeing each other for about a year when I moved to Darlinghurst; it was perhaps another year before she moved in there with me. Sometime during that second twelve-month period there occurred the episodes I have since come to call the heroin weddings. They happened like this. The sister of the friend from whom I inherited the flat in Womerah Lane was married to a Greek guy called Ed, and Ed had a mate called Bill, a Chinese, who acted as an agent for illegal immigrants. A conduit, if you like. Bill had on his books a number of young men, all Chinese nationals, who claimed to be political refugees fleeing the crackdown after the massacre at Tiananmen Square; they were seeking women to marry so as to legitimise their presence in Australia. The going rate for a bride was between $5000 and $10 000, depending on the wealth of the groom, to be paid in instalments over the period of the courtship, the ceremony itself and the divorce a year or so later. The bride had to be an Australian resident, unmarried and willing to spend time being photographed with her future husband: walking in the park, shopping, going to restaurants and so forth. Bill chaperoned these activities, photographed and paid for them too.

He was very well organised. Clothes, photos, gifts and other items of a personal nature belonging to the grooms-to-be were delivered to the houses of the brides-to-be so that, in the event of a snap visit by immigration authorities either before or after the knot was tied, the illusion of cohabitation could be sustained. The brides-to-be had to learn the history of their prospective husband's flight from China, as well as the romantic tale of how they met and fell in love; they were examined periodically to make sure they had both stories straight. The language question, a point of great vulnerability, was barely discussed; most brides- and grooms-to-be could only converse, if at all, in broken English; the rest of the time they used sign language.

There was a tame celebrant, a woman, a Justice of the Peace, who officiated, and a function centre in the eastern suburbs where all of the marriages took place. Presumably both the celebrant and the staff at the function centre were in on the deal, but this was never conceded;

they behaved at all times as if providing a legitimate service. Nevertheless, the weddings were occasions during which the appearance of things and their reality irrevocably sundered, and this was only partly because of the amount of heroin the brides-to-be consumed.

For the exchange of packets of the drug was a silent accompaniment to the other, more obvious exchanges going on. Ed, rapid of gait and plausible of manner, motor-mouthed, thin as a ghost, with a pointed face seemingly made for nosing into the cracks in doors, used to deal, and his probable original relationship with Bill was that of buyer to seller. A proportion of the funds earned thus tended to flow back via Ed to Bill to pay for the packets of white powder; and the inevitable stresses and strains of the lead-up to and consummation of the fraud were thus eased by the contents of the tiny envelopes which Ed brought around at various times in order to pamper and calm the brides-to-be.

Heroin was not a new discovery for either of us. Elle had been using it off and on for years as her recreational drug of choice. My own always casual acquaintance with it goes back many years to when I was a young student of twenty and lived in a house with an addict who, companionably, used to share with me sometimes. I have never sought it out but always taken it when it was there. At this time, when Elle said she felt like some—or, as she liked to put it, felt like being bad—I'd go halves with her. We didn't use needles. We smoked, chasing the dragon: the heroin would be made into a line on a piece of aluminium foil, the foil held over a flame until the powder melted to a brown bubbling resin giving off a thick white smoke which you inhaled through a straw, a rolled-up bank note, or a hooter made of a used piece of foil. Afterwards we usually went to bed, because there is nothing like heroin for sex. There were only two problems with the drug—it was expensive and we never seemed able to get quite enough of it at any one time. Until the heroin weddings, that is, when it flowed like milk and honey in the proverbial land.

Of the three weddings I attended Elle's was the last; and, as at both of the others, the bride was stoned, with that bright, brittle, glassy stare, that secret, inward-looking smile, that mask of serenity, the false presence, the real absence ... On the morning of the marriage

Ed turned up early at Elle's house, talking as he came up the stairs, talking when he went back down them fifteen or twenty minutes later. He brought Elle's wedding shoes, white slip-ons to go with the simple, elegant, white satin shift; white accoutrements, all hired; a cheque for a part of her fee; and, naturally, a packet of the white powder. After he had gone Elle made the first of many visits to the bathroom.

I remember her later, dressing in the Pink Room, which her flatmate and former lover had vacated some weeks before. The orange blossom of her bouquet lay sharp and sweet on the air. She was nervous and giggly and excited all at the same time, and, stepping into her brand new knickers, somehow, perhaps with the nail of her big toe, split them down the front. A gap about two inches long opened in the lace, through which a tuft of black curly pubic hair swelled. She stood there otherwise naked, laughing, in those cheap white lacy briefs with their intensely erotic hairy slit down the front. And stands there still.

I had not yet met her husband-to-be and could not quell a strange sense of alarm with respect to him—as if the forms of marriage might translate, by occult means, the facts of their disparate lives and turn them into real lovers. Wen was a slim, delicate young man, some years younger than Elle, wearing glasses and a suit that was too big for him. Like most of the other grooms he spoke almost no English, and he was accompanied at all times by another young man, slightly more robust of build, also wearing glasses, with bad skin. Clearly, I noted with relief, he was gay and this other man his lover. What happened at Elle's wedding, then, was the meeting of two couples who were very much in love, one of which was marrying one of the other.

Elle, though stoned, played the blushing bride to perfection. Even those who knew the illusive nature of the occasion were almost persuaded. If Wen, standing stiffly beside her, had not looked so startled, an officer of the Immigration Department itself might have been deceived. The warp in the afternoon came when I stepped forward to sign the register—irony upon irony, I was acting as a witness, writing my own name beside Elle's and her shy young boy husband's and her shy young boy husband's boyfriend's. As I leant forward to sign, in the sun-drenched veranda of that white-painted house above a garden full of blowsy azaleas, I felt the satin of Elle's dress against my arm and the ever-so-slight pressure of her hand on the outside of my thigh as if to say I was her real intended and this our authentic wedding. The photo taken of that moment, which I no longer have, could pass for such: I am smiling, pen in hand, bent forward over the book; Elle is beside me, lips parted, eyes bright with unshed tears, discreet, compliant, eager ... Only the stiff young Chinese man, the delicate homosexual son of a Beijing judge, adds a note of strangeness to what is otherwise a picture of lovers on their wedding day.

The rest of my memory of that occasion consists of vivid flashes, images which have lost their chronology and the narrative thread connecting them. Bill's courtliness, his impassivity, his decadence; the Chinese soccer player I talked to at the reception who told me with tears in his eyes that, although he had been in the national team at home, here in the new country he could not even use his real name, let alone play; the wedding guests, women friends of Elle's or of mine, in their bright dresses moving among the dark-suited Chinese; the charged atmosphere in which the sense of complicity we shared made us seem like players at a masque which, while false to the core, nevertheless acted out a real event.

Afterwards we returned to Elle's place to celebrate. One of our party, who had already married her China man, insisted that she would take her share of the heroin through a needle and spent the rest of the day and half the night retching; but Elle and I, like the royal couple in *Illuminations*, were sovereigns for the entire afternoon, leaning against each other as we made our way across the yard as if towards the palm gardens, and spending the waning hours, when the windows in the Blue Room went an antique yellow and light shivered along the splintery wooden floors, in an elaborate, gasping, exquisite dance across the golden rectangle of the bed.

There was no other consequence to Elle's marriage although, in the time I knew her, she never did obtain her divorce and so missed out on the last instalment of her fee. Wen went to live with his boyfriend in Melbourne, leaving behind a jacket I wore until it wore out, and once, about a year later, Bill flew Elle down for one more day of photographs; after that, she heard nothing more from either of them. As for the Immigration Department, they did eventually find out about the scam, because one night on a national TV current affairs show I saw the celebrant, that calm, elegant, fifty-year-old, a clipboard held in front of her face, ducking ignominiously into the shrubbery as she was pursued through a park by a journalist with a microphone and a camera crew; but no charges were ever laid. Later still, there was a report in the press of the arrest of the mastermind of an illegal immigration racket. The name of the man rang no bells, but he was Chinese and may well have been Bill; who knows?

It was not long after I went to live in Darlinghurst that a friend, Christopher, with whom I sometimes worked in a cleaning job, told me his sister had a problem I might be able to help her with. Annabelle was a student at Sydney University, studying English. She was due to hand in an essay on Australian poetry which, for some reason I no longer recall, she was unable to write. Would I do it for her? She was offering $200. She'd give me the topic and the reading list and I would do the rest. In the nature of things there wasn't much time to think about this before the deadline arrived. One day I went around to Christopher's place to meet her.

Both Annabelle and Christopher were English by birth but had lived for quite a few years in the Antipodes. Christopher was thin and tall, with straight fair hair falling round his face, and glasses with tinted lenses. His sister was also blonde; plump and attractive, if you like plump blondes, with a big wide face and a slow, blurred voice. They were very close, living together in a spacious ground-floor flat in Ithaca Road, Elizabeth Bay, with Christopher's girlfriend, whose name I have forgotten: she was, like Annabelle, big and blonde, and from the outset I had trouble telling which was the sister and which the girlfriend, not least because of the casually intimate affection with which all three treated each other.

It still seems odd to me that Christopher worked as a cleaner. He was one of those ultimately cool guys whose every act broadcasts the fact of their coolness. His clothes were just right, as were the places he went and the people he knew, the music he played and the drugs he sold. His life was all of a piece: he went clubbing almost every night, and that was where he sold the pills he had from some source which, sensibly, he never revealed. His sister and his girlfriend likewise spent their nights clubbing and their days—what was left of them after they rose late—reclining languidly on sofas in that elegant apartment, smoking cigarettes, drinking coffee and getting ready for the next evening's indulgences. Perhaps that was why Annabelle couldn't finish the essay. It might just have been the onerous demands of her social life.

These people made me nervous because I knew I lacked that indefinable something called cool; and they surely knew it too. They would probably laugh at my gaucherie when I'd gone. Or was that just paranoia? I sat down beside Annabelle on one of the sofas and she gave me a piece of paper to read: the essay topic required you to discuss nationalism and identity in twentieth-century Australian poetry, and included a list of poets, four of whom needed to be referred to extensively in your discussion. I scanned it ... Slessor, FitzGerald, Hope, Stewart, Wright, McAuley, Buckley, Webb, Beaver, Porter ... the names read like the anonymous roll calls on war memorials in town parks. None, with the exception of Kenneth Slessor, had I read for pleasure. But Stewart and McAuley were the co-authors of Ern Malley, weren't they, and one or other of the others must be worth a look. (I found out later I was mistaking my Stewarts: it was Harold who co-authored Ern, not the more prolific, Taranaki-born Douglas.)

Annabelle was gazing at me with her eyes wide open in her big flat face. I realised she was afraid I might turn the job down; that, despite her nonchalance, this was something she badly wanted to happen.

Well, I guess I could come up with something ... I said.

Could you? Really? That would be so cool.

She relaxed back onto the sofa and in her slow way lit a cigarette. Christopher, standing by the window, smiled at me over his shoulder. His girlfriend sighed from the other sofa.

I'm so bored, she said. *Christopher ... ?*

I'm meeting him at six, he said. She sighed again.

Well, I'll get going, I said.

It's too long ago to remember exactly what I wrote and foolishly I didn't keep a copy of it—the going rate for an essay out on the internet these days is a lot more than $200—but I do recall dropping a quote from Fernando Pessoa at the head of the piece: *That is the central error of the literary imagination: the idea that other people are like us and must therefore feel like us. Fortunately for humanity, each man is only himself ...*

I started out with Slessor's *Metempsychosis—*
Suddenly to become John Benbow, walking down William Street
With a tin trunk and a five pound note, looking for a place to eat
With a peajacket the colour of a shark's behind
That a Jew might buy in the morning ...
—in which the poet becomes, or rather sees himself in the process of becoming, a sailor footloose in the Sydney of the 1920s—
Suddenly paid off and forgotten in Woolloomooloo ...
Suddenly to become John Benbow ...
—then moved on to a discussion of the same author's Captain Dobbin: ... *having retired from the South Seas/In the dumb tides of 1900, with a handful of shells/A few poisoned arrows ...* he sits in his harbourside library reading, his head full of images of his life at sea, like the transmogrified mind of the ocean exiled ashore. Captain Dobbin logs all the boats coming in and out of Sydney Harbour and lives in the past or in books. He worships Cook and admires Bougainville but for some reason which isn't clear despises del Cano, the Basque who completed Magellan's voyage and was actually one of the first (only eighteen men survived to tell the tale) to circumnavigate the globe. The poem itself is a kind of inventory of the contents of the old sailor's mind and makes an implicit analogy between the ocean, a library and a consciousness.

It was interesting to realise how many of the mid-century, male Australian poets projected themselves into the minds of sailors, explorers, adventurers and the like. The aforementioned Douglas Stewart, in *Terra Australis,* manages to become both Captain Quieroz, who in 1606 made a disastrous attempt to establish a colony at Austrialia del Espiritu Santos in what is now Vanuatu, and William Lane, the founder, in 1891, of New Australia, a utopian socialist and proto-racist ideal community in Paraguay; Lane would later espouse militarism and racial purity on both sides of the Tasman, and become editor of the *New Zealand Herald* in which he orchestrated a campaign of hysterical exhortations towards military recruitment during World War One.

The analogy between ocean and mind is made explicit in the first stanza of *Terra Australis*:

Where in the world's skull like a moonlit brain
Flashing and crinkling rolls the huge Pacific ...

In the poem, Quieroz and Lane are both dead, both mad, sailing on through eternity in search of their doomed paradises.

James McAuley also wrote a poem called *Terra Australia,* in which the fabled continent Quieroz looked for is imagined found—*a land of similes*—within any casual reader of the poem. It is neither ideal nor a paradise, but a profoundly ambivalent place where the cockatoo *screams with demoniac pain*, the emus are *insolent* and, in the north:

Stand the ecstatic solitary pyres

Of unknown lovers, featureless with flame.

McAuley, whom I was reading for the first time as himself, turned out to be a harsh, humourless, abrasive poet who wrote with the high degree of formal control necessary, perhaps, to contain the destructive energies within. He became in later life an academic who was also a fierce right-wing polemicist and a supremely tortured Roman Catholic—none of which prevented his compulsive drinking and womanising. In his most powerful anthology piece, the autobiographical *Because*, he confesses to a *despair/Older than any hope I ever knew.*

His partner in crime, the other Stewart, Harold, was completely different. His anthology pieces were formal, neo-classic versions of Greek myths in a context only marginally Australian:

Orpheus suffered in his bliss
An arid metamorphosis.
But now Eurydice is dust
The thirsty desert of his lust ...

I couldn't relate to him at all in this incarnation, though his later career was more compelling. After writing the Orpheus cycle in the 1950s, he translated and published two volumes of haiku (*A Net of Fireflies* and *A Chime of Windbells*) which were extremely successful, selling upwards of 50 000 copies each, many of them in North America. This vast number of sales was achieved partly because haiku were popular among beats and hippies. I have a friend who recalls stealing a copy of one (they were expensively and beautifully printed books) from the Norman Robb Bookshop in Little Collins Street, Melbourne, where Stewart worked as a bookseller throughout the 1950s and early 1960s; he was behind the counter as my friend skulked from the shop and knew, John felt, that he was shoplifting. John later lost the copy and purchased a replacement from the same shop, chatting companionably with Harold as he did so.

Stewart received a grant to study in Japan in the early 1960s. He became a convert to Shin Buddhism and in 1966 left Australia for good, living out the rest of his days in the ancient capital of Kyoto, about which he wrote a voluminous and meticulous account (*By the Walls of Old Kyoto*, Tokyo, 1981) which, even though it is a poem plus commentary, is still consulted as a guide by visitors. Towards the end of his life he confessed that he had never felt Australian at all: *It's a country that repels me. I find it very alien and hostile. As a small child of five or six, I was taken to see the bush and I burst into tears of inconsolable grief and had to be taken home.* The culmination of his writing work, a 5000-line epic poem called *Autumn Landscape-Roll*, about the quest for Nirvana by Tang dynasty poet Wu Tao Tzu, remains unpublished.

There was ample material here with which to write Annabelle's essay; my main problem was that I couldn't afford to get too clever when I came, as I inevitably would, to discuss Ern Malley. I decided to take him seriously as a poet but not to write as if he were a real person. In contradistinction to at least one of his authors, Malley is an internationalist with no interest in questions of nationality; matters of identity, however, are intrinsic to his very existence. The first poem in his oeuvre, *Dürer: Innsbruck, 1495*, lifted entirely from McAuley's unpublished work, is a meditation upon authenticity:

But no one warned that the mind repeats
In its ignorance the vision of others. I am still
The black swan of trespass on alien waters.

Because McAuley and Stewart loaded clues to the falsity of Malley's identity throughout the fifteen other poems composed for the hoax, a thematic emerges, the old conundrum which has bothered so many souls: how to ascertain the authenticity of a self? This thematic is also the site of a pathology for those who pass beyond the bounds of sanity. Ern Malley sounds sometimes like a schizophrenic struggling to keep himself together; his fractured language has the extravagance and numinous strangeness of schizophrenic speech. My argument in the essay, so far as I recall, was that this incipient schizophrenia, this obsession with authenticity and identity, was Malley's true inheritance from McAuley and Stewart, who had displaced anxieties of their own into the hoax poet's poems, just as other poets displaced a similar anxiety with respect to national identity onto historical figures like del Cano or Quieroz or William Lane. In the conclusion I contrasted the poignancy of Malley's doomed search for individual identity with the empty geographical nationalism of McAuley and the other Stewart, while pointing out its congruencies with Slessor's ability to enter wholly, if temporarily, into the mind of a John Benbow or a Captain Dobbin.

It was a cheeky strategy but it worked. Annabelle got an A for her essay and was so grateful she paid me a bonus. I still remember her slow smile from the sofa when she told me her mark: it was suddenly as if she had written the essay herself, and I was—what? An admired tutor, perhaps, to whom you feel gratitude for aiding you in the fulfilment of your potential. That was fine by me. I tucked the money into my back pocket and on the way home bought from Nicholas Pounder's bookshop on Victoria Street a copy of Jon Tuska's *Billy the Kid: His Life and Legend* (Lincoln, Nebraska, 1986), still the best book ever written about William Bonnie's life, death and subsequent immortality.

✳

But if an ocean is a mind, what is a poet? The body? Those who imagined themselves to be like explorers or navigators, where were they going and why? Even when I did not much like their verse, because of my own obsession with origins I felt these poets were in some way ancestral to me, that I was following after them the way they followed after del Cano or Quieroz. At the same time I did not really understand what it meant to find a point of origin; or rather I suspected that each apparent origin point has its own antecedent, which itself is preceded by some other event in time, making of the past an infinite regression. You cannot get back to the beginning of time, just as you cannot go back to the beginning of thought: the alleged configuration of the universe fifteen billion years ago, which we see as something unimaginably distant from us, continues to beg the question: what was before? All our solutions are imaginary. As an explorer, then, I was also an Ern Malley, a concoction, a fraud, the heteronym of some unknown Pessoa. In the same way that Ern discovered his own lack of primacy in the contemplation of Innsbruck and its reflection in the postcard of the Dürer watercolour, even when I went to the furtherest limit of mind, someone had always been there before me.

Nevertheless, this obsession has not left me. I am always trying to find a point earlier than the supposed point, whether for the origin of the species *Homo* (two million years BP?), the entry of early humans into Australia (half a million, perhaps, not 40 000 or 50 000 years ago?), the first non-Aboriginal incursions onto the continent (5000 BC, with dingo aboard or trotting behind?), the European discovery (1520s, by the Portuguese?). The reason for this is not so much that earlier means more interesting—though maybe it does—as that a different understanding of the past can give us a different present and a different future, in the same way that discovery of Celtic or Spanish ancestors might go some way towards explaining an individual's characteristics or predilections. So when a friend rang and said she had a friend who had another friend who wanted someone to research a famous early shipwreck and report upon the feasibility of making a feature film out of the story, I jumped at the chance: two survivors of the grisly events in the aftermath of the shipwreck are said to have been the first Europeans to live in Australia.

It was a West Australian tale from the early seventeenth century, famous in the annals ever since. My friend's friend Trixie's friend Rick had some money from a local authority out of which he was offering $6000 for me to write the Report. Both Rick and Trixie worked in the film industry and were hoping to set themselves up as producers of the intended film; both also lived in WA, Rick at Geraldton, Trixie in Albany. My friend is a director, Sydney based, but whether she wanted to direct the film herself wasn't clear. Once she had put me in touch with Trixie and Rick she played no further part in the proceedings. Not long after, the first instalment of the money arrived and I set to work on an extended Treatment called *The Brotherhood of the Damned*.

The Vereenigde Oostindische Compagnie (Dutch East India Company) ship *Batavia* set sail from the Texel off the coast of Holland towards the end of October 1628. It was her maiden voyage. She was done out in green and gold and carried the red lion of Holland on her prow; her decks and gun ports were also painted red. She sailed in convoy with seven other ships—a war ship, three other *retour* ships, two store ships and a yacht—for the port in the Indies that bore her name and is now known as Jakarta. A *retour* ship was designed for trade to and from the east: on the outward voyage the *Batavia* carried soldiers and silver, the one to buy spices, the other to fight a local war with the Susuhunan of Mataron in east Java. She also had aboard a casket of jewels which included ancient gemstones that had belonged to the Holy Roman Emperor. There were more than 300 people on the ship, including women and children, mainly family of the soldiers.

Batavia was flagship of the flotilla, and the fleet commander, soon to be Councillor of India, was Francisco Pelsaert: not a sailor but a high official of the VOC. Pelsaert was from Antwerp in the Spanish Netherlands, educated, aristocratic and refined, a friend of the painter Rubens. The captain of the *Batavia*, by contrast, a man called Arian Jacobs, was a rough piratical sailor who had risen through the ranks because of the excellence of his seamanship. The two had met before. Pelsaert, returning home after a successful tour of duty in Agra, India, left from Surat on the west coast in a ship skippered by Jacobs. Before they sailed the two men argued violently, probably because Pelsaert insisted on departing by the due date while Jacobs wanted to linger to trade. Jan Company, as the VOC was popularly known, always underpaid its employees, yet spent a great deal of time and effort trying to prevent them from augmenting their meagre salaries by illicit trading.

The situation on board the *Batavia* was further complicated by the presence aboard of Lucretia van der Meylen, a beautiful young woman going out to join her husband in the Indies, and of the Undermerchant Hieronymo Cornelius, Pelsaert's second in command, a watchful, tortured, knowing man with a background as an apothecary and certain bizarre religious obsessions. On the passage from the Texel to the Cape of Good Hope, Captain Jacobs conceived a passion for Lucretia, which she did not reciprocate. He was more successful with her maid Zwaantie, whom he seduced with promises to make of her a gentlewoman, effectively turning her into a spy against her own mistress.

At the same time Jacobs and Hieronymo, who seem to have shared a resentment towards the authority of Pelsaert, began to conspire against him. The inciting incident was Pelsaert's rebuke of Jacobs after he struck a man while coming aboard drunk after a night spent carousing in a tavern in what is now Cape Town. The Captain and the Undermerchant decided they would look for support amongst the crew and, when the time was right, rise up in mutiny, take the ship and its treasure, and turn to piracy.

Jacobs' motivation was straightforward: the desire for revenge; greed for silver; and a kind of bloodthirsty resentment against any who dared try to put a restraint upon him. Hieronymo Cornelius, like the villain in a Jacobean tragedy, is a far more complex figure. To understand him at all, I had to learn something of the religious background, both at the time and in the far past of Christendom. Calvinism in the Netherlands was in crisis in the early seventeenth century, a crisis ostensibly resolved in 1619, when the ideas of Franciscus Gomarus triumphed over those of his rival, Jacobus Arminius. Gomarus' strict interpretation of the doctrine of predestination became the official belief of the Calvinist Church in the United Provinces and hence, insofar as there was one, the state religion.

Gomarus believed that God has fixed for all time those who are saved and those who are damned and there is nothing anyone can do about it. The Elect may be known by the blameless lives they lead; the Damned by their dissolution. Arminius held that human actions in this life can make a difference for the salvation of the soul after death. Those who live a good life on earth may go to heaven; sinners will not. This doctrine is closer to Roman Catholicism than the extreme predestination taught by Gomarus, which in Hieronymo's view mirrored the social hierarchy: the Elect have made this earth their heaven; all good things find their way to their table, onto their backs, into their vaults; and the Damned languish. Hieronymo's conclusion seems to have been that, if we are already condemned, then there is no constraint upon our action, nothing we may not do. A divine law that excludes *a priori* a proportion of humanity from the possibility of grace is not just a mockery, it is a provocation too. On our way to hell, let's enjoy ourselves while we can.

There are deep historical layers to these beliefs. Of particular interest to Hieronymo, a well-read man, were the followers of Caprocrates of Alexandria, one of the earliest of the Gnostic heretics. Caprocrates believed that Christ derived the mysteries of his religion from the Temple of Isis in Egypt. He then taught these mysteries to his disciples, who transmitted them to Caprocrates himself. The Caprocratians used incantations, had special grips, signs, words, symbols and degrees, and were said to brand their devotees with a hot iron on the buttock. They rejected the resurrection of the body but believed in the metempsychosis of souls; as in Buddhist thought, through many incarnations a soul might at length escape the prison of a body and be released into the liberty of heaven.

Caprocratians believed the world was created in error, by an evil being or beings. This is the explanation for the suffering we find around us. God exists outside or beyond the world, and is obscured from us by the machinations of these malign beings; nevertheless, there is in each of us a spark of divinity, and by choosing the right path we can reunite this spark with God who is its origin. One of the peculiarities of the Caprocratians was that they thought the way to escape the world was through it. Church Father Irenaeus wrote: *so unbridled is their madness, that they declare they have in their power all things which are irreligious and impious, and are at liberty to practise them; for they maintain that things are evil or good, simply in virtue of human opinion ... souls should have experience of every kind of life as well as every kind of action ... doing all those things which we dare not either speak or hear of, nay, which we must not even conceive in our thoughts ... in order that ... having made trial of every kind of life, [they] may, at their departure, not be wanting in any particular.*

It was in this strata of Gnosticism that Hieronymo saw analogies for his Brotherhood of the Damned. They are a remarkably persistent set of beliefs, having outlasted every attempt by the established churches to eradicate them. Hieronymo's personal connection with Gnosticism was through the Dutch painter Torrentius who was an Adamite, another sect that has survived since early post-Christian Alexandria. In common with the Caprocratians, Adamites believe you have to sin in order to escape. (In some versions this involves making love to a different person for each of the 365 days of a year in order to exorcise, individually, the 365 demons who rule them.) The Adamites reject prayer and worship, and instead hold ceremonies in places they called paradise where, naked and sinless, like Adam and Eve before the fall, they eat and drink, dance and sing. These beliefs and practices are clearly still with us. There are analogies with Freemasonry, Rosicrutionism and the kind of magic practised by Aleister Crowley.

The painter Johaness Torrentius was born Johannes Sijmonsz van der Beeck in Amsterdam in 1589. Contemporary documents and references establish that he was notorious for his unorthodox conduct and his obscene pictures. At about the same time that Hieronymo enlisted in Jan Company, Torrentius was arrested, tortured and sentenced to twenty years' imprisonment by Haarlem's municipal authorities for immorality, blasphemy and membership of the outlawed Adamite sect. At this time most of his paintings were burned. After his imprisonment Charles I of England, who admired and collected his pictures, interceded on his behalf with Stadholder Frederik Hendrik. Through the latter's good offices Torrentius was released from prison in 1630 and travelled to London bearing a few of his remaining paintings including, it seems, the allegory *Temperance,* which is now in the Rijksmusuem, Amsterdam, and the only one known to survive. Sometimes called *Still Life with a Bridle,* it was discovered in 1913 as a grocer's lid on a barrel of sultanas; Charles's brand on the panel's verso places it firmly in his collection. It was anticipated that Torrentius would paint captivating pictures for the English court but apparently he produced very little before returning to Holland, where he died in obscurity in Amsterdam in 1644.

Hieronymo's enlistment in Jan Company probably coincided with the painter's arrest and imprisonment, because both men had crossed a line that meant they could no longer live the kind of libertine life they had previously enjoyed. As Torrentius chose exile in England, so did Hieronymo exile himself to the Indies as an undermerchant. But not, it seems, in order to enter obscurity. Rather, it looks as if he was seeking a theatre in which he could put into practice some of his wilder ideas.

One of the scenes I wrote for *Brotherhood of the Damned* was a premutiny account of a religious discussion between Hieronymo and his immediate superior, Pelsaert. Pelsaert was a Remonstrant, a follower of Arminius' gentler brand of Calvinism; thus he did not necessarily believe himself to be one of the Elect, and, in the scene as written, is confounded by Hieronymo's virulent nihilism. The encounter happens on shipboard as the *Batavia,* having left the Cape with a much diminished flotilla, sails eastward across the southern Indian Ocean. The plot for the mutiny has already commenced: Lucretia has been waylaid, bound, raped and smeared with excrement by a group of masked men, amongst whom she has recognised the voice of one, Jan Evertz. The attempt to hang Evertz, which the fever-ridden Pelsaert has postponed until they make land, will be the signal for the mutiny to begin.

However, before this could happen, the *Batavia* ran aground in a group of islands some forty miles off the West Australian coast known as Houtman's Abrolhos: a strange name, derived from both Dutch and Portuguese sources, the Abrolhos must have been sighted by some unknown Portuguese navigator whose charts had been seen by the Dutch. Frederick de Houtman in 1619 rediscovered the Abrolhos (the word means *keep your eyes open*) and so they became, on the charts, 'his'. Whatever was going on aboard the *Batavia*, they did not heed the warning; probably they thought they were still far out in the Indian Ocean. Thus as surf broke over reefs ahead in the early dawn, the watchman decided the sea spray was merely an effect of moonlight on water.

The *Batavia* struck at high tide and despite all efforts to refloat her—cannon were thrown overboard, the main mast was cut away—she stuck fast. When the decision to abandon ship was made, attempts by the sailors to salvage food and water from below deck were hampered by drunken soldiery, who in their despair had broached barrels of brandy and wine and were carousing with their women. With great difficulty about sixty passengers and crew, plus some meagre supplies, were put aboard the ship's sloop and ferried by Captain Jacobs to a nearby island, later known as Batavia's Graveyard; Lucretia was among them. They were afterwards joined by another sloopload, then another, but following the first trip Jacobs refused to land any more supplies because the people ashore were already pillaging what little he had.

Meanwhile on board the foundering *Batavia* Pelsaert supervised the placing of floating buoys on the twelve treasure chests he'd had brought up from below. He then left the ship in the yawl with a group of loyal sailors and a small casket of jewels, telling Hieronymo he would return later to secure the rest of the bullion: his primary responsibility, in the Company's eyes, was of course the loot. This included two beautiful antiquities that the Dutch-Flemish artist and diplomat Peter Paul Rubens was shipping for possible sale to the Mogul ruler of India, Shah Jehangir. One was a fourth-century AD Roman cameo known as the Great Cameo of Gaspar Boudaen, depicting Constantine, the first Christian Roman Emperor; the other an onyx vase known as the Rubens' vase, cut from a single agate found in the Byzantine period and carved with images of Pan. There were also, along with chests of silver coin and the casket of jewels, cloth, wines, cheeses, trade goods and a pair of massive gates for the fortress of Batavia.

The weather was worsening; when Pelsaert tried to return from Batavia's Graveyard to the ship, he could not get aboard. He advised the drunken soldiery and their sardonic leader, Hieronymo, who had stayed aboard because he could not swim, to construct rafts to get ashore that way, then sailed in the yawl to another nearby island.

By the afternoon following the shipwreck, Pelsaert, Jacobs and some thirty others, including the ship's officers and the best of the sailors as well as the bulk of the food and water, were safe on that small island later (and still) called Traitor's Island. On the larger island, Batavia's Graveyard, were the majority of the rest of the survivors, including Lucretia and all of the other civilians. Their derisory supplies of food and water were under the armed guard of loyal soldiers led by Wiebbe Hayes, as was the casket of Pelsaert's jewels. On the *Batavia* itself, the rapidly sobering soldiers and a few sailors were building rafts. Hieronymo, one assumes, was already conniving how to come into his kingdom.

Jacobs knew they were in dire straits, and after much deliberation he and Pelsaert decided to set sail for the mainland to look for water. Pelsaert first tried to visit those on the larger island to inform them of what they were doing, but Jacobs, who did not want to be swamped by desperate people seeking to join them, prevented him. Instead, they left the yawl on Traitor's Island, with a note and a barrel of bread, and sailed away for the Great South Land. When a few desperate sailors from Batavia's Graveyard managed to cross to Traitor's Island, they took the yawl and followed the sloop; the two boats made the mainland together but found no water there. Pelsaert called it a *dry, cursed earth* and set sail for Batavia.

The situation on Batavia's Graveyard was bad and could only get worse. People continued to die from injuries sustained in the shipwreck; their bodies, and those of the drowned, were dragged across to the other side of the island. When a barrel of wine washed ashore and some of the men got drunk, a gunner named Ryckart Wouters blurted out details of the mutiny plot, adding a substratum of fear and doubt to the mix. Before one of the equally mutinous cadets struck him down, Wouters predicted that Jacobs would murder Pelsaert and throw his body into the sea. There was thus no hope of rescue.

By the time the first raft of soldiers from the stricken *Batavia* arrived, people were beginning to die of thirst. This and the next raft came without substantial supplies of food or water; the soldiers had lost them along the way. Some drank their own urine; some drank sea water and went mad; no one could eat the dry sea biscuit without water. Meanwhile, on the *Batavia* itself, Hieronymo was the sole survivor left aboard; lashed to the bowsprit, with the black screaming shapes of seabirds diving around him, I imagine him hurling defiance at the evil angels who rule this world.

It was a violent storm that saved the castaways, allowing them to gather enough rainwater to meet present and future needs. The storm also broke up the *Batavia*, driving wreckage ashore, including water, wine, vinegar, biscuit, bacon, cheeses, as well as pieces of the ship and its fittings. Among the flotsam, miraculously, was Hieronymo, still lashed to the bowsprit and more dead than alive. In my Treatment he is found by Lucretia, who nurses him back to health. If this was indeed what happened, she would regret it bitterly later.

When Hieronymo recovered, a Council was elected from among the survivors, consisting of the Undermerchant Hieronymo, the Predikant or minister of religion, the Senior Assistant Merchant and the Provost. Tents were made out of sailcloth rescued from the wreck. Supplies of bread, water and wine were inventoried and rationed and, it turned out, would last some weeks, especially if augmented by fish, seal meat and bird's eggs. Further supplies and other useful items could be scavenged from the wreck; water could be gathered by raft from neighbouring islands. They assumed the sloop and the yawl had gone to get help and would in due course return. There was nothing else to do but wait.

It isn't clear from the surviving documentation precisely when Hieronymo learned that the mutiny plot had been betrayed. Once he had, he would also have known that he could expect nothing but trial, torture, conviction and death if ever he again came under the jurisdiction of Jan Company. He was in effect already a dead man. I can still hear his laughter reverberating down the years:

This world is a theatre of damnation, he cries, *and we actors are all doomed souls. Let the play begin.*

The Undermerchant dispatched a group of soldiers under Wiebbe Hayes to another island in search of water and left them there, hoping they would die. He split the remaining survivors amongst some of the closer islands, none of which had any water. He formed a new Council from among those loyal to him, then disbanded the old. Soon the executions began, first clandestinely, later openly. With a band of murderous young men drawn from the ship's junior officers, soldiery and cabin boys, Hieronymo began systematically to kill anyone he thought might oppose his reign of terror or anyone he judged to be a burden on the limited resources. The remaining women were shared out among his men; these women were kept caged, like animals. Hieronymo himself took Lucretia as his concubine, although it is said she submitted to his advances only under the threat of death. What form their sexual relations took can only be imagined.

The mutineers became intoxicated with killing. They experimented with different ways of dealing death, and murdered at the merest excuse. People were stabbed, garrotted, poisoned, drowned, strangled, had their heads stoved in, their throats cut, were decapitated. The sick were all slaughtered together one night in the hospital tent. Women and children, even babies, were not exempt. Survivors sent to other islands were hunted down and killed if they hadn't already died of thirst and hunger. Hieronymo and his picked men salvaged fine clothes from the wreck and pillaged Pelsaert's casket, strutting around in silk stockings, garters with gold lace, rich red gowns adorned with gold braid, wearing rings on their hands and jewels around their necks. An oath was sworn among the mutineers, though it is unclear if it was signed in blood. The islands were theirs to do as they would; when the rescue mission returned, they were going to take the ship and go pirating in accordance with the original plan.

There was just one problem: those originally sent to one of the far islands to die had survived. By some strange chance Wiebbe Hayes and his two dozen or so soldiers had found themselves on the only island in the group with a natural store of water, made even more substantial by the recent rains. The water was not on the so-called High Island itself but on another one nearby which could be reached by wading through shallows at low tide. This other island also had wallabies, muttonbirds and eggs. Instead of sending the soldiers to their deaths, Hieronymo had given the only group of men who could threaten his regime the best island in the Abrolhos to live on.

When escapees from Hieronymo's reign of terror arrived at High Island, Hayes' army—about forty-five men, including a group of French soldiers—began to construct pikes and morning-stars from wreck timbers and barrel hoop iron that had washed ashore. Hieronymo, who had by now proclaimed himself Captain General, had some thirty-six men under his command, although not all of them were committed mutineers. He also possessed the only firearms to survive the wreck. Having utterly subjected or destroyed those people who did not share his views, he decided to eradicate the colony of soldiers on High Island.

There were three attempts to eliminate the renegades, all more or less disastrous. The first attack was preceded by an emissary's attempt to bribe some of the French soldiers to desert; they were offered 6000 guilders each. Wiebbe Hayes, who seems to have been both clever and resourceful, kept both the emissary and the boat he came in. A few days later the first attack came, led by one Jacob Pieters. The defenders, throwing stones from catapults, using slings similar to those used for grenade hurling, proved tougher than expected, and forced the mutineers to retreat. A second attempt followed soon after. Three boatloads of mutineers attacked from the sea. Hayes' men advanced knee deep into the water and held them off. The mutineers' two muskets failed to fire and they were obliged once again to retreat under the taunts of the defenders.

On 1 September the mutineers sent the Predikant ashore to try to negotiate a peace. Hieronymo offered wine and cloth in exchange for the small boat brought to the island by the mutineers' original emissary. His suggestions were relayed to Hayes via the Predikant and the formal negotiations set for the next day; once again Hayes kept the emissary, saying he was as much their minister as the mutineer's. Hieronymo and five of his men brought the trade goods ashore, the cloth was given over, the wine decanted from barrels into other containers, and another attempt made to bribe the French soldiers; meanwhile others of their party waited in concealment for the signal to attack. But Hayes had suspected treachery all along and set his own ambush; before the mutineer's trap could be sprung, his men sallied forth and easily captured Hieronymo and the other five. Four of them were beheaded on the spot with their own swords, but Hieronymo was kept a prisoner.

Two weeks later, the final assault on High Island began, led by the mutineers' new commander, Wouter Loos. This time they managed to get their muskets to work (the problem appears to have been damp powder) and four of the defenders were wounded, one of whom later died. Nevertheless, the attackers were again driven back, and it was at this extraordinary moment that the rescue ship, the yacht *Sardaam*, appeared on the horizon. Hayes and some of his men left the battle and, taking the emissary's small boat, rowed out towards the yacht. Some accounts suggest there was a race between their boat and one rowed by a party of mutineers, and this is of course the version I used in the Treatment.

However, alongside the *Sardaam* there was no real contest between the bizarrely robed and bejewelled mutineers and the honest soldiers; Pelsaert, who commanded the *Sardaam*, had the yacht's guns broken out and levelled at the mutineers in their boat. They were told to throw their weapons into the sea before coming aboard, which at length they did. At this point, one of their number abjectly confessed his part in the murders, while claiming it was all done under Hieronymo's orders.

Pelsaert dispatched a party to High Island to bring Hieronymo to him. The next day the rest of the mutineers on Batavia's Graveyard were rounded up. Lucretia's ordeal—after the capture of Hieronymo she had been 'given' to Wouter Loos—was over. Pelsaert then set out to look for the jewels, most of which were found in the tents of the leading mutineers, along with copies of the various oaths and proclamations Hieronymo had drawn up. At the same time, Gujarati divers at the wreck site began to recover the chests of silver, some of which could be seen glinting below in the pellucid waters. Eleven of the twelve were brought up over the next six weeks.

Order having been restored, Pelsaert confined the mutineers, bound and gagged, to Seal Island, from which he had them rowed across severally or alone, as required, for their trials on Batavia's Graveyard. When Hieronymo denied any wrong doing or blamed the dead for what had happened, he was tortured: a sealed canvas collar was fixed around his neck and water was poured in; to breathe, he had first to swallow. He soon relented, but only in order to tell more lies. His trial, which lasted a week, was characterised by a series of multiple versions of what had happened, to the point of complete confusion. Each time he was tortured, he would ask to be unbound so that he could say what really happened. Then he would construct another fiction.

His partners in crime, less subtle and less devious, did at length make full confessions. When these were shown to Hieronymo he agreed under torture that they were accurate. Then he retracted his agreement. Dutch law required that any confession extracted through torture had to be signed by the confessor twenty-four hours after the torture had ceased. Hieronymo's strategy was designed to frustrate Pelsaert and avoid legal guilt. It was only when he was filled so full with water that his belly swelled, his eyes popped and Pelsaert made it clear he would not relent but this time let him utterly drown that the Undermerchant at last acceded to his fate.

Even so, he tried to delay or avoid the inevitable execution, asking to be allowed to see his wife in Batavia first, requesting baptism and attempting to take poison. When Pelsaert allowed the request for baptism, Hieronymo said:

Nothing more? Can one show repentance of life in so few days? I thought I should be allowed one or two weeks. Then he fell into a rage, shouting: *I see you want my blood and my life, but God will not suffer that I shall die a shameful death. I know for certain, and you will see, that God will perform unto me a miracle this night, so that I shall not be hanged.*

He had a relative, an unexposed mutineer from the *Batavia*, among the crew of the *Sardaam*, who gave him the poison. But the dose was insufficient to kill him; he was forced to call for an antidote, then to spend the night in vomiting and diarrhoea.

At the end, Hieronymo refused to attend divine service with the rest of the condemned men. He reiterated his belief that there was no devil and no hell and nothing to fear from death and, at the request of the other mutineers, went first and alone to the gallows. At that moment, Lucretia came forward, lamenting the sins he had made her commit and the damage done to her reputation. In a last, paradoxical act of generosity, Hieronymo announced that she had only become his lover under threat of death and that no blame should attach to her for the things he had made her do. Then he stepped up to the block and laid down his right hand to be severed by a single blow of an axe; his other hand was also cut off; and, stumps pumping blood, he was dragged to the scaffold shouting: *Revenge!*

His last words were that he went *to seek justice in heaven, having failed to find it on earth.*

As his body twitched on the scaffold sea birds shrieked down out of the sky, their black shapes clouding the air as they had when he was lashed to the bowsprit.

One hundred and fifteen people—ninety-six company employees, twelve women and seven children—died during Hieronymo's reign of terror. Another ninety-five succumbed during the shipwreck, from natural causes, or by judicial execution, leaving just one hundred and twenty-two survivors of the doomed ship *Batavia*.

Seven prominent mutineers were executed on Seal Island; others were taken back to Batavia for further investigation and executed there. Jacob Pieters was broken on the wheel. Some were whipped or keelhauled or dropped from the yards onto the deck during the sea journey. Captain Jacobs and his mistress Zwaantie, imprisoned at Batavia and tortured, admitted nothing and were both still alive and in jail when they disappear from the historical record about two years later. Within a year Pelsaert, a sick and broken man, was dead; as for Lucretia, it turned out her husband had died during her voyage out to join him; nevertheless, she married again and, five years later, returned with her second husband to Europe, where they settled in Leyden. She remained childless but became godmother to half a dozen other children, showing that her reputation had survived the lurid events on Batavia's Graveyard.

✳

I was revising this bloody tale one evening when all hell broke loose downstairs. Male voices roaring, furniture crashing over, bodies colliding with each other and with the walls. It was all the more unexpected after complete silence there for the whole of the afternoon. I knew Jimmy was home from sea but thought he was either out or sleeping. The fight, without diminishing in intensity, moved from room to room, until I heard a cry followed by extravagant cursing. There was more violent movement of bodies, then a pause. Jimmy's back door crashed open and someone ran away. Another pause. Silence. I heard Jimmy's voice, sounding so close I jumped:

Martin, Martin, call the police, call the police!

I called them but I didn't go downstairs to see what had happened. I hung around in the kitchen, and now and again went out onto the catwalk to have a look. It didn't feel as if it was over yet. It wasn't. Soon, I started hearing another voice from the laneway, moaning.

My wallet, my wallet ... give me my wallet ...

Whoever it was was lying on the concrete just outside the garden gate and he didn't sound well. Someone, a passer-by, was with him. Someone else said they'd called an ambulance. Jimmy was locked in his bedroom, too scared to come out. I heard his voice float up from down below:

He stole my stereo. That's why we fought.

It took about twenty minutes for help to come, and all this time the guy was calling for his wallet, weaker and more desperate by the minute. I thought perhaps he was dying. While the ambulance crew were tending to him the police arrived. There were two of them. They waited outside in the laneway until the guy was stretchered into the ambulance, then came in to talk to me. I told them I'd called them because Jimmy had asked me to. They suggested I stick around, and went down to talk to him. Later they came up to see me again. We sat around the kitchen table. In all the excitement I'd completely forgotten to remove the ashtray containing the roach of a joint I'd smoked earlier. There was a moment when one of the cops looked down at the ashtray and then up at me. Perfect comprehension of what was happening flowed between us but nothing was said. They went on with the interview.

It was hard to work out exactly what had gone on. The guy—he was only eighteen, a New Zealander—had certainly made off with Jimmy's brand-new boogie box, which Jimmy had bought upon his latest return from sea; but it looked as if that had occurred after the fight and was not the cause of it. Jimmy had stabbed the guy with one of his kitchen knives, badly injuring him. I later found out that he had in fact almost killed him: if the knife had gone in a little to the side of where it did, it would have pierced his liver and he would have been a goner. After stabbing him, Jimmy had locked himself in his bedroom and stayed there until the police arrived. The guy had grabbed the boogie box and made off, only to collapse halfway down the laneway. Then he discovered the loss of his wallet and dragged himself back to the garden gate, leaving a trail of blood. The wallet was in Jimmy's place, apparently having fallen out of the New Zealander's pocket during the fight. But what had caused the fight in the first place?

The police didn't know and nor did I. It only became clear some months later. Meanwhile, the cops took Jimmy down to the station, and peace and quiet descended on our little corner of the world again. Nick came over to see what I knew, which wasn't much. Some time in the wee small hours Jimmy was bailed and came home. Next morning early he came up the stairs in a state of high excitement. His greyish-white t-shirt had a spreading bib of blood on the front and his eyes were wild.

I am not a poofter, he said, over and over. *I am—how you say?—Good Samaritan. I try to help these people.*

He even brought a photo of his son in the Philippines to show me.

I am not a poofter—I have a son—see? He had, of course, inadvertently given away the motive for the attack on him, though not the precise circumstances.

Might go to jail, he said at one point with an eerie look in his eye, as if prison were a place of opportunity, not a punishment.

But he didn't go to jail, only to court, where the prosecution faltered for lack of evidence: the Kiwi boy didn't want to press charges, didn't want to give evidence, he just wanted to go home, and in the end the case was dismissed and Jimmy walked free. He resumed his old life and, some time later, for the very first time in my experience of him, got a regular boyfriend. Troy was in his mid- or late twenties, older than most of the young men Jimmy brought home; he was a sailor himself; they were shipmates, messing together on shore. They'd drink and smoke and eat together, and go up the Cross and come back; every morning, grotesquely, they would repair to Jimmy's little bathroom directly beneath my kitchen and there indulge in an orgy of coughing and spitting, clearing out the phlegm accumulated in the previous twenty-four hours. When Jimmy went away to sea again, Troy looked after his place, sometimes sunbathing in the dusty garden wearing nothing but alarming red briefs.

And then something happened. One morning Elle and I were woken by the sound of heavy knocking on Jimmy's door in the stairwell below the bedroom window. Jimmy didn't answer; instead, he took off through the front door, as was his habit whenever trouble came to the back. But this time those seeking him were policemen, and they had been brought there by Troy. While they waited to see if Jimmy might answer or return, Troy told the cops what had happened.

He had woken from a deep sleep to find stubble rash all over his face and Polaroid photographs of his undressed body lying around the room. He was groggy and disoriented and couldn't work out why he had slept so long, because he'd only had a couple of drinks the night before. He thought he must have been Mickey-Finned. What else might have been done to him in his stupor he did not know or did not say, but he was very angry. He felt violated, he felt betrayed, most of all he felt he had been made a fool of. He and Jimmy had been mates not lovers and then Jimmy had, by an act of deceit, tried to change the rules. Troy told the police he wanted to smack him but decided to do the right thing and involve the law instead. The cops said that was all very well but it would be hard to convict Jimmy because there wasn't much evidence and they were not even sure what the charges might be. After a while they gave up and went away. Jimmy came back later when the coast was clear. I never saw Troy again.

Suddenly it was clear why there had been so many eruptions of angry young men around our place. There was the morning we woke to find three or four of them out the front throwing bricks at the house. There was the stabbed boy who must have woken up to find himself being violated by Jimmy. There was Troy with his Polaroids and stubble rash. And there were all the others who had come in a high good humour and left hurriedly, furiously or silently not so very long after. We talked to a few people about Jimmy's problem and one of them suggested putting him on the mailing list for an organisation set up by and for gay Asian males; this group met weekly on a Tuesday, and for a while Jimmy did splash on the atrocious scent and go out each Tuesday he was ashore. He even came home a few times with obviously complaisant young men. But it wasn't long before his old habits reasserted themselves: clearly he liked young, straight, Anglo boys and he liked them rough. Compliance didn't excite him, apparently, unless it was chemically induced—by what? We never found out what Jimmy used, although it may have been Rohipnol, a common, easily available date-rape drug in those days. Nevertheless, while there were more young men inveigled home from the Cross, there were no more explosions. Jimmy, if he had not learned to curb his desires, had at least learned how to be prudent in their satisfaction.

There is a coda to the story of the wreck of the *Batavia*. Having salvaged the bullion, taken on supplies of water and wallaby meat, and completed his written account of the trials of the mutineers, Pelsaert set sail from the Abrolhos in the *Sardaam*, heading for the mainland. On the coast of what is now Western Australia, two men—Jan Pelgrom and Wouter Loos—were set ashore and abandoned. They were given supplies of food and trade goods—knives, beads, bells, mirrors—guns and a boat. Their instructions, which Pelsaert read out to them on the beach, were to seek gold, silver and other articles of trade and to make friends with the Aborigines if they could. They were also told to look out for other ships along that coast. *Man's luck is found in strange places,* Pelsaert observed, before rowing back to the ship.

Jan Pelgrom de Bye, a cabin boy, was just seventeen years old. He had become as intoxicated as the others with the slaughter and had murdered a boy on Seal Island. Later he helped in the killing of a woman named Janneken Gijssen and a man called Andries Jansz. When refused the opportunity to decapitate one Coen Aldertsz (he was held not to be robust enough to wield the axe), he wept. During the period of Hieronymo's reign he cohabited with at least three married women and at the trial was sentenced to hang, though without his hand(s) being cut off first. In the face of this sentence he pleaded for mercy and, perhaps because of his youth, was marooned instead.

His companion Wouter Loos was a soldier who had taken part in the killing of the Predikant's family (his wife and all but one of their many children were slaughtered). He was prominent enough among the mutineers to be elected to command once Hieronymo had been captured. Pelsaert intended carrying him to Batavia to have his crimes investigated further, but Loos' various acts of kindness towards Judith, the Predikant's surviving adult daughter, and towards Lucretia made him change his mind. It was clearly the act of a Remonstrant, one who believed good deeds could alter the fate of a soul.

Again, the mystery of who Lucretia was rises up before us: each of the men who had coerced her into being his mistress came to her defence when nothing obvious could be gained personally by either of them. Hieronymo went to his death cursing God but praising Lucretia; Wouter Loos' gallantry aboard ship could only have been inspired by respect for the character of the woman he had demeaned. She must have been as remarkable in her way as the doomed apothecary.

Nothing further is known of Pelgrom and Loos, although their fate reverberates down the succeeding years of Australian history. These bloody Dutchmen were the precursors of the convicted felons transported less than two centuries hence from the British Isles to Botany Bay and to the other convict settlements founded subsequently: Port Arthur, Hunter River, Moreton River, Swan River, Norfolk Island. If, as Robert Hughes claims in *The Fatal Shore* (London, 1987), transportation was an attempt by the ruling class to export whole strata of society, relocating those already damned by God in a literal hell on earth, then Pelgrom and Loos were the original inhabitants of that inferno. But not the only ones: there are those who claim that a blue-eyed, flaxen-haired strain repeatedly manifests among the Aborigines of that coast—near the modern-day site of Kalbarri, where the Dutch castaways' arrival on land is commemorated at Red Bluff by a cairn with the inscription: *It is believed the first permanent landing of white men in Australia was recorded here, at the mouth of the Wittecarra Creek.*

I finished the Treatment, proofed it, printed it, wrote a covering letter and sent it off to Rick in Geraldton. Afterwards I walked from the Potts Point Post Office back up Macleay Street to the Cross and on, heading towards Oxford Street for some reason I no longer recall. It was a blue day in early spring, not too hot, clear and still, with just a hint in the air of the torpid summer to come. Strolling along Forbes Street in the shadow of the old sandstone walls of the former Darlinghurst Jail, now an art school, I entered one of those silences you sometimes come across even in big cities. There was no traffic in the street, and the distant roar of motors from the busy roads before and behind faded to a murmur. None of the residents in the St Vincent's Caritas Centre were lounging, as they usually were, in the sagging armchairs on the deep verandas of the institution. Nobody in the street either until I saw coming towards me on the footpath two figures, a man and a girl. He looked like one of those superannuated hippies you still see sometimes, while the girl, perhaps twelve, I took to be his daughter. But as they came closer I realised it could not be so.

The man was dressed in a leather jerkin and tight black trousers tucked into antique ankle boots, and wore a round hat on his head; I felt sure he carried a knife. She, not a girl at all but a child-woman prancing at his side, had on a fantastical dress made of patchwork and no shoes on her feet. They were both grimy, the dirt of years etched into the tanned skin of their faces and their lean brown arms. I began to feel afraid. There was a roaring in my ears that had nothing to do with the muted din of the city. As they came closer I knew I could not, should not, look at them. The roar crescendoed as we drew abreast of one another and I could feel rather than see the strange predatory glitter in the man's eyes, the wicked gleam of the child-woman's, whose precocious white breasts showed through rips in her motley.

All of the hairs on my neck rose up as they passed and soundlessly went on. I had to stop myself breaking into a run; I had to suppress the urge to turn and look after them; my heart was going like billy-o in my chest. But when, judging them to be ten or so paces past me, I did look back, there was no one there. No one on the footpath, no one crossing the road, nobody anywhere. I was only now passing the entrance to the art school so they could not have gone in there; nor could they have gone anywhere else unless into thin air or, improbably, into the massive sandstock walls of the old jail. I walked on, full of relief at surviving what felt like a close encounter with something old, corrupt and malevolent out of the criminal past of the city. The sound of the traffic returned, I heard my own footsteps scuffing the pavement and saw, at the police precinct ahead, the unimpeachable reality of a couple of constables entering the station with cups of takeaway coffee in their hands.

The fate of my Treatment was no less obscure. Months after I sent it off to Geraldton I received a cryptic card from Rick. There was a Larson cartoon on the front: somewhere out west, a doctor is bandaging a cowboy's arm while, next to him, sits a ventriloquist's dummy shot full of holes. The doctor is saying:

You're gonna be OK, mister, but I can't say the same for your little buddy over there ... the way I hear it, he's the one that mouthed off to them gunfighters in the first place.

Rick apologised for the delay, said they were very happy with my work and would soon attend a meeting to formulate the company that would develop the script. He promised a detailed letter once a few loose ends were tidied up. I never heard from him again.

Incredibly, and despite the wonderfully dramatic nature of the events, none of the many and various proposals to film the *Batavia* story has yet come to fruition, although there have been many books on the subject, both fiction and nonfiction and, in 2004, an opera. Meanwhile, the ventriloquist's dummy who cannot keep his mouth shut and ends up drilled full of holes still makes me smile.

III

Voyage

When in the mid 1990s Jimmy Bonus went to live in Rooty Hill, Nick sold the house in Womerah Lane (for $350 000; it would be worth a million now); after looking around at the available options, Elle and I decided to leave the centre and move to the margins. It didn't make sense to pay twice the money for half the space, which is what we'd have had to do to remain in the inner city or the eastern suburbs. We looked south, in the north-west and to the north before settling on a house at Pearl Beach, a small village near the mouth of the Hawkesbury River that forms the northern boundary of Cumberland County in which is the City of Sydney. When you walk up the strand at Pearl Beach, from its further end you can see, past Lion Island and across the wide mouth of the Hawkesbury, Palm Beach, the northernmost of the northern beaches of Sydney. You might even be able to swim there if you were fit and desperate enough. You can certainly row—I know someone who did.

It was a shock moving out of the city. Almost as soon as we did Elle went away to work on a film shoot, leaving me entirely alone in a place where I knew no one. As is the way of such things, one job led on to another and then another and in the end she never really came back at all; or rather, she came back only to get her things. I heard much later that she had fallen in love with a grip or a gaffer or perhaps a best boy and they had gone to live in Kalgoorlie. Or was it Coolgardie?

The residual romanticism I still felt about so-called country living did not answer the circumstances I found myself in. I was lonely and bored, with too little to do. There are only so many bush walks, coastal walks, swims, trips to the waterfall you can take, and I soon began to feel time weighing heavily upon me. It was the evenings that were most difficult. I worked at my desk in the mornings and, after the requisite smoke, went out exploring in the afternoons, making my way up Green Point Creek to its source, walking along the spine of the Hope Range as far as Gad's Hill, exploring the stone carvings on the tessellated shields behind the Warrah Trig or clambering round the greasy rocks at Middle Head to where the cliffs fell 400 metres into the jade-dark waters of the Hawkesbury; but at night I had nothing to do except read, listen to music or watch the grainy television our landlady had left along with most of her beach furniture in the house. I began to drink quite heavily, sometimes a bottle of wine a night, with the consequence that I would wake queasily next morning, headache still throbbing beneath the fog of the pain killers I had taken, eyes small and piggy in the mirror, face collapsed in sad lines of loneliness and defeat.

After a period of living like this I realised I was falling into habits I could not sustain either financially or physically and decided to mend my ways. I restricted myself to a bottle of wine, or maybe two, on weekends, and during the week drank only beer. This was not especially hard to manage, because there wasn't a liquor outlet at Pearl Beach: if you had no car, as I did not, you needed to carry your supplies around the point of Mount Ettalong or else catch one of the infrequent buses over the hill and down the Old Bog Road. So long as I did my shopping while still in the throes of that puritanical self-loathing many drinkers feel the morning after, I could automatically, as it were, restrict my intake to one or two beers in the evening. That reduced my options to dope, music, TV or my library.

I began to hate the television, not just because it was as snowy as one of those novelty scenes you turn upside down then right again to watch the flakes settle on the cityscape within, but because most of the programmes and all of the advertisements were inane. At one time I used to be able to get stoned and watch TV for hours, but this facility has left me. On the other hand, getting stoned and trying to read was hopeless: I would end up staring for minutes at a time at a single sentence, unable to understand its actual meaning or contain the wild cascade of speculation it set off in my head. So I restricted my intake of dope as well, to a single after-work middle-of-the-day smoke, and in the evenings turned unstoned to my library which, as all good libraries should, contained many books I had never read. I stacked a dozen or so of these on the kitchen table where I ate my meals and decided to read through them one by one. They had, after all, each represented some kind of rush of enthusiasm, curiosity or appeal at the time I had acquired them: these traces must surely still exist in my mind, waiting to be reinforced.

Among those I chose was one I had bought at Antiquarian Books all those years ago: *The Secret Discovery of Australia* subtitled *Portuguese ventures 250 years before Captain Cook* by Kenneth Gordon McIntyre. McIntyre's thesis is that certain maps drawn at Dieppe in France in the mid-sixteenth century show the northern, eastern and parts of the southern coastline of Australia in such detail that someone must have sailed those shores. His candidate for the man who made this primary European voyage is a Portuguese, Cristavão de Mendonça. After two other failed Portuguese expeditions—one to the Cape of Good Hope and the other to Brazil—attempting to intercept the renegade Portuguese Fernão Magalhaes, now working for the Spanish crown, Mendonça's voyage was part of a second wave designed to apprehend the interloper within the confines of or round about the Spice Islands themselves. Magellan was hoping to show that those fabulously rich islands fell on the Spanish side of the Line of Demarcation established under the Treaty of Tordesillas of 1494.

Mendonça, according to McIntyre, was to attempt to intercept Magellan should he take the south-eastern route across the Pacific and was thus ordered to search the Isles of Gold: that is, Australia. In 1522, with three caravels—as large a fleet as Columbus took on his first voyage to America—he set out from Portuguese India, sailed through the Straits of Malacca, east along the archipelago as far as the Arafura Sea, threaded Torres Strait, and then proceeded down the east coast of the Great South Land as far as Warnambool, west of where Melbourne is now; here one of his ships was wrecked in a storm. A second ship may have been blown by the same or another storm across the Tasman Sea, coming ashore at Ruapuke Beach, fifty kilometres south of Raglan on the west coast of the North Island of New Zealand. The third returned intact to Goa to tell the tale. Mendonça himself was later Governor of Ormuz at the head of the Persian Gulf.

Both lost ships are recalled in local legend: at Ruapuke and at Warnambool there are tales of strange ships that appear and disappear in the sand dunes; it is sometimes said that the Korotangi, a bird carved out of green serpentine, probably from Sulawesi, and a *taonga* of the Tainui tribe, came from the caravel lost at Ruapuke. The so-called Mahogany Ship of Warnambool was seen at half a dozen different times by different observers during the nineteenth century. It is associated further with a set of five keys said to be of ancient manufacture found a little to the east at Corio Bay in 1847 and subsequently known as the Geelong Keys. Charles Joseph La Trobe, the first Governor of the state of Victoria, had some of these keys in his possession and wrote a long report upon them before giving them to the Mechanics Institute, which unaccountably lost them. It is conjectured that these keys would have unlocked, in La Trobe's words, *a box or trunk, or seamen's chest*. The third piece of physical evidence McIntyre cites is a ruin at Bittangabee Bay on the south coast of New South Wales: roofless walls made of local stone, rubble and seashell mortar, which might be the remains of a sixteenth-century Portuguese fort: did Mendonça winter here in 1524?

McIntyre also discusses another early Portuguese voyage: that of Gomes de Sequeira, who had previously sailed north to the Carolines and the Marianas. In 1525, on a trip from Ternate to Sulawesi, he was blown off course: *They did not know where they were, but ran all the time in the direction of the sunrise. They could not stop where they were; and, relying on God's mercy, they ran before the storm, keeping the wind on their stern for they could not risk any other course. In this way they ran three hundred leagues* ... McIntyre speculates that the *round island* Sequeira found when the gale blew itself out, and which he named *Ilha dos homens brancos* or the island of pale-skins, was the Timorlaut island of Tanimbar. A second island, barren where the other was fertile, might have been Croker

Island north of Darwin, or even a part of the Arnhem Land coast; others have suggested Prince of Wales Island, further to the east. It is possible that Sequeira visited and mapped most of the island groups in the Arafura Sea east of Tanimbar as far as Cape York, including the Kei and Aru Islands and sections of the coasts of New Guinea and northern Australia. When the Treaty of Saragossa in 1529 redrew the Tordesilla Line at a cost to Portugal of 350 000 ducats, most of Australia was included in her ambit. Probably they were less interested in acquiring the island continent than they were in securing the back passage to the Spice Islands discovered first by Mendonça, then by Sequeira: Torres Strait.

In my view, McIntyre proves his case insofar as such a thing can be held to be proven; the cartographical evidence is particularly persuasive. But in establishing the primacy of the Portuguese as European discoverers of Australia, what has he shown? Why, indeed, this peculiar obsession with primacy? These are not rhetorical questions, because I share the obsession, as do many others, with finding out who was first, which was earliest, what lies behind. McIntyre's book, which is scholarly, sober, meticulously constructed and, so far as possible given the subject matter, disabused of all the wilder aspects of historical romanticism, is nevertheless a profoundly romantic work. He is aware of this: at one point, discussing Mendonça's primacy over Sequeira, he remarks dryly that in discovery there are no prizes for getting there second.

It isn't just that there is something enticing about overturning orthodoxies, though that is surely a part of it. Another aspect is the sense of wonder some like to cultivate: the same emotion we indulge when telling ourselves about the vastness and grandeur of the universe is invoked when we contemplate our past. A third strand, related to the first, is our desire for novelty, our need to think the unthought, feel the unfelt, even though, in this late age, it can seem that there is little that remains to be thought and less to be felt. A fourth might be a need to be involved in some kind of mission, to have a puzzle to solve, a mystery to find out about, a quest.

A consequence of these several aspects for quest junkies is that no sooner is one mission accomplished than you are casting around for another: to Edward Dorn's speculation—*Is a man/Without quest/A dangerous sign*—I would have to answer yes. Without quest I become vulnerable to the ever-present temptations of substance abuse, with their inevitable negative consequences; without quest I become dangerous both to myself and others; without quest I am prey to ennui, self-loathing and worse. This time I was lucky: in the beguiling labyrinth of McIntyre's book I found another figure to obsess over, Manoel Godinho de Eredia, the discoverer of the unknown land of Nuca—or Luca—Antara.

Eredia enters McIntyre's narrative courtesy of a Portuguese map found in 1946 in the National Library of Rio de Janeiro by a Dr Mota Alves. This map, dated 1602, shows a part of the island of Flores, the whole of Timor, several other smaller islands in the Timor Sea and two unknown lands, one called Luca Antara, the other Ouro or the Isle of Gold; this latter island McIntyre identifies as that part of the Kimberley in Western Australia now known as Brunswick Bay. Also depicted on the map are sailing routes between these various islands. It seems clear from the Alves map that Portuguese visited at least Western Australia during the late sixteenth and early seventeenth centuries.

Recently, however, this interpretation has been challenged. In a closely reasoned, detailed and persuasive paper published in *Cartography* in December 2003, independent scholar Noel Peters argues that Ouro and Luca Antara as depicted in the Alves map actually represent the Tiwi Islands of Melville and Bathurst, north of Darwin. Peters is perhaps on less secure ground when he suggests it was Eredia himself who carried out the survey of the Tiwi Islands, since there is no direct evidence on the map, or anywhere else, as to who the voyager was; but, it seems, someone did go there and map the islands.

Who was the wonderfully named Godinho de Eredia? McIntyre describes him thus: *Eredia was an eccentric and confused enthusiast, fired with a vision of the great continent in the south, call it Nuca Antara or India Meridional or Java-la-Grande or what you will, who obtained permission to go exploring down that way, but because of circumstances beyond his control never got there. Nevertheless, he drew maps of his Promised Land* ... In the same paragraph he mentions a book of Eredia's called *The Declaration of Malaca*. I was doubly fascinated: first by the name, whether Luca or Nuca Antara, and second by the existence of Eredia's book. I decided to find out all I could about the name and, if possible, obtain a copy of the book.

This was in the early days of the internet, at least as far as I was concerned, and there were not many hits for Nuca Antara. Disturbingly, several of them led to the (probably non-existent) Nuca Antara News Agency operated by a certain Franz T. Schineis. Schineis disseminates anti-Semitic propaganda throughout the world, and appears to be Adelaide-based; he is a neo-Nazi, racist Holocaust denier who believes Australia is controlled by Jews and Freemasons. His espousal of the name Nuca Antara, translated by him or one of his followers as Neck of Antarctica, is partly because the initials N. A. coincide with those of National Action, Australia's peak racist organisation, but also because of his promotion of a completely different history for the country from the one we all know: *The official forgery is based on the pseudo-discoverer Captain Cook, a Buckingham Palace stuntman.*

It was worrisome to find myself in company with fanatics like Schineis; I didn't want to share any part of my obsession with him, but what could I do? He and his cohorts had already laid a claim to the name and nothing I could do would make any difference to that. I put him out of my mind for the moment and continued looking through the other hits on the list: they all, I quickly realised, led back, circuitously or directly, to Eredia and his book, which was more commonly known as *Description of Malaca, Meridional India and Cathay* and included among its appendices the enticingly titled *Report on the Golden Chersonese*.

A copy of *Declaracam de Malaca e India Meridional com o Cathay,* written in Portuguese and published originally in Goa in 1613, was discovered by a Belgic scholar named Leon Janssen in the Bibliothèque Royale de Bruxelles and republished in facsimile with a

French translation in 1882. This had been, in its turn, Englished by J. V. Mills, B.A. (Oxon), an official of the Malayan Civil Service, whose translation was put out in Kuala Lumpur by the Malaysian Branch of the Royal Asiatic Society in 1930. This edition had recently been reprinted by the MBRAS, in 1997, and copies were available. I immediately set in train the process of buying one. This involved quite a lot of to and fro-ing via email before I was in a position to send $US60, *being payment for reprint no. 14: Eredia's Description of Malaca* to a certain Datuk Haji Burhanuddin bin Ahmad Tajudin, the Honorary Secretary of the Malaysian Branch of the Royal Asiatic Society, 130M Jalan Thamby Abdullah, Brickfields, 50470 Kuala Lumpur. The book was despatched by sea and took ages to arrive, leaving me in a fever of impatience for which there was no remedy, only distractions.

When at length it did come, it was wrapped in brown paper and covered with postal and Customs stickers that made it seem as if it had come not just over seas but out of the past as well. It was a pale-blue hardback 339 pages long, with Eredia's actual text taking up only about a third of the volume; the rest consisted of many notes by J. V. Mills and appendices of various kinds. The current editor, Cheah Boon Kheng, had confined himself to a modest introduction of just two pages, leaving the rest of the book to Eredia and Mills. As well as text there were numerous illustrations poorly reproduced in facsimile—mostly maps which looked to be of places on some other planet than ours, but also landscapes, street plans, drawings of fortresses, plants, boats, a waterspout and portraits: one of Afonso de Albuquerque and another of the Basque Jesuit missionary Francis Xavier which, it turned out, because portraits of the saint are rare, was one reason for the careful preservation of a copy of Eredia's book in the repository at Goa.

Among the line drawings was a self-portrait showing Eredia as a man of medium height with cropped hair, a moustache and a small pointed beard in the Spanish style (the kingdoms of Spain and Portugal were at this time united under the rule of the Spanish King Philip III, to whom Eredia had dedicated his book); robed, with his left hand on his hip and his right resting on a globe, he has directly under the palm of this right hand the rough outline of a piece of land

with the words *Luca Antara* written upon it. *Luca*, not *Nuca*: my relief
was indescribable, especially when I read elsewhere in the book Mills'
advice that every time Eredia writes the name of this fabulous land
he writes an initial L, never an N. How the mistake crept into almost
all subsequent literature on the subject (not that there is much of it)
is unclear. As for me, I forthwith abandoned Nuca Antara to the neo-
fascists or anyone else who wants it; and became an ardent prophet of
its sister land, that land of light, perhaps even the light of Antares, the
red star whose name means the antipodes of Ares—the opposite, that
is, of the god of war.

It was hard not to like Eredia, the *Descobridor*, as he styled himself.
He contributed to the volume a short autobiography, written in the
third person, from which I learned that he was the son of a Portuguese
father, one Juan de Eredia Aquaviva, and a Bugis mother; she was the
daughter of the King of Supa in Macassar, baptised into the Catholic
Church as Dona Elena Vesiva *at the request of the Kings of Macazar acting
on the advice of the aforementioned Juan de Eredia.* This—both the falling
in love of these two and the baptism of the Macassan princess—took
place in 1545 at the port of Machoquique, immediately before Juan and
his bride sailed back to Malacca, where Manoel was born on 16 July
1563. (When Eredia writes Macazar he means the island of Celebes,
now known as Sulawesi; Machoquique was midway on the west coast
of this great island and the Kings of Macassar were, famously, of the
people known as Bugis.)

There is another tale behind these bare facts, given elsewhere in
the book by a Father Francisco Luis: the Portuguese, he writes, had
mounted their 1545 expedition from Malacca to Sulawesi, once again
at the request of the Kings in the Province of Buguis in Macazar, in order to
admit them to the church. However, continues Father Luis, *when the
time came for the junk to return to Malaca, at the moment of embarkation ...
there occurred a disturbance and a riot in which weapons were displayed, because
Dona Elena Vesiva had secretly embarked on the junk in the company of Juan
de Eredia, to whom she had become attached or affianced against the wish of
her parents. As all gathered on the shore at daybreak with arms in their hands
in quest of the Portuguese, the Administrator, in order to avoid a conflict which
might have fatal results, then and there gave orders to raise the sails of the boat*

*and weigh anchor and set out … the affair made … people who had been baptised
so offended with the Portuguese that they broke with them and the Portuguese lost
their friendship.*

Twelve years later, in 1557, Dona Elena wrote to her cousin
Tamolina, Queen of Machoquique, in an effort to repair the breach
so made. This attempt was successful; a Portuguese ambassador
was sent to Macassar, and trade in spices, aromatics, rice and grains
resumed. Dona Elena herself died after a short illness in 1575 at the
age of forty-five … which means that she was only fifteen years old, a
child bride, at the time of her abduction—for what else could it have
been?—by the Portuguese in 1545.

Manoel was educated at the College of the Company of Jesus in
Malacca, then, aged thirteen, travelled *at his own expense* to Goa where
he was received into the seminary and studied grammar, arts, the
philosophical and other sciences, and mathematics. At the completion
of his studies, in which, he writes of himself, *he displayed great aptitude*,
he was received into the Company of Jesus and became a teacher of
mathematics; however, he did not remain a Jesuit for very long: he had
a natural inclination for making discoveries and was released from his vows
by his Superiors in the year 1580.

Employed subsequently as Cosmographer Major of the State, he
drew up *some very excellent maps of the oriental Indias and of Asia, replacing
the old drawings in the world-maps and atlases by new chorographic represen-
tations of Cathay and Meridional India*; it was, he continues, these maps,
submitted to Philip III, King of Spain and Portugal, which led to the
Instruction given in Lisbon on Valentine's Day 1594, *to effect the Discovery
of Meridional India*. (Discovery in this instance means something more
like colonisation than actual finding; clearly the Portuguese knew
already where it was.) There must have been some delays, because
Eredia did not receive the commission based upon this Instruction
until 1601, when he set out forthwith for Malacca, Meridional India
and immortality—as well as a twentieth part of any revenues accruing
from those states he managed to take possession of and incorporate
to the Crown.

But as soon as Eredia arrived back in Malacca he was distracted
from his purpose. There was a guerrilla war going on on the

peninsula—as there had intermittently been for the whole previous century of the Portuguese occupation—and in the early seventeenth century the *Malaios* were being particularly troublesome. At the same time the Dutch, who took every opportunity they could to foment opposition towards Estado da India, were gearing up for a direct assault on the port; it was their blockade of Malacca in 1604, when Eredia's expedition was supplied, provisioned and ready to sail, which ended his hopes of glory.

Both before and after this catastrophe Eredia's ships were engaged in clearing the southern channels of corsairs. His energies were also given to building a fortress at Muar in the Straits of Malacca; sinking ships; firing villages and palm groves; and helping to storm and take the citadel at Johor. At the same time he was actively charting the straits with a fleet of twelve galliots and sixty smaller boats—charts from which maps were later prepared—and exploring the inland of the Malay peninsula itself where he found, in his own words, *many mines of gold, silver, 'calem' (= tin), copper, mercury, alum, saltpetre, lead, iron, and other metals besides minerals and precious stones including emeralds, diamonds, topazes and crystals, as well as new fisheries for seed-pearls and pearls.*

At some point this frenetic activity took its toll and Eredia fell ill, apparently with beriberi. He returned to Goa where, notwithstanding letters of exhortation from kings, viceroys, admirals, counts and even the Pope, his projected voyage to Meridional India finally lapsed. He appears to have lived out his life there with his wife, his daughter and at least one grandchild, a girl (his only son had died years before, aged thirteen, *of convulsions*). All of his writing was done in Goa; after an early life of strenuous adventure he appears to have retired to his study and lived his last years among books, papers and maps.

These writings are extensive and bizarre. As well as the *Description of Malaca, Meridional India and Cathay*, there is the *Report on the Golden Chersonese or Peninsula, and on the Auriferous, Carbuncular and Aromatic Isles (translated from an old manuscript in my possession)*; the massive and elusive *Treatise on Ophir, Concerning Tharsis and Ophir in the Ancient World, the Voyages of Solomon and the Region of Arsareth, Tartaria*; a *History of the Martyrdom of Luiz Monteiro Coutinho*; and, in 1618, a *Mappemonde* which was evidently his last work and also one of the few of his maps to have survived. Luca Antara is drawn on this map, and beside it is written: *Discovered by M.G. Eredia in 1601*. Haunted to the last by the fabulous land he never entered, Eredia died in Goa not long after his Mappemonde was drawn.

He was not a man entirely to give up his dream, however. Among the appendices to the main text of the *Description of Malaca* is a short piece, just half a dozen pages long, called *Report on Meridional India* and subtitled *Discovered By M. G. De Eredia in the year 1610*—how so? The report begins: *Meridional India comprises the continental land of Lucach which reaches southwards beyond the Tropic of Capricorn and beyond the Antarctic Circle as far as the Pole, and from there extends as far as the land of Parrots, the region of Pithacoru: it includes the Java major wherein Beach is situated, or Luca Antara, and the Java minor which yields spices and other neighbouring islands such as Petan, Necuran, and Agania, all prolific in riches and gold and other metals and minerals, as well as cloves, nutmegs, white and red sandalwood ...*

Eredia recounts earlier voyages to this land, drawing upon Ptolemy and Marco Polo, before describing what appears to have been an actual voyage, by one Francisco de Rezende of Malacca, *in a junk driven out of its course from Timor.* They were not permitted by the natives of that land to disembark but did manage to recover some gold from water up to their waists. Eredia believes a native boat that came ashore at Balambuan in *our Java* in 1601 was from the same place; modern authorities have identified this as the island of Sumba. Subsequently, *Chiay Masiuro, King of Damut, Prince that he was* set out from Balambuan towards the south, and after twelve days sailing reached an island of 600 Spanish leagues in circumference where he was entertained by the *Xebander* or Governor and saw *much gold, cloves, maces, nutmegs, sandalwoods and other spices and aromatics and riches.*

This island Eredia identified as Luca Antara and, upon hearing Chiay Masiuro's account, *gave secret instructions to a servant of his, disguised and unknown, to go to Java (containing Mataron, Bantan and Sunda) to acquire more accurate information about this expedition on the opposite or Southern coast of Java in the great Bay of Fishermen; this servant joined the fishermen and crossed in six days to the coast of Luca Antara.* Upon his return he wrote to Eredia, in a letter dated 14 August 1610, that having followed the land for three days he disembarked *on a coast which was deserted, for I was not observed by any stranger, and I and my companion on the shore were the only inhabitants; I remained there three days and confirmed the truth of Chiay Masiuro's account ...*

This anonymous servant, then, who fell ill upon his return to Mataron and about whom nothing else was written, is the source for Eredia's claim to have discovered Luca Antara in 1610. Having quoted his letter in full, Eredia passes on to a consideration of the renewal of trade between Luca Antara and Java, moribund for over 300 years—that is, since Marco Polo's time. He also gives account of other lands: Lucach or Beach, and Pithacoru, the land of Parrots, which he speculates may be one and the same as, or at the very least contiguous with, Luca Antara. At Lucach, it was said, lived a race of badly clothed white people who had no iron but only weapons of wood, and some Portuguese, descendants of men from two ships lost off the Cape of Good Hope in 1503. And there too were the requisite gold, spices, jewels and so forth which Portuguese explorers swore they found in the most unlikely places, including, for example, on the shores of Espiritu Santo where Quieroz was.

I was immediately entranced by the tale of the unknown, loyal servant's voyage to Luca Antara and determined to find out all I could about it. In fact, I wondered if it would be possible to fabricate an account of this voyage in such a way as to give it not just credence as a work of fiction but the unmistakable aura of truth, but decided, reluctantly, that both historical novel and nonfictional re-creation were probably beyond my ability to write. I settled instead for a simpler alternative: more research and an account of where that research led.

The first thing I did was compose a letter to Datuk Haji Burhanuddin bin Ahmad Tajudin, the Honorary Secretary of the Malaysian Branch of the Royal Asiatic Society, asking him if he or any of the members of the society had made a special study of these events and, if so, what conclusions they had come to. I was not confident an inquiry such as this would be answered at all and certainly did not expect the Datuk to respond quickly; so it proved. When he did, it was a polite, formal letter suggesting I address any queries about Eredia to the editor of the reprint, Cheah Boon Kheng, in Penang.

Again with no great hope of success I sat down and did precisely that; but Cheah Boon Kheng responded with somewhat more alacrity than the Datuk and, what's more, he had something to say. I quote from his letter:

... with respect to your inquiry as to any scholar who might have concerned himself directly with Eredia's servant's alleged voyage to Luca Antara (wherever that was!), yes, there is one I know of who has researched that particular matter in depth. He is a former student of mine who goes by the name of Henry Klang, and he presently resides, I believe, in Melaka, as old Malacca is now known. Unfortunately I do not presently have an address for him, however, I will endeavour to procure one for you. While I do not wish to be indiscreet, nor discouraging, I feel it is my duty to inform you that Mr Klang has at times suffered from an illness, one of whose manifestations is a fervent belief in speculations which are clearly delusory—while hastening to add that, in these delusions, he is a danger neither to others nor to himself. Mr Klang was once a promising scholar, and still possesses many of the skills and qualities of a scholar; but I must warn you that you cannot rely entirely upon everything he says ...

Of course I wrote back immediately to Cheah Boon Kheng thanking him for his interest and expressing the hope that he would indeed be able to put me in touch with Mr Klang, but it was some time before I heard from him again, and when I did it was not by letter but by email: a very short message which informed me that Henry Klang was indeed in Melaka, that he would appreciate it if I were to contact him *in the matter of Eredia's servant*, about which he had assembled some fascinating speculations—that word again—but that our conversation should proceed by email. And there was his address. I sat down straight away to write to him.

Now came the most frustrating part of a process that had, all things considered, gone quite smoothly up until now. Every day, sometimes several times a day (sometimes several times an hour), I checked for emails, but no reply came from Henry Klang. This went on for about a week, at which point I decided the contact had not been made or the search was in vain, or—as the scholar in Penang had intimated—Klang was ill or insane. I gave up waiting and turned to other things.

I resumed my exploration, if that is the word, of the local area, going for long walks in the bush, deliberately leaving behind whatever paths there were and heading off instead into the trackless wastes like one who wished to lose himself entirely. The dry sclerophyll forest of eastern Australia, with its endless pink, yellow and grey sandstone, its scarps and tumbled shelves, its angophoras, turpentines and other gum trees, its prickly shrubs, its fugitive, delicate wildflowers, its songbirds and honey-eaters, parrots and lyrebirds, lizards and snakes became my habitat too as I bush-crashed in a kind of frenzy, sweating, climbing, falling, recovering, eaten by flies, torn by thorns, barking my shins, with leaves in my hair and spider webs clinging to my cheeks. I felt constantly that I was about to find something rare and strange, though what this was I never quite knew. Those places like primitive oases, where stubby, ancient palms grew among the rocks of dried-up watercourses, were the nearest I came to answering this feeling.

After a week or perhaps two of this 'exploration', one day I walked out onto a high flat ledge of rock overlooking the Hawkesbury and saw that it was inscribed with the dim outlines of whales, dolphins, turtles, sunfish, sharks, and beings with upraised hair or head dresses and big genitals between their skinny legs. From there, on that line of cliffs which defines the northern bank of the river as it flows into Broken Bay, you can see the whole panorama of the system with its humped bush-covered headlands, its long snaky inlets, its wide blue waters crossed by random white lines of boat trails and deeper, more subtle flows of tidal warps or riverine currents; and in the giant hush rising from below I paused and sat and wondered what on earth I was doing.

It was as if I had determined to replace my quest for knowledge of the historical discovery of the land with a search for some other reality in amongst its contemporary biogeographical expression; but there was a disturbing subtext to this, for the oblivion that had overtaken the makers of the rock art had, it seemed, become part of my ambition as well. Belatedly I understood that, since I lived by the sea and any casual walk inevitably led back to the littoral, to lose myself in this wilderness was impossible unless I went directly inland—and I was as unwilling to do this as I was to give in to the temptation I sometimes felt to swim out towards the horizon until, exhausted, I sank beneath the waves.

Faced with my inability to make such an irrevocable move in either direction, I remembered Henry Klang and the hopes I had of furthering my knowledge of early voyages to Luca Antara. I hadn't even been turning on the computer, let alone looking at emails. I left that rocky shelf, made my way to the nearby fire trail winding down through switchbacks to the village, and walked straight back home. There I switched on and logged onto my server and found waiting for me, among sundry pieces of dross, an email from H. Klang with the subject line: *The Voyage of António da Nova.*

Dear Edmond, it read, *I am in reception of your email about Luca Antara and who was the person who first came into that land. His name is António da Nova and I am possessing the unique and only account of his voyage. Do you perhaps read Portuguese? It is a very great labour for me to turn this manuscript into English, many are the years now that I have worked without money or any other kind of help just to let the world know these things. I do this for love alone, so that people may learn what wonderful things there have been happening in the past, and will turn away from their selfishness and be admiring true hero deeds from yore ...*

It was a long letter without a great deal more of actual substance; but the news that there was a voyage and an account of it, and the name of he who led it, was enough to banish my incipient despair. I read through Klang's email several times and then began to formulate my reply. He clearly needed careful treatment, was some kind of isolate, perhaps even a paranoiac, who had to be approached with circumspection. I decided to adopt a detached and scholarly tone, to put myself forward as responsible, disinterested, above all calm.

Dear Mr Klang, I wrote, *Thank you for your email. That is indeed exciting news about da Nova and his account and I wish you all the best in the course of your scholarly task. Unfortunately I do not speak or read Portuguese so can be of no help to you in that respect. I could however perhaps be of assistance in the preparation of any English version of his account—I am a professional writer of many years' experience, have worked as a teacher of English as a second language and been awarded an MA with first class honours in English Language and Literature* ... and so on.

The hope that Klang would send his translation to me in whole or in part was a very long shot indeed, but I figured that he was someone who clearly needed help with his English grammar, should (and why else would he be doing what he was doing?) publication be his ultimate aim.

His reply was not long in coming:

Esteemed Edmond ... it began, *you are giving me strength just when my heart is failing ... you cannot know how hard it is being for me to do this thing alone and without any help from anyone. The only ones who are trying to help me are desirous of wanting to steal my work and saying it is their own* ... and so on, with no commitment to any collaboration with me.

Well, why would he? Who was I? A voice out of the empyrean, a fellow nutter perhaps, at best a fellow traveller. Our e-conversation continued in this vein for some time until I found the courage to ask him directly if I could see something of what he was working on. This was of course the crucial moment, and I half expected him to break off the contact then and there.

Given the pace of our correspondence thus far there was in fact a slight lull before he replied to my request:

Dear Edmond, he wrote, *I cannot agree to sending you the words da Nova has written, not until I am finishing my translation, otherwise it may fall into the hands of wicked people because in these days it is sad and true to say there is no honesty and everyone is just out to make themselves rich* ...

My heart sank. I'd blown it. Whatever it was he was sitting on would never come to me now.

He continued in this maudlin and paranoid fashion for some time before suddenly, near the end of the email, he changed his tune:

However, it is seeming to me that there is a way which you can be helping me, because I am writing abstract of da Nova's book to interest publishers to give me advance and I would be liking to interest publishers in Australia because Australia is Luca Antara and also scholars here in Malaysia are all crooked liars who steal your work ...

Yes, I wrote back, *yes, yes, yes, I will be helping you with abstract* ... But the documents Mr Klang subsequently sent to me could not by any stretch of the imagination be described as comprising an abstract. Precisely what they *were* is still not clear to me even today. They may be translations from the Portuguese of the alleged author, António da Nova; but if that is so, the translations are partial and incomplete, with no warrant at all of accurate correspondence to any original. I think it more likely that Henry Klang was summarising da Nova in his own words rather than offering a version; but this depends upon the supposition that there was an original document to summarise, and I cannot offer any credible evidence that this is so. Which brings me to the third possibility: that Henry Klang made up the passages of the *Voyage of António da Nova* that he sent me, which means that, in reproducing them here, I am reproducing a work of fiction.

Of course I tried to establish the status of the attachments to the emails that arrived irregularly from Melaka, but Henry Klang, in his besotted state, simply ignored my questions. He could only talk about the voyage in the same extravagant terms of those excerpts from his emails I quote above: da Nova's journey was an example of the kind of true and wonderful heroism which has gone out of the world; anyone who opposed him (Klang or da Nova) was some kind of evil goblin; the world was teetering on the brink of the ultimate confrontation between good and evil and only the example of someone like da Nova could save the good ... While I looked forward to these erratic bulletins from beyond the horizon, I came to dread the scrambled paranoid letters which came with them and indeed soon ceased to do more than scan them briefly before turning to the narrative itself.

This narrative is what follows: the two dozen or so pieces of writing Klang sent me, preserved in their original order with the breaks conforming to breaks between emails. I have made minor changes to grammar and syntax which, while they do not alter the thrust of what is written, do perhaps here and there change the tone. I have done this because I believe it would be wearisome for a reader to have to experience da Nova's voyage in the ubiquitous present-participle construction of Klang's prose. I have also, so far as I have been able to, corrected the spelling. Otherwise the material is as it was sent to me.

As to permissions, I have done all I could to secure the right to reproduce Klang's material; however, as I shall relate later, despite all my efforts I have so far been unable to come to a sensible understanding with him. If and when we do I will of course make the appropriate arrangements regarding payment, acknowledgement and so forth. Those who find my methodology dubious might reflect on the fact that Klang sent the material to me in order to facilitate publication of his work; and this I have surely done.

Da Nova writes that in the year 1610, at the time of the pancoraba or change of monsoon, when the winds die or revolve fitfully about the compass for a month or more until the great nor'-westers begin to blow, he made his way by ship from Malacca to the Bay of Fishermen to meet an old man by the name of Rindi, a friend of Manoel Godinho de Eredia. This Rindi was from south Sulawesi, sometimes called Macassar, as was Eredia's mother, who was a princess of the Kingdom of Supa on that island. Rindi, who had fruit plantations inland from the sea on Sulawesi, was unlucky with snakes, once almost being devoured by a huge python and on another occasion soon after finding an equally large snake in the rafters of his own house. He was told by the village shaman that he would die in a snake's belly if he remained on land and so went to sea instead; he served on one of the ships Eredia used on his surveys of the coast north from Malacca, and the two men, the cosmographer and the common sailor, became friends because of their shared place of origin. Now Rindi had retired to the Bay of Fishermen in the Kingdom of Mataram to the east of the great island of Java, and Eredia sent da Nova to him with instructions for Rindi to find a boat and a crew to sail him to Luca Antara.

Da Nova, arriving at the Bay of Fishermen incognito and in the evening, walked out along the white road to the north of the port until he saw in the scimitar dusk a sign figured on the door of a house: a snake with its tail in its mouth. By the sign he knew this was the place; he knocked on the door, was admitted, and spent that night and several subsequently as the guest of Rindi, who was an old man, and his equally ancient wife Sadria. During this time da Nova did not go out once, but Rindi was very busy finding the boat in which he would make the voyage and crewing it with men who were both competent sailors and trustworthy men, not an easy task in those days nor indeed in any of the days that have followed.

Mataram is in western Lombok, in those days divided into squabbling states ruled by Sasak princes, who were about to fall under the power of Balinese from Karangasem. Sasak women wear black sarongs, held in place by a long scarf trimmed with brightly coloured stripes, and short-sleeved v-necked blouses; with little jewellery and no gold. The men also wear black. Sasak peasants adhere to the mystical Wektu Telu version of Islam and are organised into irrigation associations like those used in Balinese wet rice cultivation.

Mataram consists of four towns: Ampenan, the port, where there is an ancient community of devout Muslim Arabs; Mataram itself, the administrative centre; Cakranegara, the trading centre; and Sweta, the market. Rindi lived a little to the north near a community of Bugis fishermen from which he hoped to recruit da Nova's crew; the Bugis were ordinary Muslims but the majority of the local people, as Rindi's wife Sadria explained to da Nova, are Wektu Telu.

Sadria was a midwife and was frequently called out to attend to a birth. She said the Wektu Telu believe that during birth four siblings escape from the womb: blood, egg, placenta, amniotic fluid. The afterbirth has to be treated with care and respect or else the four siblings would cause harm to the child. Offerings were made and the afterbirth buried, after which the child was scattered with ashes. When it was 105 days old there was a ceremony for the cutting of its hair; as the boy or girl grew older, other formalities were observed. Though these were not her beliefs Sadria respected them nevertheless, for it was her livelihood and anyway, as she said, one set of beliefs is the same as any other set, since there are only three certainties: we are born, we live, we die.

Wektu means *result* in Sasak, while *telu* means *three* and refers to the mixing of Balinese Hinduism, Islam and animism. Everything is a trinity: Allah (God), Mohammed (the link between God and man) and Adam (a being in search of a soul); the sun, the moon and the stars;

heaven, earth and water; head, body and limbs; creativity, sensitivity and control. The three duties are belief in Allah, avoiding the devil and helping others. Wektu Telu do not observe Ramadan, merely fasting and praying for three days. They do not pray five times a day but whenever and wherever they feel the need of prayer: hence all public buildings have a prayer corner or a small room facing Mecca. They do not abstain from pork either, believing everything is good that comes from Allah.

After death Wektu Telu bodies are washed in the presence of a holy man, then wrapped in white sheets and sackcloth before being placed on a platform while the Koran is read and people pray to the spirits of ancestors. In the cemetery the body is interred with the head facing Mecca while the Koran is read again, first in Sanskrit, then in Arabic. Carved wood, for a man, and decorative combs, for a woman, are placed on the grave. There are ceremonies on the 3rd, 7th, 40th and 100th days after death. After 1000 days holy water is sprinkled on the grave and the wooden offerings removed and replaced by stones. A low hill covered with gnarled frangipani trees not far from Rindi's house was where the graveyard was. Small headstones stood under the trees.

From the back of Rindi's house da Nova could also see the volcano Rinjani. By mid-morning on most days it was shrouded with cloud. Within, Sadria told him, there was a green crescent-shaped crater lake called Child of the Sea and on the north-east side of the crater hot springs which were very good for healing skin diseases. On the full moon at pancoraba worshippers threw jewellery into the lake and made offerings to the spirit of the mountain. Da Nova stared up at the mountain and wondered: he was schooled by Jesuits in Malacca but sometimes felt stirring within him some older faith than the rigorous disciplines inherited from Europe. Besides, he was unwell from the restricted diet on the long sea voyage from Malacca; and also full of trepidation about the expedition before him. The burden of secrecy placed upon him by his master was almost insupportable, since he did not clearly understand the need for it: his mission was so insignificant as to appear negligible. On the other hand, he supposed, if they really were to find the fabled Land of Gold, that would perhaps justify the

clandestine nature of the quest. Perhaps he too was a man in search
of his soul?

Rindi found a boat and its crew but then announced that he would not
be coming along. Da Nova pleaded with him but Rindi said he was too
old and wished to die on land, not at sea.

But who will direct the sailors? Da Nova asked.

I will bring the nakoda to see you tomorrow, Rindi replied.

There are twelve crewmen on a Bugis *prahu*; the *nakoda* is the captain
and there is usually another man who is a kind of supercargo, responsible for the trade goods, whatever they are, and for looking after the
crew, considered as a body of men not just sailors. However, in this
case it seemed there was no one filling the role, which was why da Nova
wanted Rindi to come along; but the old man would not.

The *nakoda's* name was Tandri Dewa; he was a young man, even
younger than da Nova was, handsome, smiling but with something
evasive in his manner, a way of looking away which did not inspire
confidence. The first thing he said to da Nova was that a voyage such
as the one proposed made no sense: Bugis *prahu* were trading vessels,
yet here they were, carrying nothing, to no known destination, with
no idea of the goods they might find to bring back with them and so
make a profit. Da Nova reiterated what Rindi had already said: they
would be paid in gold for the voyage, half now, half upon their safe
return, and anything they could find or trade for along the way they
could have to add to the profit of the expedition.

Tandri Dewa glowered and muttered, so da Nova showed him some
of the gold coin that would be his once they embarked and he seemed
to calm down. However, da Nova could not allay his distrust of the
man, even suspecting that he might come back in the night with other
men and try to steal the gold he was carrying. After Tandri Dewa had
gone, da Nova and Rindi buried half of the gold under the floor of
the house and covered it with mats; the remainder da Nova wrapped
around his body in preparation for the voyage that would begin the
next day. He was still feeling ill but not so ill as when he arrived, for

Sadria had been feeding him soups full of healing herbs, which he ate with balls of sticky rice and strings of dried beef.

After they had buried the gold Rindi and da Nova sat outside the house and talked; while they were talking, unaccountably, since it was night, a hooded cobra undulated through the white sand of the road towards them, then reared up its head and hissed. Both men stood and da Nova picked up a stick to keep off the snake, but Rindi stayed his arm.

See, it is going, he said quietly. *And so am I.*

He said the snake was a sign or rather a messenger and that death awaited him if he remained on Lombok; perhaps if he accompanied da Nova he would also be going to his death but he preferred to meet his end rather than wait for it. Sadria scolded him and wept, saying she would never see him again; but the old man had decided, and he comforted her and made himself ready to go.

Bugis sailing is surrounded by superstition. A new *prahu* is built from a tree that has been called out of the forest. It will have a grain of rice and a piece of tree root placed inside the main joint of the keel; this tree will be of a kind which grows straight down so that the boat will always be connected with the land. Eyes of gold dust and white will be painted on either bow so that the *prahu* can see, and a hole drilled in the keel of a new boat and oil poured through it—for luck. Once they were launched by being rolled into the water over the bodies of seven women in their first pregnancy; and even today every new voyage is approached ceremoniously.

The leaving of the land ceremony is called *Nuang Ase*. A white cock and a black goat were sacrificed on the beach: the black goat of the earth, for stability; the white cock of the sky, for courage. Then a feast was held on the *prahu*, the only time women and children were allowed aboard. They came in their beautiful dresses and ate the goat and the cock and all the other foods, and then went back ashore. The top-men were somersaulting in the rigging, then sliding down the shrouds with the ropes between their toes as the *prahu* turned away from the land.

These were the *anuk prahu*, the children of the *prahu*, as the crewmen
are known. It is important to begin the voyage on the auspicious day
chosen but not important to sail very far. The *prahu* eased south down
the arid rocky west coast of Lombok until it came to a beach where it
anchored offshore so that sand could be carried aboard for ballast.

Da Nova, who was by instinct and training a scholar not a practical
man, had little to do. They had given him a small compartment made
of woven palm fronds on the deck of the boat in which he could
sleep and do his writing; it was infested, as was the whole boat, with
rats, bedbugs and cockroaches. He noticed that no one, not even
Tandri Dewa, seemed to give orders but that everyone was content
to perform whatever task suited his mood. Among the company were
two boys, only about ten years old, called Amir and Mansur, who were
simultaneously cooks, washers up, barbers, lice pickers, deck swabbers
and general do-everythings. These boys were the most friendly to da
Nova, bringing him things to eat and offering small comforts when
they could; but Tandri Dewa, who had smiled so much when da Nova
handed over the first instalment of the gold, now only scowled and
looked away whenever he saw da Nova looking at him. And da Nova
did not know what it was he had done.

There were thirteen men aboard counting da Nova and Rindi, who
was the supercargo; the *prahu* had two masts, two steering oars, one
barrel of water at the base of the mizzenmast from which everyone
drank. The helmsmen's platforms were placed far back at the stern
and low down so that the men frequently got wet and would fall into
the sea if they went to sleep on the job. In the bow was a caged rooster
whose task it was to look ahead for obstacles in the water and to cry
out when it saw something. The half-submerged trunks of palms or
of other trees floating just below the surface are the biggest danger.
They were blue-water sailors, guided by wave patterns, seaweed, bird
droppings and other flotsam; and they navigated more by watching
the water than they did by watching the sky.

The morning after they took on the sand ballast they sailed on
round the base of the island of Lombok and along the south coast;
but when the pale shape of Sumbawa appeared on the horizon ahead,
Tandri Dewa changed course to the south-east as if he did not want to

go near that island. Da Nova found him there on the deck and asked him why. He smiled and shook his head.

We don't go to Sumbawa, he said. *Too much trouble.*

What kind of trouble? da Nova asked.

Tandri Dewa looked contemptuous.

We are Bugis, he said. *Anyone can see that, when we have our black sails flying. Except at night, when we carry no lights!* And he laughed. *Our brothers are in the north of Sumbawa, at Bima, where the Bajau, the sea gypsies also live. But in the south*—he gestured towards the paling blue line on the horizon—*they would kill us if they could. We go to Sumba to buy sandalwood.*

Da Nova did not know what to say. He felt stupid and powerless. His orders were to sail to the south even though he knew that most ships kept to the northern coasts of the chain of islands stretching into the east. The Portuguese, the Dutch, the local traders, whether Bugis or not, all preferred the mostly shallow inland waters of the South China Sea to the wild depths of the Indian Ocean. Nor was there anything in his orders about trading, yet he did not see how he could possibly countermand Tandri Dewa's intention to look for sandalwood. His only power was strapped around his waist, or back in Mataram, buried beneath the floor in Rindi's house. There was no other reason why Tandri Dewa or anyone else should do what he wanted. He returned to his small house and sat and wondered.

Here he was joined a little while later by Rindi, who had great broad hands, muscular arms, thighs like posts except he was bandy almost beyond belief, with the face of an ancient monkey and no hair at all on his head. Rindi sat down and nodded and smiled and then began to prepare betel nut for them to chew—the green stalk of *sirih*, which is male, like a penis; the nut or *pinang*, which is female, like ovaries; the lime, or *kapor*, which is semen. The lime reacts with other juices in the mouth to cause the characteristic flood of red saliva which, when spat out, Rindi said, depositing a great gob onto the deck, is returning the blood of childbirth back into the earth. Or in this case the sea, he added reflectively, watching it trickle across the wood.

After a while he pointed in the direction of the islands to the north and chanted softly:

Bima, Sape, Dompu, Taliwang.

Da Nova did not know what these words meant.

These are the names of the Majapahit cities of Sumbawa written in the Nagar-
akertagama, the old man said. *I have been in these places, there you find pictures*
of men with the heads of elephants carved into rocks and other signs that no one
can read any more. Footprints of the gods can be seen in the stones. It is said the
first king arrived in a boat from the west, was shipwrecked, and there on the beach
took a serpent, naga, for his wife. The people are descended from snakes.

He made a hissing sound.

The Nakoda, he whispered, leaning forward, *does not want you on this*
ship. If he finds sandalwood in Sumba, he will throw you into the sea and tell
everyone that you drowned.

But he has agreed to take me to Luca Antara, said da Nova, hating
himself for his naivety, hating his vulnerability even more.

Rindi shrugged.

Who knows where this place is? I have been sailing these seas for fifty years, and
I have never heard of such a land. If it exists, we would know of it.

It is east of Timor, said da Nova, but the old man shrugged again and
said such a statement made no sense, since Timor itself means east,
so that all it said was east of east. The two men sat in silence listening
to the creak of the joints in the wooden boat, the sighing of the sails,
the soft abandonment of the wake as they hissed through calm waters.
Then Rindi said:

I am a friend of Manoel Godinho de Eredia, which means I am your friend too;
I will do whatever I can to help you, even though this is a voyage into madness.

And da Nova thanked him and tried to give him a gold coin, but
Rindi was offended and said he did what he did out of loyalty to
Eredia, not for money. And then he went away, leaving da Nova to
sit and think and later write his thoughts in the Journal he kept. Later,
and later again, Rindi returned and told da Nova many things which
he wrote down in his book as wonders.

The wind blew steadily from the west, the weather stayed fine, the
crew were happy insofar as you could tell and soon the blue outline
of Sumba was in view on the starboard bow up ahead. There was a

problem with the mast, Rindi told da Nova, but they would fix that when they came to Waingapu on the northern coast somewhat towards the east of the island. Here they would take on sandalwood in exchange for the gold da Nova had given in payment for the voyage; after which they would go perhaps to Ende, the great port on the south coast of Flores. Bugis *prahu*, Rindi explained, have their masts stepped onto the deck, not through to the floor of the hull; dismasting can domino one into the other; or a mast might fall vertically through the decks, cannoning through the hull and sinking the boat very quickly. Their *prahu's* mainmast had rotted where it was stepped into the deck.

Coming up to the land they saw it was wide and flat, with emerald valleys and sweeping hills and dense stands of sandalwood and cinnamon trees. Granite megaliths sealed the graves of nobles buried with their slaves and horses. A beautiful scent drifted out over the water towards them, the aromatics of cinnamon and sandalwood. They passed white sand beaches where horses and cattle wandered. The people tending them wore black sarongs. Behind, through trees, the high conical thatched roofs of houses rose up like palace towers. The crew of the *prahu*, full of excitement, were working her towards the land, calling to one another from the rigging like birds. Tandri Dewa stood in the bow, watching ahead. Rindi sat cross-legged on the deck outside da Nova's shelter.

Have you been here before? da Nova asked.

Yes, Rindi said, *many years ago when I was just a young man, I came here. What is it like?*

It is a very old land. It is an island now, but once it was a mountain of a great country that is now under the sea. This country was also called Sumba, and this island, along with Timor, is a remnant of it; but Sumba is older. There are no volcanoes here. Some people say a great ladder once connected heaven and earth and that is how they came to Sumba. Others say that the first people came over a stone bridge from Flores. I have seen in their villages stone boats in which they also said they sailed; but who has ever sailed a stone boat?

They worship their ancestors and are in love with stones. Their temples are built of great carved stones balanced one on top of another and they bury their dead under such stones within their villages. It is said that the great sailor, Sindbad, came here on one of his voyages, but I do not know which voyage it was. He came here for sandalwood and left behind horses; and Sumba is still the best island for horses. Sumba horses are small, strong, handsome. The land is dry and grassy, especially in the north and east, where the sandalwood grows.

The people look like Indians—dashing, tall and turbaned Sumbanese men like Indian princes. There are Muslim Endenese settlements on the north coast and also people from Savu. There are Chinese merchants and Arabs at Waingapu, where we are going. I have heard a saying in this place: all the way from Sind to Sumba. Sind means sea, it is where your word India comes from; Sumba is Sumba, the ancient land. All the way from Sind to Sumba means from one end of the earth to the other. But that was before ...

Before what? asked da Nova.

Before your people came, said Rindi.

I am only half Portuguese, said da Nova. *My mother was a Kling.*

I know that, said Rindi. *But in you your father's blood rules.*

Da Nova wondered if Rindi was right. His father had been a common soldier and his mother an ordinary woman of her people; they were very different, both from their fellows and from each other. His mother, small, dark, with long straight black hair and eyes like forest pools; his father tall and pale with reddish hair, freckled skin and eyes of such a pale eggshell blue they seemed transparent as the draining sky at evening. What brought them together? His father, like any other Portuguese soldier, meant to spend his time in the east gathering wealth which he would then take back to his country and use to set himself up on the land. His mother was never part of this plan: she was to be his companion only for as long as he remained in Estado da India.

There was no subterfuge. Like him, she understood the arrangement to be temporary; again like him, perhaps its transitory nature suited her. He remembered them best in the evenings, when his father sat out on the veranda reading his Bible and his mother, her cooking done, squatted as she preferred on the step nearby and, as the first fruit bats swooped into the maluka trees that gave the city its name, looked up at her husband, smiled and shook her head in wonder at the sight.

This man, she would say, *will you look at him reading? Always the same book, and yet he is never tired of it.*

And then he would sigh and lower his Bible and look patiently at her before resuming his silent reading. As for her, she never renounced her own religion and maintained the household shrines as diligently as he read his Bible and said his prayers; neither did she ever show the slightest inclination to follow him in his beliefs or even find out what they were. By the same token, her heathenism, as he called it, did not seem to bother him, even though it was a rejection of his faith as well as a denial of the paradise he expected to be admitted to eventually, presumably without her.

For all that his father never did gather up his booty and return to his village north of Oporto, just as, while he lived, his mother did not go back, as she often threatened she would, to the village of her people in the west. Instead, bickering gently, indissolubly joined at the heart, they stayed together in the little house behind the mosque at one end of the bridge over the river where all the godowns were until one day he took a fever and died, leaving what riches he had gathered to the Jesuits for his son's education; and then she left him and did go back to her people in Sind where the Klings come from.

It was in the afternoon. As they neared the port at Waingapu the excitement among the crew died and Tandri Dewa began to look worried. No boats had come out to greet them and there seemed to be nothing going on on the dusty roads running down to the shore and then along by the wharves. There were only a few small boats moored offshore and a strange yellow haze was in the air. Tandri Dewa sniffed and gave the order to heave to. They anchored some distance from the land and waited, scanning the shore.

Something's wrong, said Rindi.

Two men were sent ashore in the *lipa lipa* they used for such things. They were not away long and came back paddling the canoe fast through the water. They said they had seen bodies on the roads, skulls dangling from trees in the middle of the town.

They are called andung trees, said Rindi. *That is where they hang the skulls of their enemies.*

These were fresh, the men said. *There were bodies on the road. We saw a child but he ran away. The Arab houses are all closed up and the Chinese are too. Something bad has happened.*

Tandri Dewa spoke sharply to them:

Did you not ask anyone?

There was an old man jangling amulets beneath the tree, muttering incantations and looking at the entrails of a chicken slit open and spilled before him. We waited for him to speak. He said it is a war of clans, that one clan has stolen the gold heirlooms of another and that the feud will go on for twenty years; today, they are contending on the grounds behind the town, and everyone has gone to the fight or is hiding in their houses.

They looked at Tandri Dewa. He did not know what to do. Suddenly he seemed like a young man without experience. Different members of the crew spoke up: some wanted to go ashore armed and see what they could find in the town. Others said it was bad luck and they should go elsewhere, to Ende to find trade goods or to Timor for sandalwood. Nobody knew how long the mast would last before repairs were needed. All this time Tandri Dewa did not speak but listened and thought. Rindi, likewise, said nothing. Then Tandri Dewa said they would spend the night aboard the *prahu* and go ashore in the morning to see what they could find. If it was safe they would repair the mast and then, if there was no sandalwood to buy, go to Timor.

During the night they saw fires on the land and heard the wailing of women coming across the water. Also the sound of horses, galloping through the dusty dark roads of the town and the cries of men in an exaltation of rage or joy. Some of the crew stood looking towards the shore, their eyes glistening with expectation; others huddled on the deck, sleeping or trying to sleep under their sarongs. Tandri Dewa did not sleep, spoke to no one, and no one spoke to him. Da Nova lay in his shelter, trying to see what the future held for him, but nothing came to mind. He was woken before dawn by Rindi, who took him by the wrist and drew him out on deck.

Look! he said.

Da Nova looked at the sky which was everywhere black except where the fires showed on the land. There was a damp stillness in the air, a flash and then a faint mutter in the west.

We will have a storm, the old man said. *See, the Nakoda is worried.*

Tandri Dewa was going from man to sleeping man, waking the crew. The flashes of lightning in the west were becoming brighter and more regular, the thunder mutters louder and closer together. Then the wind arrived, first with a faint sigh like that of a sorrowful god who must nevertheless begin the work of destruction, then with more severe intermittent gusts, finally building to a steady scream amidst which warm pelting rain fell.

By this time the anchor had been raised and the boat cleared towards open water. As soon as they were out in the strait they were picked up and thrown eastward before the gale. Five days and nights they rode the storm, with the rotten mast whipping back and forth so violently as many as five men were needed to hold it in place so it didn't break; these men were at the same time clinging to the lee mainsail. The *prahu*'s short timbers, designed for flexibility, moved so violently they let water come in, which had to be bailed by hand. It took four men to manage the steering oars bucking in their harnesses. The *prahu* squirmed and stretched like the spine of a fish. Sails split with sounds like guns going off and had to be sewed up on the spot. There were no guard rails or rigging harnesses or ratlines and the crew scaled the masts barefoot, clinging to the spars with their legs alone.

All this time the twelve men aboard, including the two boys, worked as one; even da Nova, who had no real skills as a sailor, made himself useful at simple tasks requiring only a pair of willing hands and a modicum of intelligence; and at last, on a grey and ragged morning, the storm blew out and left them battered but unbroken somewhere out in the Timor Sea.

They had been blown past Savu, that low bare island where the people wear a cloth of black or dark blue stripes interspersed with flowers and reptiles and push boats out into the sea as offerings. And they had passed Roti too, whose people cut chunks from live buffalo to eat and otherwise subsist on the products of the lontar palm, which gives them wood for houses, furniture, musical instruments, mats, baskets, cigarette papers and a fresh juice tapped from the trunk, boiled to a syrup and mixed with water. Nor were they snared anywhere else in that net of islands running south and west from Timor, and likewise they did not see that big land with its honey bees and sandalwood, its beehive-shaped houses, its salt mines, its crocodile gods, its circle dances and its one lofty peak called Ship Rock where fanciful Portuguese said Noah's Ark had come to rest after the flood.

Instead, as the last vestiges of the storm blew away and the wind died and the sea itself changed from the turbulent roaring monster it had been to a sullen and oily stillness, while great streams of plankton miles long like banded yellow sea snakes drifted by, they realised they were becalmed. A high bright overcast sky was mirrored perfectly in the polished water. There was no wind to blow them onwards; no fish to be caught; nothing to eat except ground corn with salt and a stew made from barnacles scraped from the side of the *prahu* itself. It became hot, then hotter. The deck began to dry and crack and the crew would throw buckets of sea water over it a dozen times a day. Rats and cockroaches proliferated, although no one knew what they lived on. In the water barrel slimy things crawled in the slimy water. What fresh water they had caught or was left after the storm was soon gone. One day they managed to catch and kill a seagull and ate it all, even its feet.

The men set lines and lay listlessly about on the decks, too tired and bored even to talk to one another. They said the *prahu* was unlucky and probably everyone aboard her would die. Those maintenance tasks possible for them, stranded as they were in the blank yellow ocean, were done lackadaisically or not at all. Everyone waited for night to fall, when it was a little cooler, a little less oppressive, but when time dragged even slower than it did in the day. One night they saw high above them a white light arcing down in the sky: it halted, turned bright green, then rose again in a different direction at lightning speed before disappearing; and then they were afraid, all of them, even Rindi who did not fear anything; but da Nova said it was just a meteor, a lost star or some such, though even he wondered how a meteor could change colour and rise.

And then the crew began to mutter about the unlucky voyage they were upon and some of them looked sideways at da Nova and cursed him in their hearts, while others blamed Tandri Dewa, saying he was too young and inexperienced and should have done from the start what he was hired to do and not gone off looking for sandalwood in Sumba. Even the gecko that lived in the *prahu*, which everyone took to be a lucky sign, because while there was a gecko aboard it was thought no harm would come to them, disappeared and could not be found. The rooster in his cage at the bow became thin and dejected and seemed to feel the hungry looks that were directed at him, though no one could really imagine making much of a meal out of him.

The discontent on the *prahu* was alleviated when a small shark was hooked on one of the set lines. It was pulled thrashing aboard and, while two men held it to the deck, a third severed the spinal cord in the neck. This shark made a feast for all thirteen men and boys aboard; it was cut up and its flesh cooked in the big pot with a little of the ground corn that remained, while the liver and the kidneys were put to one side and fried and given to Tandri Dewa and the fisherman who caught it, respectively.

Still no wind came, still the battered *prahu* lay like a painted ship on a painted ocean; the muttering among the crew resumed, although now it seemed that all the men aboard, with the exception of Rindi, blamed da Nova for their situation. Some, thinking that once he was no longer aboard their luck would change, wanted to throw him into the sea. Rindi stayed by da Nova, sitting cross-legged on the deck outside the shelter where the explorer lay as if defying anyone on board to approach. The two boys, who liked the old man and saw nothing wrong with da Nova, did not know which way to turn, spending much of their time curled up among the ropes at the bow of the *prahu*, staring out to sea and saying nothing at all. Meanwhile Tandri Dewa paced at the stern, shooting black looks at Rindi and wondering what to do: he knew the fragility of his own authority, knew that a single act or circumstance could turn the men now gathered sullenly behind him into enemies.

It was at this moment that Rindi rose and with great solemnity, watched by all of the crew, went below decks. It was a *coup de théatre*; everyone watched the empty deck, waiting for the revelation of his return. He returned and summoned Tandri Dewa who, looking more than ever like a young man out of his depth, did not know whether to choose defiance or compliance. In the end curiosity won out and he went below with the old man. Again the crew waited; when the odd couple returned, the young man leading and the old one behind, Tandri Dewa was holding something in his hands: a small model of the *prahu*.

Look, he said to the crew, lifting it high so that it could be seen. *See this talisman? Somehow during the storm it was turned around and has been facing backwards all these last days. This is why our luck has deserted us and why we have been unable to further our hopes.*

Then he, as stately in his turn as Rindi, went forward to the bow of the *prahu* and there placed and fixed into position the little *prahu* with its bow forward, facing the way ahead which was a way into the unknown. And then Tandri Dewa pointed ahead and said:

Kaju Djawa is the name of the land that lies over this sea. I have heard the old men talk about it, when I was a boat's boy like our two boys here. I was hired by this man, António da Nova, to take him to Kaju Djawa, which he calls Luca Antara, and I agreed and accepted gold and set out. But, as you know, I did not want to go there directly, but first to find sandalwood in Sumba or Timor and only later, or perhaps not at all, sail for Kaju Djawa. There is nothing to be traded on that coast except a sea slug which the Chinese esteem, but which stinks and must be dried and smoked and this takes time and men and equipment we do not have.

However, our luck is pointing us that way and we must also find somewhere we can fix our mast; so I am saying to you, shall we do this thing? If the winds return, shall we sail for Kaju Djawa, even though there is nothing there for us except the thin glory of going?

The crew shuffled and murmured and then one of the foretop-men asked: *If we go to this land, how do we return?*

And Tandri Dewa said: *I do not know, never having sailed this way before.*

Then he looked at Rindi.

And Rindi said he had never been in these seas before either but he had heard that the *prahu* who came for sea slugs on this coast afterwards sailed north to Aru, where they also found turtle shell and *cendrawasi* and such; and if they were to sail to Kaju Djawa, that would be the way to return, by going north and seeking those islands where the *cendrawasi* lived, and trading gold for them, and replacing the lost sandalwood with these and other goods.

After Rindi had finished speaking nobody said anything; and as that crew of silent, hungry men lay out on the creaking deck of the *prahu* in the middle of the yellow metal sea, under a white metal sky, torpid, immobile, like a company of the dead, the scream of a gull came distantly upon the air and they looked into the west and saw clouds where before had only been haze; and just at that moment the merest breath of wind fanned against their faces, and they hoped.

But Rindi turned to da Nova and said quietly that he did not trust Tandri Dewa and that, whatever happened, and even though for the moment they were all one, they must always be on the lookout for treachery from him, because he was a man uncertain of himself and thus one who could not be relied upon to act in any predictable manner. And then he too looked into the west, from which the breeze was now blowing steadily enough to be caught in the sails, which bellied forth in the direction of the unknown land, and the *prahu*'s timbers groaned and the *prahu* herself, slowly, reluctantly, like one waking from a deep sleep, began to move.

And da Nova stood up and went to the side of the *prahu* and looked over and there in the water below saw a vision: it was a city of high towers with turrets and pennants flying, pavilions of golden teak housing the court dancers, minstrels, high priests and god-kings. Sheets of gilded copper covered the stone walls and towers of the city; parasols, banners and tapestries of delicate silk coloured the dim-lit galleries and antechambers; finely woven mats of aromatic grasses lay over the stone causeways; and round about it were orchards and gardens where caparisoned elephants waited and white horses galloped over green fields.

Then, as he watched, out of the city gates, as if to a festival, a great crowd of people came, richly dressed in jewelled robes, the women beautiful in their gowns of silk, the men turbaned and armed with daggers and swords, the children running and playing. And he stretched out his hands as if to touch this vision but as he did so the motion of the *prahu*, gathering speed, clouded the surface of the sea at the same time as that great crowd of people, overcome by fear of some unseen calamity, turned and tried to run back into the city; then all dissolved in a mist of waters as if it had never been.

Three days passed. They began to near land. A swirl of screaming birds rose above sparsely vegetated low islands—frigate birds, boobies, terns nesting over guano deposits as deep and rich as loam. They saw gulls seizing eggs from unattended nests amidst the unbearable cacophony and stench of thousands of years. There were islands made of metal, rust-red, great tears of colour leaking from outcrops of pure iron ore. Others were just a drift of coral sand over which the perpetual ocean broke. None of these places were suitable to stop and make repairs.

Night fell as they neared a rocky high island that looked more promising as a mooring place. A full moon rose blood red over the enormous land they sensed ahead of them. The tide rose faster and higher than they had ever known it to do; the light of the moon yellowing as it climbed laid down a golden staircase on the water. They hove to and prepared the *prahu* for a night at anchor. In the rich waters of that coast they caught many fish which were cut up and stewed in the big cooking pot so that everyone ate as much as they wanted, even da Nova, who was, in the festivities of survival, given a place in the circle along with all of the others.

They woke to a glassy sea, rose-coloured cliffs, a blue sky. The glossy black shapes of hump-backed whales made silvery paths in the light of the early sun. Yellow and black banded sea snakes, sleek, poisonous-looking, swam around the *prahu*. As they sailed closer they saw, inside the cliffs, the opening of a sea cave. One of the *lipa lipa* was lowered and four men—da Nova, Rindi, two sailors—paddled in. Looming above them, painted on the cave walls above the water line, they saw huge beings staring down at them. They were yellow and red, male, with big genitals, big hair, white faces, round eyes, long noses but no mouths; they wore neck pendants, slatted gowns, and enormous two-tiered headdresses like woven baskets upended, with two great dark brown horns above. As they gazed in awe at these godlike beings they heard the soft hiss-splash of large animals entering the water nearby, and turned and paddled back to the *prahu* as fast as they could; but the big saltwater crocodiles who guarded the images looked lazily after them and did not follow.

The coast they had come to was crumpled and creased, notched with mangroved estuaries, deep bays, sandy beaches, plunging cliffs and rocky headlands, stony islands, innumerable hidden reefs, treacherously strong and unpredictable tides—the biggest in the world. As if in a dream, dumb with wonder, they sailed up a gorge and saw thousands of pinky-mauve jellyfish like clouds in the water. There were rocky, fern-filled clefts, sandstone walls getting higher, prawns and fish and sharks and dugongs, slide marks left by crocodiles in the mud. The majestic river cut an enormous straight path through a rugged sandstone plateau to empty into an almost enclosed basin with high bluffs whose pink-orange cliffs reflected in the water. Cascades of water flowed over black basalt where weed grew like long green tresses: hanging gardens. But the land, beautiful in the distance, was unremittingly harsh up close and they could find nowhere to stop. They turned and sailed back out to sea.

North, towards evening, they came to another bay of empty mud and salt flats, broken near the coast by a network of meandering watercourses lined with mangroves and bathed in delicate pinks and blues at sunset. Five rivers debouched here, and in the lee of a line of low red cliffs they found safe anchorage at last, fresh water and, seemingly, timber enough for their needs. Da Nova insisted on going ashore with the watering party. As the small dugout slid into the sandy shore he leapt over the side and, thigh-deep in the warm clear sea, waded in and fell to his knees on the beach and raised his arms above his head.

Here, he murmured to no one but the land. *Here I am.*

He heard the men crying out and went to see what they had found: a turtle stranded by the outgoing tide in a small pool behind a rocky barrier. They killed it and took it back to the *prahu* and that night everyone ate turtle soup.

Next day a dispute broke out amongst the crew. It was about how to fix the mast. Some of them felt that it should be removed from its slot in the deck, the rotten portion cut off, then reinstalled; others wanted to get wood from the land to make splints which would then be driven into the slot to support the base. Those who advocated the latter course pointed out that it was easier, quicker and would mean they could go back to Timor sooner; the other party felt that their plan was safer and did it matter if they spent some extra days here? Tandri Dewa took no part in this discussion but only listened, looking sometimes speculatively over at the old man, Rindi, who was by now recognised as the wisest man aboard even by those, like Tandri Dewa, who did not like him. But Rindi turned to da Nova and suggested they go ashore and look for signs of people and of the kinds of things to be found in this land.

Behind the beach lay a long narrow lagoon full of water lilies with blue flowers over round pale green leaves. As they walked, small crocodiles sun bathing on the banks slid into the water. Da Nova paused but Rindi said only the saltwater variety was dangerous.

How do you know that? da Nova asked. *Have you been here before?*

The old man smiled and did not reply. They walked on, passing under trees full of roosting flying foxes and coming into an area where sparse bushes and shrubs grew among great drifts of soft, talc-like dust between red rocky outcrops. Climbing up to the top of one of these low eminences to get a sight of the country, they found a series of great three-toed footprints in the solid rock and wondered. It was as if some giant creature had passed this way when the rock was soft as sand and left its mark.

Beyond was a wide plain where, at sparse intervals, strange bulbous-trunked trees grew. The young ones had smooth grey bark that shone like polished metal; the old ones were gnarled and wrinkled as elephant skin. The biggest were sixty foot high and of a girth that was wider than that. All of them, young and old, were leafing and blossoming here at the beginning of the wet, creamy flowers unfolding to reveal long stamens and letting a sweet smell waft across the plain. They went closer and found one with a double trunk carved with spirals, chevrons, grids and other devices. They knew then that there were people in this land, and looked around and wondered what kind of people these might be.

It was hot, the sky an incandescent blue, the sun white; on the horizon purple thunderheads grew, the air thickened with humidity and the choruses of insects made a solid wall of sound beating in upon them from every side. In amongst the bottle trees were slender, weirdly eroded limestone rocks many feet high like petrified warriors from some old war. The landscape seemed suddenly strange, threatening, totally inimical to people such as they were. They saw skinny yellow ravenous dogs which slunk away then circled around and came and followed them a little distance behind. Rindi found a plant with pods like a pea or a bean whose red seeds, he said, were used as weights and counters on Sulawesi.

Look, said Rindi, pointing to a small bush near where they stood. It was some kind of hibiscus, a pink, four-petalled flower with a black stamen; beneath it grew white snowflake lilies with round green leaves edged in red and split on one side where the flower grows; and beneath that some kind of snake, iridescent in the blank, hot light, slithered away through the soft dust. Everywhere there were ants, busy with the work of destruction and construction. Even though the men sifted the sand and broke off pieces of rock where they could and collected pebbles, nowhere did they find anything they could take as a jewel, or an ore that might contain precious metal.

They turned and went back towards the sea; before they had gone more than half a mile the clouds rolled in, thunder roared, lightning flashed and the rain began to plummet down in sheets like glass, breaking where it hit the dust and the shards bouncing and leaping up. They were drenched immediately but it seemed to them that the parching dryness of their time becalmed in the Timor Sea was receiving recompense from the skies, and so they walked undaunted on through mud streams and sudden rills until they found the sea again; and saw, strangely, ahead of them a ragged bunch of lithe brown men, almost naked, hauling a tree they had felled down towards the shoreline to be used in repairing the mast.

Da Nova never knew how it was that the faction advocating fixing
the mast with splints won out over those who wanted to shorten it.
Nor did he ever know what course Rindi would have preferred. It
seemed as if a kind of silence had descended upon them, as if the
harsh enigmas of the land they had found placed some interdiction,
not just on their speech but on their thought as well. That night after
the rain cleared and the moon rose and the sky filled with the stars
of the southern heavens, they saw from the deck of the *prahu* fires
burning inland—not the vast conflagration of a bushfire but wavery
pinpoints of light from cooking or perhaps signal fires.

Tandri Dewa came to talk to Rindi.

Did you see any signs of people while you were ashore? he asked.

We saw a tree with carved bark, said Rindi. *Some dogs. Nothing more.*

In your stories, what is said about those who live in Kaju Djawa?

I have no stories, Rindi replied. *Why don't you ask the young man?*

So Tandri Dewa asked da Nova what he had heard about the people
who lived in Luca Antara, and da Nova replied:

*It is said that this land is inhabited by a white race, resembling Spaniards;
they are badly clothed, wearing shirts woven from plant fibres; as arms they carry
wooden staves, for they have no iron. They also have darts for hurling, but no bows
or arrows. They enjoy all kinds of foods that they gather from the country around
them and also meat from animals that they kill with their weapons. Even though
they are poorly armed, they are still dangerous, and not so very long ago used their
staves to kill some Dutchmen who came ashore looking for water. So my master
Manoel Godinho de Eredia wrote to me. And I believe him.*

Tandri Dewa gazed at da Nova for a long time.

And what did your master tell you of what goods may be found in this land?
he asked at last.

And da Nova replied, as if chanting a prayer memorised long ago:

*The countries produce great quantities of gold and metals and minerals, clove,
mace, nutmegs, sandalwoods, the herb 'birco', which is red dye wood, and ivory; they
contain elephants, rhinoceros and many animals and birds, rare and valuable, as
well as all kinds of provisions.*

Tandri Dewa remained silent, gazing at da Nova; then he smiled
softly to himself, a smile that was derisive and sceptical though not
aggressive, the smile a devious man smiles at one who is naive, a smile

of superior cunning, a treacherous smile. Da Nova did not notice this smile or if he did he did not understand it; but Rindi saw it and knew it for what it was and later, after the disaster had struck, he recalled it to da Nova and identified its occasion as the moment when Tandri Dewa decided to betray them: for who could believe that the country da Nova spoke about was the same as the barren shore where they lay?

By midday on the next day the mast was repaired and Tandri Dewa announced that they would sail early the following morning and go north, as Rindi had suggested, to seek the islands where the *cendrawasi* could be found. The afternoon was to be spent preparing the *prahu* for the voyage and looking for food: their stocks of corn were low and they had been living for the most part on the fish they caught which, on these rich shores, were not hard to find.

It was while he was addressing the crew, who were all lounging on the deck in whatever shade they could find, or else in the full sun, that Rindi touched da Nova on the knee and pointed to the land. There, in silhouette, on the top of the low red cliffs running along the back of the beach where they were, stood a man holding a very long spear upright, against which he leaned, with one leg raised and bent so that the foot rested on the inside calf of the other. This man had a wide mane of hair that caught in the sun behind him, and reminded da Nova of the painting of the gods they had seen in the sea cave. He seemed to be alone, and since no single man could threaten a company such as they were, it was odd how fearsome he seemed, standing still and silent and anonymous above them.

Tandri Dewa sensed the interruption, paused, looked, then everyone on board looked where he looked and as they did so the man on the cliff let his leg slip down to the ground and lifted his spear and turned and faded behind the hill; and no one on the *prahu* doubted for a moment that his skin, rather than being white, was as black as any skin they had ever seen; even those black men who sometimes came trading out of India were not so black as this man was.

After that no one wanted to go ashore to look for food, saying that in a land as poor as this, what food could they find? But Tandri Dewa said there were the large hopping animals they had seen, rich in meat, which could easily be brought down with one of the two guns they had on board, and that he would reward with gold any man who came back with one of these animals; but still no one would agree, saying they were fishermen, not hunters, and that there was plenty of fish and they could look for corn or rice or some such when they reached the islands where the *cendrawasi* were; and in the meantime would be happy with what they had. So Tandri Dewa gave up and turned his attention to the *prahu*.

But da Nova gazed at the red cliff where the black man had stood and wondered; and then he said to Tandri Dewa that he would go ashore and try to make contact with the people, to see if they were friendly or not and also what trade goods they had, since that was the reason for his mission and he would not feel right about turning and sailing away without trying to talk to the people; and would Tandri Dewa give him one of the guns and set him ashore in the *lipa lipa* so that he could fulfil his mission? And Tandri Dewa smiled his smile and said that he would.

Then Rindi said to da Nova that he did not trust Tandri Dewa or his smile and that, if he went ashore, the *prahu* might sail away without him. But da Nova said that Tandri Dewa would hardly leave one of his guns behind, nor would he forfeit the gold that he wore round his waist, nor that which awaited him back in Mataram, since there had been so little profit from the voyage so far; also there was still a chance they would find some riches, gold or jewels, in Luca Antara and while that chance remained Tandri Dewa would act like an honest man. Rindi shook his head and stayed quiet; but when da Nova climbed down from the *prahu* into the *lipa lipa*, the old man went with him, saying he would carry the musket; and so they went ashore.

They walked south along the wide shore towards the cliffs where they had seen the man standing, then climbed up a small ravine, scrabbling over crumbly sandstone, pushing through dry, thorny bushes, eaten by flies, until they reached the top and looked south and east. The land went on forever, a red waste dotted here and there with the great bottle trees and dusted with the green of shrubs or with patches of yellow cane grass. In the distance brown bluffs loomed, between which they could trace the bed of a great river far to the south. There was no smoke anywhere and no sign of any people; but great flocks of big white birds rose and wheeled in the blue air, and distantly they heard a barbarous chorus of voices harsher and more metallic than the voice of the crow.

Da Nova felt suddenly unsure of his mission: what could he, one man, accomplish in the face of this huge and barren land? How could he trade with people whose language he did not speak, who might not even want the things he could offer, nor offer anything of value to him? And if, as he sometimes thought, he was a man in search of his soul, how would he find it in this waste of emptiness? He caught his breath and felt his heart begin to hammer at the temerity of his undertaking and the impossibility that it would ever reach fruition; and it was at this moment that Rindi touched his arm and said softly:

Look.

Da Nova looked and saw below the *prahu* with its black sails raised turning in the blue water, the steersmen at their oars and the foretop-men aloft, Tandri Dewa in his usual spot towards the bow, gazing seaward. He heard a cry come over the water, the thin, piercing voice of a child calling something, goodbye perhaps, as a breath of wind bellied the sails forth and the *prahu* leapt a little in the water as if eager to go. Never had da Nova felt more desolate or more foolish as he did at that moment, having ignored all the signs, even the old man's warning, in favour of his own mad quest which was, he saw suddenly, a quest for nothing, nothing at all. He sat down and would have wept if Rindi had not said to him:

Everything that happens, happens for a reason. It is because we do not always know that reason straight away that we make mistakes. Instead, we should wait and see why it is that we have come to this land and what it holds for us. If you despair, we will both die. But if you rouse yourself, and look north, and go with me, we might yet find what we are looking for.

And da Nova was ashamed and recovered himself and stood up,

and the two men, the one old and the other young, both unknown, climbed down from the cliff and began to walk north along the great wide sandy beach which went forever under the sky until it met the blue line, pale as thought, of a far distant headland. Towards evening, as the sun drowned in the western sea and the great kaleidoscope of the sky began to shift through the spectrum, on a small rocky outcrop reaching down onto the sand they saw one of the hopping beasts sitting upright and immobile, looking out to sea as if admiring the sunset, which Rindi shot with the gun, making a sound so loud it echoed up and down the shore; and then they built a fire and butchered it and roasted the meat and sat eating in the lee of the rocks like the last people on earth; until night came and they slept.

Days passed. They walked. First along the shore then, when they reached a bluff, inland. It was hot all the time, the flies were terrible, thunderheads built through the morning and let go torrents in the afternoon, with great flashes of lightning and a snapping and booming like cracks of doom. They could not keep the gun dry in these downpours and in the end abandoned it as useless, throwing it down in the sand and leaving it there to rust and to perplex those who, days later, found it lying there. They ate the meat of the wallaby while it lasted and drank rainwater or water from the many furious rills that ran through the sandy waste after a storm. When the meat was nearly gone, they used pieces of it as bait to attract fish, which Rindi caught with his bare hands in deep pools at the back of the beach; they broke shellfish off the rocks or dug them out of the sand.

Yet for all that they were getting weaker, especially Rindi, who was old and tired and no longer possessed the undirected energy of youth, which wants to live even in the absence of any reason to live, just as it wants to go even in the absence of any destination. A morning came when he woke where they had lain down to sleep under a bottle tree and said he could walk no further. Da Nova would not leave him, and sat beside the old man, squinting into the interior, where all he could see was billowing cane grass, flowering bottle trees, grey evergreens and distant brown bluffs. It seemed like the end. They had been walking for perhaps a week, but that week felt like a year. Neither of them could remember what it was like on the *prahu*, nor why they had left, nor why they had come. They felt constantly they were being watched yet they never saw another living soul. At night distant fires told them they were indeed not alone, yet who these people were and why they did not approach they could not say.

They sat there for one whole day, hardly speaking, weak, eaten by flies, almost delirious, until in the evening, as the great red sun appeared suddenly in the west below the dark looming of clouds, Rindi, who was dozing with his back against the tree, woke with a start as at some noise.

There, he whispered, pointing to where the stems of fine grass parted as a snake undulated towards them: a sleek snake with a soft satiny iridescence of skin, brown with olive-green lights in the scales. It was a python of some kind, two yards long, and seemingly unaware or unafraid of the two bedraggled humans under the tree. Rindi breathed out slowly, making a sighing sound. The snake seemed to hear him and stopped only a few feet distant and raised up its head. They saw its tongue dart out, testing the air; they saw the lid slide across its yellow eye and back again; they felt in their hearts how alien all things reptilian are to men; yet they also felt they were kin to the snake, for in all that desolation it was a living being as they were. Rindi sighed again. The snake dipped its head, dropped languidly to the ground, and slid unhurriedly past them and away into the grass.

I will die tonight, Rindi said. *The snake has come for me.*

Da Nova tried to say it was not so, but Rindi could not be persuaded otherwise.

You will go on, he told da Nova, *you will survive and return and tell your master about this Luca Antara, which is unlike any other land under the sun. But I will remain and mingle with the earth of this place and become part of it and never leave.*

And da Nova shook his head and wept and held the old man in his arms, and after many hours fell asleep in this fashion; and when he awoke in the morning Rindi was stiff and cold beside him, having died in the night just as he had said that he would. And da Nova wept some more, and lamented, and decided he would not leave that spot but would die there beside his companion, no matter what.

He scraped a shallow grave in the red sand and heaved the old man's body into it, covered it and stood before it and said some few words that made no sense, then sat beside the grave for the rest of the day, trying to keep off the ants and the flies and the other feeders upon carrion which appear as if by magic as soon as the spirit departs from the flesh. Black crows sat in the branches of the bottle tree, croaking gleefully to each other in anticipation of a feast; a great eagle with a tail shaped like a wedge circled above, then another, then another; lizards crept out of the grass and looked at da Nova as if wondering what he was doing there; and he thought that he no longer knew. For he had no more food and no water either, was faint and weak and not inclined to try to help himself; when all of a sudden and without warning—perhaps he had dozed, or fallen into unconsciousness—he looked up and saw a man standing before him not ten yards distant: the same as he who had stood upon the low red cliffs where the *prahu* was anchored, or another just like him, with black skin and scarcely any clothes, holding a spear that was twice as tall as he was.

This man, when he saw da Nova start awake and try to stand, beckoned to him with a sweep of his arm and held up a small woven bag in which there was something which might have been food or water; da Nova managed to stand but could not walk but only swayed, leaning for support on the tree trunk; so the man came closer and took from the bag some berries which he gave to da Nova to eat; and they were sweet and delicious and answered his thirst as much as his hunger. Then the man gave him some roots to chew on, and when da Nova had eaten those he took him gently by the arm, raising his hand to his mouth in the gesture one makes while drinking and trying to pull him away from that spot. And da Nova at first resisted but then gave up and let himself be led, and followed the man where he went, slowly but determinedly north, on a path only he could see.

That afternoon a great storm broke over them as they walked, with thunder and lightning and rain so heavy it was like a solid wall of water. The man pointed to a rock shelter not far off and took da Nova's arm to guide him there. It was in one of the many rocky outcrops to be found in this part of the land, for they had moved away from the sea, and were now in a rough, sandy country with many ravines which were wearisome to cross and furthermore, now that the rain was falling so hard, had turned into wild rivers foaming and roaring on their way to the coast.

The rock shelter was a high overhang among enormous boulders, easily large enough for two of them, and dry as well. Sheets of water cascaded over the lip of the rock above them and ran harmlessly away down towards the stream bed below; but the sand at their feet was brown and dusty and there were places where fires had been made. Da Nova looked at his companion. The man smelt of animal fat and smoke. His black hair was tangled in a great mass over his brow and his face was bearded; his eyes were large, deep set, like great brown liquid pools. His body, long and lean, was streaked here and there with red or white paint of some kind, and he wore nothing but a loin cloth. He felt da Nova examining him and turned and smiled: his two front teeth were missing but the rest were large and brilliant; da Nova, embarrassed, dropped his eyes and looked away. He felt the strangeness of the man as a kind of affront and could not understand how to communicate with him or why they were together at all.

The man said some words in his own language, perhaps referring to the wildness of the weather and the need for them to remain where they were; then he took from the bag suspended at his belt the means for making fire and from the back of the shelter kindling and dry wood which some previous wayfarer had left there; he lit a fire and made signs to da Nova to remain where he was, then went out naked into the rain, for what purpose da Nova could not imagine. He was gone for some time. Da Nova fed the fire and looked out at the falling rain. He stood up and stretched and walked around the shelter, going right to the edge of the dry part and cupping his hands and drinking the water that fell into them. After a time he noticed on the back wall of the shelter some marks in black and red and went and looked more closely at them.

They were paintings of men and women dancing, wearing elaborate tasselled headdresses, belts and bracelets and bangles, with woven devices falling from their armpits, and attended by figures of animals. Some were strangely distorted, with long thin bodies bifurcating into two heads, while others were bent over and resembled animals themselves, and others had the fantastical forms of underwater plants, as if they had grown up among kelps and other seaweeds on the ocean floor. As da Nova traced their outlines with his hand and the rain roared outside the shelter and thunder rolled and lightning flashed, he seemed, just for a moment, to be looking back into some antique antediluvian world of great elegance and sophistication which had flourished here and left behind these enigmatic dancers as the only token of its existence.

He was so entranced by his speculations, imagining the dancers as refugees from that great city now lost under the sea, that he did not hear the man returning until there was a thump of a body falling onto the sandy floor and a mutter of protest at the state of the fire. He turned and went out again into the rain, leaving behind at the fireside the dead body of a small dragon or a large lizard he had killed; da Nova looked fearfully at it, feeling more than ever that he had strayed into a world of such peculiarity as to be unaccountable in terms of anything he had known before.

The man came back with more wood and built up the fire until it blazed; and when the embers within had reached a stage he considered satisfactory he grunted and picked up the dragon and laid it bodily on the fire to roast, then sat crouched alternately watching the progress of the meal and his companion, da Nova, through the flames. After a time the man tapped himself emphatically on the chest and said: *Warri Warri*, which da Nova understood to mean that was his name; so he placed his own hand on his chest and said: *António*; and then they entertained themselves repeating each other's names and laughing at their mistakes until for the very first time each felt himself to be a friend of the other, and companionable, indeed human, in all that wilderness of rain and wind and stone.

And then Warri Warri stood up before the fire and made a long speech, pointing to the north where they were going and then at da

Nova and then to the north again; and after a time da Nova understood him to be saying that where they were going people such as himself, with white skin, lived, and that was why Warri Warri was taking the trouble to go with him, to return him amongst people of his own kind. So he stood up himself, and nodded and bowed and placed his hand on his heart and extended it to the other man to show his thanks, while his courtly shadow danced with the antique dancers on the wall behind him and Warri Warri smiled and poked at the dragon with a stick to see if it was ready; and it was, and they ate, and da Nova was amazed at how succulent the flesh of the dragon was, for he had never eaten anything like it before. And after they had eaten, Warri Warri raked the embers of the fire together and put on more wood and sat cross-legged in front of it and began to sing in his own language, while da Nova stretched out in the soft sand and slept; and outside lightning flashed and thunder rolled and rain pelted down as if it would never end.

It would be tedious to relate all the details of their travel north, through country harsh and durable as metal, which never varied, or varied only slightly, so that da Nova did not see the changes until he realised he was no longer walking through the soft red dust of the desert but had reached a watery land of long-legged cranes Warri Warri called *brolga*, high-stepping in creek beds past pools where masses of lilies grew and flowered a bright light blue on the meniscus of still waters kissed by dragonflies. Here there were red termite mounds leaning like the ruined towers of miniature cities, yellow elephant ear wattles, red *kurrajong* flowers, palms of one kind and another including the pandanus palms da Nova had seen in the islands, and pink *nulla nulla* flowers like red clover.

In the distance, for two whole days, they saw on the skyline a great city of stupas, eroded by aeons into the shape of rounded beehives; but when da Nova plucked at the arm of his guide and wanted to go there, Warri Warri shook his head, signing that there was nothing there, and continued on the path that only he could see. Another day they came to the rim of a vast crater in the ground, miles across, and walked along its western ridge, with da Nova marvelling how such an enormous hole came to be in the ground; but Warri Warri pointed to the sky and showed how some great rock had fallen here a long time ago and made the hole; and then they went on.

Living on the food that Warri Warri gathered as they walked along, or from animals he hunted and killed when they crossed their path, drinking the water of springs and soaks he would never have found by himself, da Nova felt himself growing leaner by the day; his clothes turned to rags and fell away and his skin, already dark because of his mother's people, burned an even darker brown; while his beard, which he had not been able to clip or shave since leaving Mataram, grew long and ragged, and his eyes became faded and far-seeing like those of a man much older than he was.

Each night Warri Warri would lead them to some sheltered spot where they could make a fire and cook, if they had caught anything; or if they had not, simply sit and eat whatever vegetable foods they had found that day, or whatever meat might have been left from the day before. On one of these nights, when da Nova felt himself slipping away from everything he had ever known and been—the clever boy in Malacca, the youth educated by Jesuits, the apprentice mathematician, the junior cartographer—as if about to shed a skin and come forth as some new and shining thing, Warri Warri touched his arm and pointed ahead and spoke to him earnestly in his own language, which da Nova still did not understand, although now and again he recognised words that had become familiar through repetition; he looked into the man's bloodshot, cloudy eyes where it seemed the smoke of a thousand fires had gathered and thought that he saw there relief and gladness and also a kind of weariness, as if this long journey had somehow distracted him from whatever it was he was doing before. And da Nova realised the man was telling him they would arrive at their destination soon, perhaps the next day, perhaps the day after, and that the place they were going to was beside the sea. And also that then he, Warri Warri, would go back into the desert and resume his other life.

Sure enough, the next day da Nova smelt salt on the air and the day after, having camped in the lee of a pile of round boulders like giants' marbles, when they crested the rise, there before them lay a great gulf of blue, with islands that were paler blue out in it, and nearer to where they stood a river flowing into the sea and by the river mouth a collection of small huts from which the smoke of cooking fires rose past the tamarind trees that grew there, and some longer buildings from which smoke also arose; while moored off the river mouth there were two large boats which looked like *prahu*, along with many small canoes; and people passing to and fro in the settlement, going about their business.

Da Nova looked greedily down at this scene, then turned to Warri Warri and embraced him, inhaling the man's peculiar odour of smoke and dragon fat, and slapping his thin shoulders with his hands. Warri Warri seemed shy and backed away and looked as if he was saying goodbye and going, which da Nova did not want him to do and tried to persuade him against; but Warri Warri signed that the people down at the river mouth were not his people but strangers and might not welcome him and anyway he had other things to do. And da Nova remembered the silver St Christopher he had worn on a chain around his neck during all these far travels and took it off and presented it to Warri Warri, who had often admired it in the days they were together. And he, much pleased, put it about his own neck; then they said their farewells and Warri Warri went, fading back down the hill so that in a minute or two it was as if he had never been. While da Nova took a breath and squared his shoulders and began to walk down towards the settlement by the river.

The first living thing he saw as he approached the village was a cat: a skinny tortoiseshell which left off chewing something unrecognisable at the side of the path to mew querulously at him. There was a line of shacks leaning unsteadily together, facing out to the sea where the two *prahu* and the many *lipa lipa* were moored or, in the case of some of the canoes, pulled up onto the muddy shore where pelicans loitered. There was a heavy smell in the air, a sweet, smoky, rotting sea smell which came from the long sheds on the other side of the line of shacks and made da Nova gag.

The first person he saw was an ancient Chinese man squatting in the dirt in front of one of the shacks, smoking a pipe and looking incuriously at his ragged, bedraggled figure. The Chinese took his pipe from his mouth, spat into the dirt at his feet, then pointed along the road. In front of another shack, sitting in a roughly made chair, was another man, also smoking. Da Nova walked along towards him, noticing as he approached that this man had a square green bottle of Dutch gin beside him which he drank from the neck, and wore what had once been a European shirt. He was old, much burned by the sun and the wind, and did not look up once as da Nova came towards him.

Da Nova stopped. Now the man turned to look at him with faded blue eyes nested deep in a web of lines beneath startling eruptions of facial hair. He looked him up and down twice and then silently handed him the gin bottle. Da Nova took a mouthful, almost choked, recovered, swallowed and gave the bottle back. He watched the man's skinny throat jerking as he drank, then sighed and recapped the bottle and put it down in the dust at his feet.

Sit down, he said, in Portuguese.

Da Nova, almost overcome to hear his own language spoken after so long, looked around for somewhere to sit but found nothing.

Estrela! The man yelled. *Bring the stool!*

There was a scuffle from within the house, a pause, and then da Nova saw a plain wooden stool appear past the piece of dirty cloth which stood for a doorway to the shack; it was held in a pair of elegant mahogany-coloured arms, but he could not tell to whom these arms and their graceful hands belonged. He took the stool, murmuring thanks and catching a brief glimpse of white eyes in the gloom within before the curtain fell across the doorway again. He sat down next to the man.

My name is António da Nova, he began, *and I have come to Kaju Djawa as a discoverer and trader, looking for goods to buy and sell.*

You're not in Kaju Djawa any more, the man said. *This place is called Marege. The Land of the Seven Rivers ends over there* ... and he waved his arms in the direction da Nova had come.

I did not expect to find one of my countrymen here, da Nova continued, *in this far-flung perilous place.*

Countryman? The man said, and laughed. *I am not your countryman. I have no country.*

How so?

Because I, sir, am a degredado: do you know what that is?

Da Nova knew; but he did not know what to say. As always with such men, the cause of his banishment hung over him like an invisible cloud. What had he done?

And how long have you lived in this ... Marege?

Forty years, said the Degredado. *I came out of the west, from island to island, looking for a place where no one knew what a Portuguese was, or how to speak the language we speak; and I did and have lived here amongst the people of the land and the Macassar-men who come here in perfect freedom for all of that time; but now you have found me; as I have always known someone would. I knew this day would come, and with it my death.*

The man raised the bottle to his lips and drank again and then offered the gin to da Nova; and after that he took up his pipe again and lit it and began to smoke, looking out over the sea. Two men in a *lipa lipa* were paddling from one of the *prahu* towards the nearest of the long smoke-sheds. A pelican landed on the brown water, throwing up a double wake of white foam as it hissed to a stop. They heard the creaking of crows in the tamarind trees. Da Nova wondered again who was in the house.

You did not say your name, sir, he said.

The Degredado glared balefully at him.

No, sir, I did not.

The two men sat in silence. Da Nova felt the strangeness of his life like an atmosphere around him; he swayed on his stool, made frail by the gin and the exigencies of the long journey to this equivocal station. The Degredado saw him falter, recover, falter again, watching him speculatively, as if waiting for the inevitable collapse.

Estrela! he called into the shack again, and this time da Nova saw with a last flare of consciousness before the faint took him a dark slender young woman wearing only a sarong about her waist come through the stained curtain towards him; and as he fell sideways towards the dirt, she and the Degredado together caught him, an arm

each, and lifted him up and took him inside to the hot darkness of the
shack and laid him down on a bed there.

The fever lasted many days: how many da Nova never knew because
he could not count them himself and those who tended to him had
no desire, or was it no means, for reckoning the passing of time in that
manner. The woman, Estrela, came and went before his feverish eyes
like a vision, bending forward out of the hectic red mists with a bowl
of fish soup for him to sip or placing some morsel of cool sweetly
sour tamarind pulp upon his lips or wiping the sweat from his brow
with a wet cloth; while all the time, even in the remotest extremity
of his illness, he somehow retained awareness of the old Degredado
muttering and drinking and spitting out the front.

Sometimes in his delirium Estrela appeared to him like an animated
version of one of the dancing figures he had seen on the cave wall
in Kaju Djawa. It was an image he had not been able to forget: a tall
slender figure with a round head, bangles at elbow and wrist, a tessellated skirt worn low on her hips, bent slightly at her lissom waist,
kicking one foot carelessly in the air as she danced. It amazed him how
the painter had been able to give such moving energy to the still figure
on the rock wall; now, he was amazed at the stillness he felt at the core
of Estrela's being, she who appeared before him always in motion.

Sometimes he tried to talk, to tell her about the life he had led in
Malacca when he was a boy and living with his father and mother; but
she would place her forefinger on his lips and *Sssshhh* the way you
do to a child. Sometimes he thought she was his mother and that the
man out the front was his father, reading the Bible to himself, and
not the Degredado muttering the words of old songs over and over
to himself. Sometimes he became convinced he was dying, sinking
deeper and deeper into the velvet redness which was his illness until,
at the very last moment, as red turned to black and the dark towers
rose all about him, he would rouse himself and cry out and wake up
bathed in sweat; and then Estrela would come to him, murmuring and
soothing; and he would lie back, heart hammering, and wonder what

kind of world he had returned to.

Then one morning he opened his eyes and in the instant knew he was better. He was lying in a kind of hammock, watching splinters of light jag through cracks on the wall opposite. There was a bowl of water by his bed and on the table opposite he could see the remains of a meal of bread, fruit and fish. There were two doors: one led to the road, the other out the back of the house, from which the smoke of the cooking fire came. It seemed there was no one there: no Degredado sitting out the front, no Estrela working in the back. Da Nova leaned up on his elbow, took the water bowl and drank from it; then he tried to get up.

The red tide rose again in his eyes as he stood swaying next to the bed for a moment before crashing full length onto the dirt floor, narrowly missing the table edge. There he lay, looking directly at the desiccated pod of a tamarind that had somehow fallen to the floor and been forgotten: a procession of tiny ants carried off the moisture that remained in the fruit. He gathered his strength, then pushed himself up on to all fours, grasped the table with one hand and pulled himself upright again. This was how he was when the Degredado walked in from the road.

Ha! he said. *It lives, it breathes, it walks.*

He had a bottle in one hand; with the other, he gathered up the flat piece of unleavened bread on the table top and leered at da Nova.

You may join me for breakfast if you wish, sir, he said with a derisive bow of his head and then went back outside again.

Da Nova lurched from table to doorway, pulling the curtain aside, wincing at the daggers of light flashing off the sea over the road outside. He covered his eyes and made for the stool on the other side of the door from the Degredado's chair. It was not until he was sitting hunched up there in the cataleptic sun that he realised the state he was in: a skinny, almost naked, bearded man with yellow skin through which the outline of his bony ribs pushed. He looked like one of the dogs they had seen in the desert.

I hoped you would have died by now, the Degredado said, disappointedly. *But it was not to be.*

Your daughter saved my life, da Nova said.

I know, I know, the Degredado replied. *How will you ever repay her?*

And he looked queerly at da Nova, who felt a sudden chill, even in that bright sunlight, pass up his belly into his chest. He was so far from home, so close to death and yet, at the very moment, as the old reprobate glared at him, he knew what he would do, how he would repay the debt of his life, how he would get back home and even what he would do once he had: at that moment his soul, which he had come all this way to find, revealed itself to him as that part of himself which could not die; and the reason it could not die was because it did not belong to himself, but another. He looked away from the Degredado and up the delirious road with its shifting sands and saw her coming, a basket on her hip, towards him out of the haze.

Every morning the Degredado (who liked to joke he was in truth *degradado*, 'made vile' by his exile) took his stick and walked down to the boiling sheds where the men from the two *prahu* were working. They collected a kind of sea-slug from the shallow waters offshore, boiled them with papaya leaves in sea water, buried them, dug them up, washed, dried and stored them, by which time they looked like sausages rolled in mud and thrown up a chimney. These sea-slugs, called trepang, were accounted a delicacy by the Chinese, who would pay large amounts of money for them in Macassar, some for their own use there but more to be sent on to China itself, in exchange for silks, porcelains and gold.

The Degredado, her father, Estrela explained to da Nova in antique and halting Portuguese, was the agent ashore for this trade, with the respect of both the local people and the visiting Macassans, each of whom paid him for his good offices: the local people in kind, giving him meat, fruit and seeds to make bread, and whatever else came their way; while the Macassans gave him trade goods of various kinds which he then gave on to the local people: knives, choppers, coins of silver and gold, textiles, porcelain, rice brandy, tobacco and betel. Though in truth, she said, it was mostly just the iron, the cloth, the tobacco and the betel that the people valued, not the other things.

She had taken to crouching by his bed if he was reclining, or squatting down next to his stool if he sat outside, talking softly to him in a close and confidential manner, telling him all sorts of things, like one who has a whole lifetime of conversation built up as if behind floodgates, which now opened and spilled out into da Nova's rapt and voracious listening. Her father was left off a Portuguese ship somewhere in the islands to the west of where they were, not for anything he had done, except that he was a New Christian and suspected of continuing to practise his old religion in secret, though in fact he was neither Christian nor Jew but an unbeliever, and maybe that was why he was exiled in the first place. Degredados were taken on Portuguese ships and purposely put ashore to act as de facto agents of Estado da India, and this was her father's lot; but he would not comply with this demand and moved east, always east, until he landed up on this bare shore with a wife he had found in the Tanimbars, a woman as obstinate and tenacious as he was himself, who gave birth to her, Estrela, and then died before she had properly grown up. So determined was her father to have nothing more to do with his countrymen, she said, that when, some years before, a Portuguese ship explored the two large islands to the north, he had gone with her into the interior and remained there until it sailed away again.

Where does he get the gin? da Nova asked, fearing that there were Dutchmen nearby.

The men from Macassar got it from a ship that wrecked in the Banda Sea, she said, *whole crates of it. He has been drunk since.*

She paused and looked him in the eye.

What will you do when you are better? she asked. *Will you go back from whence you came?*

Yes, da Nova said, *I will return and tell my master what I have found.*

There was a catch in the breath of the girl Estrela, who could not have been more than sixteen years old, and beautiful, but also innocent, wild and strange, with a look about her of someone out of an old tale.

Take me with you! she said. *My father will never let me marry, or have a life of my own, or see the world, for he wants me to stay here always and look after him.*

How then can I take you? da Nova said. *I wish to travel on one of the prahu, but they do not like to sail with women aboard; and if your father does not agree then there is nothing to be done, for both those on shore and those on ship will be against us.*

I can sail as well as any man, she said. *And with you as my companion they will let me aboard.*

And your father?

My father already believes you will take me away; he saw you coming in a vision or a dream, and told me about it. He hoped you would die; now that you are getting stronger, he does not know what to do; he would kill you, except for me. You are not safe here.

When do the prahu sail? da Nova asked.

They go to the market at Aru as soon as they are finished here. Not long.

One week, maybe two. Will you take me with you?

Da Nova looked at her and knew that she did not love him but only saw him as a way out of where she was to the larger world; and he did not care, because he thought if he helped her she might in time come to love him; and even if she did not, it hurt him to think of leaving her here to live out her days in ignorance and monotony, whereas if she came with him he could look upon her day and night and know that she was beautiful. So he said yes to her question and they began to plot with each other, first to quit her father, the Degredado, and second to find some way of going aboard one of the *prahu*. And now da Nova undid the belt that circled his waist, which he had never taken off, not even in the extremity of his illness, nor when he was weak and faltering in the desert, and took from it gold and showed it to Estrela and said that they could give some to her father and some to the *nakoda* of one of the *prahu* and in that way escape. And Estrela's eyes glistened and she reached out one delicate finger and touched the gold, as if she hardly knew what it was or what it could do, then kissed da Nova once on the mouth; and in that kiss he knew he was bound to her fate forever, even if she was not bound to his; and so it proved.

He offered the Degredado gold, half of all that he had, which was not much considering, but still gold. It was evening. The tide was out and the sands glittered with mica under the dying sun, which turned the river red as if it ran with blood. On the other side, the local people, who often camped there, were lighting fires to cook their evening meal, and their cries came across the water like the cries of animals while their tall, thin, black figures moved in and out of the trees and between the fires and their dogs barked or fought and crows quarked round about.

What use is gold to me? he said. *She is my daughter, my blood. You think you can buy her off me?*

The gold is payment for your kindness. What else can I give you?

And what else can you take?

She has asked if she can come with me. I have said yes. But I will not do it against your wishes.

The Degredado drank, spat, and was silent. The Chinese from up the road, who never spoke but spent his days in somnolent communication with himself, passed on the way to the shrine of the sea goddess at the river mouth, left there by forgotten sojourners from the Flowery Kingdom, where he went every evening to pray. The Macassar-men were paddling back to their *prahu* after the day's work, calling to each other in voices light like birds. Estrela was moving round out the back of the shack, preparing food and listening for any clue as to what the men were talking about.

My wishes, he said at last. *What do you know or care of my wishes?*

Da Nova did not reply.

I came into this land forty years ago. I have walked all over it, that way, and that way, and that way. It is vast, unimaginably vast, like another world. And older than anywhere else I have been, older even than India. When I first saw the kinds of people who live here, I was revolted, because they lived like beasts, without houses, or cultivations, or any of those things that make us human. Later I realised they lived this way not because they knew no other but for a different reason. Which was that they are uninterested in the material world as such, or rather, do not see it as material. Everything here has a shadow life, every path has a secret destination, each insect or bird or animal or person traces some figure that is part of a larger figure, which we cannot always see, but sometimes we do. I mean the shape of things to come.

The Degredado paused to drink again.

If you go into the west, where you came from, you will see gallery after gallery of paintings of dancing men and women ...

Yes, said da Nova, *I have seen ...*

... and if you ask the local people who did these paintings, they will say they do not know, not them, some other people, people who were here before. But once I met a man who told me a different story. He stood on one of those high sea cliffs and pointed into the west, past the many shoals and islands, and said that formerly there was a great land here, of which the islands were simply the mountain tops; and in this land lived many peoples, some black, some brown, some yellow, but no white people. And there were palaces and kingdoms and gardens; but all this went under the sea, drowning many people, while others took to their boats and sailed away, and still others climbed to the highest land they could find and stayed there waiting for the sea to go down. But the sea never did go down ...

Da Nova remained silent and thought, remembering the city under the sea he had seen when they were becalmed, with its white, dreaming towers, its emerald gardens, its hieratic animals and antique humans, all turning and running as if away from some terrible disaster.

The dancing people in the paintings were made by those people, who are the same people who live here now, though many of them have forgotten, not out of stupidity or neglect but because the time between then and now is so long, how could they not forget? But some among them remember the past, and these are also those who remember the future. And I am one of them.

You remember the future? da Nova repeated.

Yes, said the Degredado. *I do.* He held up the square heavy bottle of Dutch gin so that the last light of the setting sun caught and spun in the viscous liquid. *This is the future,* he said. *To forgetfulness!* And he laughed and drank and offered da Nova the bottle, but he did not drink.

White man out of the west, the Degredado said, *who came to me first in a dream, I do not want your gold nor anything else you can give me. Take my daughter and go, with my curses on your head.*

And he stood and finished what was in the bottle and threw the bottle down and then took his stick and walked off up the dusty road the way the China man had gone without another word or a backward glance or anything. And da Nova watched him, thinking he might fall but he did not fall; until Estrela came from the house, having heard everything, and they began to plan their departure from that place.

The *nakoda* on one of the *prahu*, Bendra, an older man who reminded da Nova of Rindi, for half the gold agreed to take them back with him. He asked only that Estrela dress as a man, not in order to deceive the crew but so that those they met along the way did not think there was a woman aboard and try to take advantage of her. As for the crew themselves, Bendra said they would do as he told them to and that he would tell them that there was no bad luck in taking Estrela aboard because she was a woman such as the old tales tell of and thus like someone not of this world; but he made it a condition that da Nova and Estrela did not lie together, at least during the first part of the voyage.

She said goodbye to her father outside the shack on the morning of their departure while da Nova stood a little way off, waiting, trying not to look like he was looking or listening to what they said to one another. The Degredado had either finished the gin or was not drinking; he had exchanged his usual dirty sarong for a clean one, green with golden dragons on it, was wearing a different shirt, had shaved and seemed almost like a gentleman. He gave his daughter a keepsake to put around her neck, kissed her on both cheeks and then held her briefly against him. He was weeping. Estrela murmured something that da Nova could not hear, apart from the word *Tanimbar*, and said that she would surely be back someday. The Degredado pushed her away then and told her to go and not to come back because he would not be here and what else *was* there here but desolation? Then he turned and went back into the shack without once looking at or speaking to or otherwise acknowledging da Nova; which is how he had been ever since they had talked about leaving while the sun was setting over the river.

They sailed north to the Aru Islands. Bendra's *prahu* was unlike Tandri

Dewa's in every respect, since he was an old and experienced *nakoda* and his crew obeyed him without question; or they would have, had he issued orders, which he almost never did, since they already understood perfectly what was expected of them. It was an uneventful passage through calm seas, but difficult for da Nova and Estrela because of Bendra's prohibition, which had the effect of putting the idea before them in such a way that they were both tantalised by the possibility, rapidly becoming a certainty, that they would one day become lovers. As they passed day by day and night by night through languorous seas towards those wild flat islands fringed with vast green mangrove swamps, the heat in their bodies grew so that they could scarcely look at one another without feeling an almost unbearable desire to join lip to lip, breast to breast, thigh to thigh.

Every year fifteen big Macassan *prahu* from Surabaya and Macassar and Goram and a hundred smaller boats from Kei, the New Guinea coast and outer Aru arrive at the entrepot of Dobo, which is on a spit of land jutting out from Wamar village in the Aru Islands. There are Chinese, Bugis, half-cast Javanese, Papuans, men from Ceram and Timor ... a motley, ignorant, thievish yet oddly peaceful bunch. They come for dugong tusks and teeth, coral, cassowary claws, bird feathers, pearls (especially black pearls), the best mother-of-pearl in the world, sea-slugs, dried sharks' fins, birds' nests worth their weight in silver, tortoiseshell, timber and ornamented woods, and the *cendrawasi* or bird of paradise. They also come for Papuan slaves captured by raiding parties on the mainland to the north. In exchange, as at Marege, they offer knives, choppers, swords, Dutch coins of silver and gold, textiles, Chinese porcelain, rice brandy, tobacco and betel as well as muskets, small brass cannon, elephant tusks and Javanese brass gongs.

At Dobo there was a line of wooden houses thatched with sago palm leaves and, in amongst the trees, da Nova saw the sun glinting off the tiny golden dome of a mosque roof. The sandy roads glistened with mother-of-pearl; there were pet cassowaries and tree kangaroos that came when called. On their first night ashore, at the house of a Chinese the *nakoda* knew, they ate antler marrow soup, the basted claws of the cassowary bird, sharks' fins and beche-de-mer; and then da Nova and Estrela were shown to a small hut right out on the end of the sandspit where the village of Dobo is.

It was here that António da Nova and Estrela the Degredado's daughter first lay together, on a night during which the rain did not once stop pouring from the sky, so that the roof beneath which they moaned was as if sodden with their cries, and water dripped everywhere except into the very middle of the hut where the bed was; but it is doubtful if they would have cared even if the flood had burst through the door and carried them out onto the rainy ocean, so mad were they for each other after their long, strange, unspoken courtship on the *prahu*; and on that night or on one of the nights that followed, as they waited for the wind which would sail them west to the Kei Islands and beyond, da Nova wrote, his son was conceived, of which more will be said later.

The men of Aru live under the rule of their elders in villages of ten or twenty houses, fish with iron-tipped arrows, and grow corn, yams, sugar cane, vegetables, rice. They wear strips of white or blue calico as loin cloths or sarongs and put horseshoe-shaped combs as wide as their heads in their frizzy hair which they lighten with lime; and adorn themselves with armbands of shell and brass wire, ornaments of gold and silver. They carve wooden posts sculpted with spirits in the form of lizards, crocodiles and snakes. When an important man dies all his wealth is destroyed; even the precious gongs are broken up and thrown away. The body is placed on a bier, covered in fine clothes, and Chinese porcelain set underneath to catch the drips of fluid, which is mixed with arak made from sago or rice and drunk by the mourners.

The men go diving for the gold-lipped oyster in murky, current-torn water, with a lung full of air and a line to the *prahu* above. They swim ten yards or more down, suffering frequent nosebleeds as they surface, and finding a pearl every 50 000 shells—a pink, black or yellow monster, perhaps as big as a pigeon's egg. The shell goes to the *nakoda* of the *prahu* but the diver keeps the pearl. They build fishing traps a hundred yards long, using vertically planted stakes interwoven with different fibrous grids to filter the catch by size and shape. In this way they take sawfish, shark, manta ray, crocodile, dugong, whose tears are bottled to make love potions. Some of the people live like sea gypsies in wide, flat-bottomed boats, sleeping and cooking in covered huts between elaborate carvings crowned with bunches of cassowary feathers at prow and stern.

The *prahu* da Nova and Estrela sailed upon did not wish to linger to Dobo, since they already had a hold full of trepang; but they were hoping to pick up some of the *cendrawasi* that are found there and take them back to Macassar. These birds, which have their own trees where they dance for ten minutes at dawn and dusk, are sold, minus their legs, by weight to the Chinese for their beautiful plumage. They are related to crows, their cry is loud, urgent and hauntingly plain, with a hint of self-parody, and they return and mate in the exact same dancing tree in which they were first conceived.

Da Nova and Estrela joined a party going to take some of the *cendrawasi*, sailing down the salt rivers that run between the islands of Aru in dugout canoes, then landing and walking through a jungle with iridescent beetles and moths, giant ferns and fan palms, trees towering from arcing roots as if growing upside down, bristling with orchids and bromeliads, where you find seashells occupied by the arboreal hermit crab; and spent a damp and uncomfortable night there. In the morning, deep in the jungle, they saw the bark of the dancing trees glowing silver as the light gathered and the first shaft of sunlight igniting a fire of shimmering gold as sixteen birds eighty feet up fibrillated their tails, then froze, then quivered again, hopping about the drab hens, ravishing them indiscriminately along with gnarls and other protuberances in the trees.

The Aru Islanders took some birds and cut off their feet and preserved them in the way that they knew, and Bendra paid for them with da Nova's gold, explaining that they were to the Chinese a symbol of transcendence and immortality; while in Europe, as da Nova knew and told Bendra in his turn, people believed them to be legless and to mate and hatch their eggs on clouds and live on the dews of paradise.

Coming up to the Kei Islands with a fair breeze astern, they saw a *kora kora* full of pirates from the Sulu Sea rowing into the wind like men possessed. The old *nakoda*, Bendra, steered away to the south as soon as he saw them, both because he was afraid of them and also because they were most likely fleeing a Dutch ship, for when the Sulu pirates are pursued by warships they turn directly into the wind and row for their lives. They kept a sharp lookout to the north for the rest of that day, but did not see the pirates again nor any Dutch or any other ships at all.

By late afternoon they were picking a way through the Watabello reefs with the top-men shouting directions from the masthead. They passed by villages of wooden stilt houses made of driftwood built on flat coral sand interspersed with scrub and low forest. As night fell, and they found anchorage off a quiet bay, the fishing men of the village paddled their canoes out past the reef to make a necklace of lights offshore, with each man, alone in his dugout, singing as he fished, one hundred yards from his nearest fellow.

The people of Kei are like those in Aru, with wide noses and frizzy hair and black skin; but their rulers, the Mel Mel, are fairer, with straight hair and Malay features, who say they come from Bali. The best timber for boat building is found here and the best boats are made here in this white-sand, jungled paradise. They trade these vessels for brass guns, gunpowder, cloth, axes, Chinese ceramics, knives, rice brandy, and use tobacco as small change. They also make copra and *agar-agar* from seaweed, collect mother-of-pearl, prepare trepang and sharks' fins. They eat cassava, sweet potato and fish from the sea; using underwater rattles made from coconut shells on rattan hoops, they call sharks and harpoon them. Millet is grown for use in ceremonies.

Their canoes have carved bows and sterns rising to six foot peaks decorated with shells and cassowary feathers. Gongs and cannon are used for bride price—da Nova saw two large, exquisite drums carved with strange figures like those called *Dongson* in Malacca and other places. He saw also a five yard long stone shaped like a ship in which

the ancestors of the Mel Mel sailed from Bali. At Watabello men fell
into trances and ate glass, pierced their cheeks and pectorals with
bamboo slivers, sewed their mouths closed with thread and bashed
each other on the body with boulders. Here is found the great bird-
winged butterfly of Kai Besar, seven inches across, with velvet black
and brilliant wings, a golden body, a crimson breast. Here too, in the
forests of Haar, is a fruit pigeon twenty inches long, bluish white, its
wing backs and tail an intense metallic green with gold, blue and violet
lights in it, coral-red feet, golden yellow eyes. There is a quicksand lake
and an orchid garden. The leatherback turtle is the sacred vessel of the
spirits and ancestors.

Such wonders da Nova collected and wrote down in his book, but
there was no time to explore further for Bendra had only stopped here
to get water, since the cask on the deck had sprung a hole and been
repaired during the voyage from Aru, but most of the water had been
lost; and as soon as they had taken water aboard and paid the local
people for it he wanted to go, for he said he had urgent business to
transact in Tanimbar, which was the same word da Nova had heard
spoken between Estrela and her father when they parted and also the
name of the island from which Estrela's mother came. And for these
reasons da Nova did not wish to go there and asked Bendra why did
they not sail straight to Macassar or Mataram or even to Malacca?

Bendra said it was because the jewellery of the people of
Tanimbar, especially their gold jewellery, was the best that there was
and he thought he could persuade them to part with some in exchange
for the *cendrawasi* that they had got in Aru; for although the *cendrawasi*
would fetch a high price in the markets to the west, the gold of the
Tanimbars was worth even more because it was so rare and so rarely
parted with. And while they were talking thus Estrela listened with a
rapt and apart look on her face, and da Nova knew she was thinking
about her mother and her mother's people and that, if and when they
went to Tanimbar, he might lose her and never see her again.

For although she loved him in the flesh he still did not think that
she loved his soul or whatever it is that a woman loves in a man that
makes her want to follow him to the end of the earth; for when they
lay together he often saw that same look in her eyes, rapt and apart,

and at such times she would not say what she was thinking about but only smiled as if she felt sorry for him and stroked his head and kissed him and told him not to worry, it was nothing, just dreams. And all this time, da Nova realised when he looked back on it, it was their child she was dreaming, dreaming it into life just the same way all of her ancestors down the long years had dreamed their children into life, and so on down the generations, men fathering children and women dreaming them awake.

In the Tanimbars the people also say their ancestors came in ships from the west and that the ships are still there in the islands, stone ships with spirals on their prows, carved like the wooden prows of the sea-going boats they still use. Some say the villages are themselves ships, sailing west. The helmsman lives on the east side of the square, at the stern; the bailer lives in the middle and the pilot's house is in the west, at the bow.

These islands are low, forest covered. The people have frizzy hair but Malay features: fine athletic men with intelligent expressions, rich chocolate skins and flowing manes of gold-hued hair bleached with coconut and lime and bound up with a kerchief; they are also head-hunters, sometimes cannibals, and one village is always at war with another. The people live in high huts on stilts, entered through a trapdoor below. Central house pillars are carved with ancestral figures. They fish in six foot long canoes and grow sweet potatoes, cassava, beans, corn, onions and leaf vegetables. Ironwood and another yellow wood is gathered and sold to make dye. The lontar palm, called by them *koli*, is used to make a palm wine called *sagero* and distilled to make a brandy called *sopi*. The islands are split north and south into rival kingdoms; the main port is Saumlaki on Yamdera, and this was where, on a grey still morning, the *prahu* came. They saw the silver dome of a mosque with a red band around it amongst a jumble of flat-roofed buildings overlooked by palms and heard the cry of the muezzin float across the water.

Bendra went up to the headman's house to discuss trading matters while the crew rested in pleasure houses at the port and da Nova and Estrela made their way to her mother's village, which was Sanglia Dol. Here is a monumental stone staircase fifty yards long and rising thirty yards, with a carved human head at the bottom and at the top, the *natar*, a raised stone platform with the flowing lines of a boat more than a hundred yards from bow to stern, ten yards in beam. Its prow faces the western sea and here ritual offerings are made to the god *Ubila'a* prior to raids on other villages or renewals of alliances. At Sanglia Dol the megaliths are inscribed with spirals from which other spirals spring in an infinite regression going back, like the Nias of Sumatra, the Toraja of Sulawesi, the people of Flores and Sumba and the eastern Moluccas, to the ancient Dongson culture.

Estrela did not know how to speak more than a few words of her mother's language but they were enough for the people of the village to understand who she was. Some of them anyway recognised her by sight as her mother's daughter; the older women could remember her mother's departure with the *ferenghi* all those many years ago. They took her and da Nova into the biggest of the houses and gave them food and drink and summoned the men from the fields or from their fishing and that night held a ceremony in honour of the ancestors.

Women in sarongs wearing ivory bracelets, ancient beads made of Venetian glass, *cendrawasi* headdresses, necklaces of chalcedony, gold filigree earrings, swayed under flickering lights in the courtyard in front of the stone boat. Men in grey coats with their heirloom jewellery concealed underneath strutted to and fro, flashing their ornaments in the firelight—gold pendants with thick chains and clasps adorned with human faces, horns, boats, half moons, turtles. Later, after prayers and palm wine had been offered, the Treasure Baskets were got down from the eaves of the houses and opened and the treasures displayed one by one; their stories were told, who owned them, where they came from, what their owner did. As well as gold ornaments beaten out of Portuguese or Spanish or Dutch coins there were objects of porcelain, ivory, beads and carved tortoiseshell combs. Estrela and António, along with all of the others who had viewed the sacred objects and the objects themselves, were rubbed with coconut oil to calm the spirits before the treasures were put away again.

They slept that night in a house where oiled human skulls sat on shelves about the walls, and under the gaze of those mute survivors of ancestral wars Estrela told António that this was where she would stay and have their child and bring him up, and would he too like to settle and stay here with her and become a man like the men they had seen that evening. And da Nova sighed and was silent. He thought of the clifftop villages they had seen on their way to Sanglia Dol, with high double palisades of sharpened bamboo stakes; of the human arm hanging from a tree, the gibbeted heads and other limbs kept as trophies after public dismemberments; the savagery and splendour of the Tanimbars; and did not know what to do.

Estrela lay sleeping next to him in the bed so that he could feel the soft rise of her belly alongside his own. He lay there all night waking and, when the village roosters began to crow before there was even the slightest sign of the coming dawn in the darkness of the house, got up and walked outside and watched the stars fade in the sky, and knew what he must do. He went back in and woke Estrela and told her he would go back to the *prahu* and sail with them and return to Mataram to see Sadria, the widow of Rindi, and then go on to Malacca to make his report to Manoel Godinho de Eredia of all that he had seen and done on the journey to Luca Antara; and after that he would be free to return to her and live out his days in the Tanimbars, if that was what she wanted him to do. And she kissed him and put her arms around him and they made love there in the dawn under the empty eyes of the skulls.

Afterwards da Nova rose and dressed and said goodbye to her and returned to Saumlaki where Bendra, having failed to persuade anyone there to part with their jewellery, was eager to set sail and go; and the *prahu* sailed on the flood that morning, going west towards Flores; and António da Nova never saw Estrela the Degredado's daughter again.

They passed to the north of the south-west islands where many have never seen an *orang barat* or white man; Roma and Damar, volcanic islands where there are hot springs and nutmeg grows and the tree from which the resin called *damar* comes, which is used to varnish paintings; Barbar, where they grow corn and keep elephant tusks, whose nutmeg trees the Dutch would cut down not many years hence; Luang and Sermata, home to a rich, seafaring people who concentrate on trade, whose women weave *ikat* fabric for export instead of planting corn and where Bugis traders come once a year looking for mother-of-pearl and trepang and other reef products; the Leti Group, where caste is displayed by length of sarong or loin cloth, they make ancestor statues of wood and a man moves to his wife's parents' house and the children bear her name; Kisar whose people have reddish-blond hair, follow Islam and there are old, unique textile designs with bright colours and stripes, animal, human and bird-with-rider themes and a special cloth, in dark blue or black, featuring a tree of life and a man with upraised arms; Wetar where beeswax used for casting jewellery is found, as well as gold, and where people from the neighbouring islands come in their *kora kora* for heads.

These islands are mostly raised coral limestone: barren, infertile, hardly forested; in the dry season the people drink the sap of the lontar palm. They have many rituals to bring rain, from sprinkling water on children to lavish dances. They are ancestor worshippers. They believe heaven is male, earth female, and that rain is sperm. Their rain dances sometimes go on for months and usually require that a head be got from Wetar, about whose people many cruel jokes are told.

So Bendra told da Nova, and he wrote it down in his book, but they did not stop here, nor did they stop at Solor, Adonara, Lembata, Pantar or Alor, the five islands off the eastern end of Flores. These islands are volcanic specks separated by swift, narrow straits. At Lamakera on Solor the people hunt whale sharks, while at Lamalera on Lembata they hunt sperm whales. Lamakerans are aggressive and scream profanities during their hunt. Lamalerans are peaceful and sing as they kill their whales, singing them to death; they say they came in their *prahu* from Lapan Batan, a small island in the strait between Lembata and Pantar, destroyed in a volcanic eruption. They have kept all the names of the *prahu* they arrived in, down the generations, even when it is replaced it is the same *prahu*; and a *prahu* is mourned like a person if it is lost.

Then they passed by Flores, that land of impenetrable mountains,

V-shaped valleys, knife-edge ridges, earthquakes, volcanoes and the coloured lakes of Kelimutu which mysteriously change hue. Today one is turquoise, the next olive green, the third black; a few years hence, they were blue, maroon and black; while earlier still they were blue, red-brown and café-au-lait. Young people's souls go to the green lake, old people's to the turquoise, and thieves and murderers to the black lake, Bendra said. Here the first people came a very long time ago to hunt the pygmy stegadonts and the giant turtles, perhaps to extinction; here sandalwood was taken by traders from Java and China; Tomé Pires says sulphur mined from under the volcanoes came also from Flores to Malacca. The Macassarese and the Bugis control the sea lanes north of Flores, and the Bugis have their own ports on the island where they bring gold, coarse porcelain, elephant tusk money, *parang*, linen and copperware, and exchange it for rubber, sea cucumber from Maumere, sharks' fins, sandalwood, wild cinnamon, coconut oil, cotton and fabric from Ende.

Nor did they stop at Komodo where the deeply shelving Indian Ocean meets the shallow waters of the South China Sea and whirlpools and rips, violent and strong, surround the island. Here are small dragons, *ora*, which grow into big dragons, *komodo*, like an amphibious, land-dwelling shark, eleven feet long and five hundred pounds in weight with twenty griffin-like talons and layers of serrated backward-sloping teeth. These dragons eat pigs, deer, goats, buffalo, horses, men: they knock their prey down with their tail, then rip the stomach open with one slashing bite and devour the intestines while the animal yet lives. Their mouths carry a virulent poison to which there is no known antidote; even a minor wound will fester and stink so that, days later, the dragons can locate and track down their victim by smell alone.

From the deck of the *prahu* as they sailed past to the north, as close as Bendra dared to take them, da Nova saw the jagged, congealed heart of a sleeping volcano, mysterious valleys of prehistoric vegetation, the borassus palm, seventy feet high, with mop tops, at the edge seam of the world. Birds of prey circling slowly in the air told where the komodo were feeding. On the plains of Poreng, trees swarmed with six inch-long flying dragons; there were kapoks with trunks containing cluster pouches from which fluffy white cotton burst, megapodes building their mounds, green jungle fowl, drongos, sulphur-crested cockatoos whose harsh cries floated across the water.

There is only one village there, Bendra said; they are exiles from Bima, sent here as a punishment for nameless crimes. They live from the sea, catching squid in their twin-sailed catamarans in the pearly coiling waters of Slawi Bay where whales and manta rays heave. Four hundred impoverished souls in one dusty road of houses built on stilts, with goats and chickens corralled underneath in the day, then gathered up the steps into the house itself at night to keep them safe; graveyards encrusted with cairns and coral heads to prevent dragons eating the corpses; and a single spring where fresh water bubbles forth.

After Komodo they passed by to the north of Sumbawa without landing there either and then, on a quiet morning under a pearl-grey sky from which a light rain fell, they slipped soundlessly through the viscous water into the port of Ampenan; and here da Nova left the *prahu*, though not before giving the rest of his fee in gold to Bendra who was happy with the transaction and fond of his passenger too although he did not understand why he had left his pregnant wife behind on Tanimbar. And then the *prahu* sailed north for Macassar and da Nova walked down the white road to Rindi's hut with the snake with its tail in its mouth on the door to tell Sadria everything that had happened.

When he had told her how her husband had seen the snake and died on the bare red plains of Luca Antara and they wept together, da Nova dug up the rest of the gold where it was buried under the floor of Sadria's house and, keeping only what he needed for the long journey back to Malacca, gave the rest to her, for which she was grateful and thanked him.

Then da Nova returned to Malacca and sat down in his father's house to write his report to send to Manoel Godinho de Eredia who was in Goa; which he did in full, and, insofar as the first part of his voyage was concerned, entirely from memory, since his Journal was lost when Tandri Dewa sailed away; but he still had his notes from the return journey with Bendra. And this writing he did despite persistent illness, for his travels and all of the exigencies he had faced along the way had broken his health and he who had left as a young man full of energy returned as one who has seen too much and gone too far; and those who had known him before hardly recognised him so different did he seem.

And after he had written his report and sent it he waited for some reply from his master in Goa but no reply came; and he made preparations for his return to Tanimbar to see Estrela and their child who was always on his mind and why should it not have been; but his health was still poor and also Dutch incursions into those waters year by year made it more and more dangerous to go, so he delayed his departure until he had news from Estrela; and the news when it came was not good. And then he did receive word from Goa that his master had died; and he remained in Malacca.

Meanwhile at Sanglia Dol on Tanimbar a child was born to Estrela, a boy who took after his grandfather, António's father, for he had red hair and pale skin which was accounted a great wonder amongst the people; and the news spread as far as Solor where the Dominicans were, and one of them came to see and took the child by force and returned with it to the fort they had there; and Estrela was bereft and cursed the black friars; but later she married again from amongst her own people and had many children, though none pale and redheaded like her firstborn; and she lived to a great age and was accounted a woman of wisdom, known to all as Estrela da Oriente or star of the east, because that is where she came from.

In after years, as the Dutch tried again and again to take the fort at Solor, the Dominicans sent Estrela's boy to Malacca for his own safety and also to attend the school they had there. And in the tenth year of his age the boy met his father for the very first time and they knew each other and were glad. And when da Nova died not very long afterwards the boy, whose given name was Luca, after the lost continent, if lost it was, inherited his property, which was only the house behind the mosque and a few bits of furniture. And when he was grown, Luca married a woman of Malacca and they had a long and happy life and many children, one of whom, a daughter, married a Kelang man; and these two were the far distant ancestors of myself, Henry Klang, who has in his possession the only known copy of the Book of António da Nova, here summarised in abstract, about his voyage into the land of Luca Antara and his return therefrom.

IV

Return

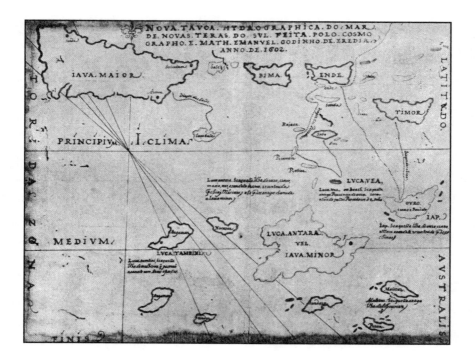

We flew across Australia at four in the afternoon with the sun seemingly stopped in the western sky ahead, as if our air speed approximated the rate of rotation of the earth and we were hung up there immobile with our local star. There was cloud over the littoral, but once we passed the Blue Mountains, the vast land stretched out in hallucinatory precision 12 kilometres below, the dusty green of the plains merging into the dusty brown of the scrub with the dusty red of the centre beyond. I saw the lunettes of Willandra Lakes where the Mungo skeletons were found; the great reverse-tiered hole in the ground where yellowcake uranium is mined at Roxby Downs; khaki lakes fed by now-dry watercourses intricate as capillary systems; parallel lines of endless ridges; the Great Sandy Desert criss-crossed with broad pink and grey horizontals, verticals and diagonals like a Franz Kline painting.

Every now and then we entered bands of cloud and everything ghosted to white; the land came back below like the surface of some other planet than ours: salt pans, salt-like ocean waves, deserts like seas, pinky-red, olive green, black-brown. Along the edge of one of the patches of green a bushfire was burning, a line of flame below a plume of smoke that I thought at first was a tornado or a dust storm. The enormity and strangeness of the vista induced vertigo: what had it taken to explore, let alone settle, this terrible emptiness? The odd little collections of houses we sometimes passed over, with two roads leading out in opposite directions and a third to the airstrip, seemed the loneliest places on earth.

Later, to the north, thunderheads massed in flotillas over the gulf, partially obscuring the view. We crossed the West Australian coast near

Broome into another vastness, the Timor Sea. Hours after that, when
the sun had at last begun to sink, the pale cones of volcanic peaks
showed through clouds ahead. We flew right over the crater of one
of them, purple and black and lava streaked, but I could not work out
which island it was: Sumbawa? Lombok? Bali? Then we were crossing
eastern Java, another volcano with jungle lapping upwards around the
cone and, beyond that, the lights of the great seaport of Surabaya just
coming on. Darkness rose over the Java Sea; one of the last things I
saw before it did was a tiny Qantas jet, miles below and to the right,
a toy plane toiling through the gathering gloom towards what destination?

I was on my way to Kuala Lumpur on a perhaps absurd quest to
try to determine the status of da Nova's, or Klang's, curious text. It
was clearly a fiction of some kind, but what kind? Was it an amateur
writer's somewhat clumsy re-telling of a real story and hence related to
a real document? Or was it entirely made up, a tale based on nothing
more than a vague and eclectic reading of old and not-so-old books?
I did not know; sometimes I felt I had written it myself, though that
was probably only a result of my editorial labours with the eccentric
English of the enigmatic Henry Klang.

When I completed my edit of the material I emailed it to
Mr Klang's address; it did not bounce back, but neither did I receive
any reply. I sent a follow-up query, again without result. I waited. There
was nothing else to do. Time passed. I thought I might forget about it
all, move on to other things, but the opposite happened. The mystery
drove all other thoughts out of my head, drove me to distraction; I
thought about it constantly; and when, fortuitously as I thought, a
cheque arrived for some film work I had completed the previous year,
I came to a decision: I would buy an air ticket and fly to Malaysia, go
to ancient Malacca (now known as Melaka) and see if I could find Mr
Klang.

On the face of it this was a mad idea: to spend several thousand
dollars to go to some crumbling backwater in search of a man who

perhaps did not exist, with only an email address as a clue to where he might be found. Nevertheless, it is what I decided to do; and, to console myself against the absurdity of the quest, reasoned that I had always wanted to see Malacca, that once great city and hub of the world, a place, in Tomé Pires' words, *at the ends of the monsoons, where you find what you want, and sometimes more than you are looking for.*

The other part of my plan was, after Malacca, to try to see some of the real places mentioned in that deceptive text, as if I might thereby come a little closer to the reality, or unreality, of the tale: Mataram, where da Nova's voyage to Luca Antara allegedly began; those islands of Lombok, Sumbawa, Flores which he had skirted to the south; Waingapu on Sumba where some of the crew had briefly landed; the eastern lands of Kaju Djawa, or the Kimberley, and Marege, which is Arnhem Land. This was an ambitious schedule and I was not sure if I could accomplish all of it. Sumba is remote and hard to get to; and I already knew I did not have time and money to visit both the Kimberley Coast and Darwin and had to choose between them. I opted for Darwin, which I had never seen, the place perhaps where the old Degredado lived and where the Australian portion of da Nova's adventure ended. The fact that it turned out to be cheaper on the return leg to fly Denpasar–Darwin–Sydney than it was to fly direct seemed to validate this decision, so I went ahead and booked. My ticket with Malaysia Airlines was actually to Denpasar with a stop-off in Kuala Lumpur; from Bali I intended to travel east over land and sea as far as I could in the time available before making the return, on Garuda Airlines, to the place I had already begun to call, at least in my mind, Luca Antara.

The *Rough Guide* I was using described a hotel called the Coliseum in Kuala Lumpur's Little India, just north of the Colonial District, as having a bar that was *deliciously seedy, oozes atmosphere and full of exotic characters,* so I decided to go there. The high-speed train from the airport took me to the central railway station, from where I caught a taxi to the Coliseum. It was about nine in the evening when the cab let me off outside the plain, double-fronted, two-storey building on a busy street. I pushed the glass doors open to a room full of collapsed furniture and not much else. A fan turned lazily in the roof; a bored cashier on a low seat looked up at me as I came to the bar. I asked about a room; he gave me a key and pointed to a swing door at the back.

Don't you want to look at it first? he said.

Okay.

Through the door there was a flight of stairs to a long open landing with toilets and bathrooms at the far end and a few rooms at the street end. Washing was pegged out on a line on one side of a partition splitting the landing. A cat with half its tail missing skittered away over a low wall. I unlocked the dark varnished door of number four and walked into a high, oblong room with dark varnished wood panelling on the walls, and dark varnished furniture: a desk, a chair, a dresser, a wardrobe. The bed was a low metal double with a thin foam mattress and two hard foam pillows. There was a sheet over the mattress and a single piece of *ikat*—handwoven cloth—for sleeping under folded up at the foot. In the corner by the window overlooking the street was a wash basin and mirror plus a thermos of boiled drinking water. There were dirty checked curtains over the louvered windows and various bizarre and hopefully superannuated electrical fittings on the walls. I peered outside: a line of tiny green illuminated stars was strung across the street. The room pleased me. I turned on the ceiling fan and went back down to tell the desk clerk I'd take it.

At a street stall opposite I bought a packet of Gudang Garam, Indonesian clove cigarettes or *kreteks*, and, back at the bar, ordered a beer. There was only one other patron, a man with a great oval head and bloodshot eyes resembling a darkly ruined Paul Gauguin. He was drinking spirits with beer chasers, chain smoking, and smiled sardonically into his ashtray. He caught my eye, raised his hand:

Where from?

I told him. He laughed softly and shook his head. A pause. Then he raised his hand again:

Welcome.

The Coliseum was twinned with a movie theatre in the adjoining

building where they showed Bollywood epics, Kung Fu films and senti-
mental Chinese love stories. Both theatre and hotel dated back to the
1920s when the British still ruled, and seemed to have preserved most
of the modus operandi from that far-off decade. All financial transac-
tions were processed by the cashier at the bar, meticulously receipted
and spiked, then filed. You ordered your drinks at the bar or from
one of the many young male waiters wearing grubby white shirts and
dark trousers; but if you wanted to eat in the restaurant opening out
in the next-door room you had to order through the maitre d'. In the
back of the restaurant was a smaller room, like a cafe, where the staff
hung out and where their families or other regular patrons ate. The
whole place was unbelievably shabby, with a patina of greasy grime
over everything—furniture, table cloths, cutlery, glassware, crockery,
walls, ceilings, waiters. As I was finishing my beer and cigarette one of
the staff began inserting metal bars across a side door that led out into
an alley running down between theatre and hotel. Another produced
a startling array of chains and padlocks and began securing the front
door. It was ten o'clock. Time for bed.

Next morning I was awake in time to see the fairy lights outside
the window blink off at 7 am. The street stalls across the road were
unpacking, ready for the day's business. Downstairs, the bar and
restaurant were still locked up, but there was a way out through the cafe
and the kitchens at the back. I had breakfast at a Chinese place further
down the street and read an English-language copy of the *New Straits
Times* over my coffee afterwards. There had been a murder in Melaka:
a middle-aged Taiwanese woman living in a high-priced condo in one
of the satellite suburbs had been hacked to death in her home with,
it looked like, a machete. Her teenage daughter was in hospital with
head wounds. There was no sign of a forced entry but the woman's
jewellery was missing.

My first task was to find an internet cafe. Passing by shops selling
silks, carpets, clothing, books, I left the main street for the stall-
cluttered alleyways behind. It was already hot. The cafe was cool
though, air conditioned, the usual collection of plywood booths, each
with its IBM clone gently humming. I sent an email to Henry Klang's
address, saying I was in Malaysia and would be arriving in Melaka that

very afternoon; I hoped he would be able to find the time to see me
and discuss further *our mutual enterprise*. I don't know why I always fell
into a parody of business English when I wrote to him, but it seemed
irresistible. Nor had I any great hopes that he would respond, yet it
was necessary to go through the motions, make the required moves. I
hit send, disconnected, paid and left. I wanted to have a look around.

Kuala Lumpur, which means *muddy estuary*, is only about 150 years
old. It began in 1857 as a staging post for Chinese tin miners at the
confluence of the Gombak and Klang Rivers, very close to where
I was staying. I crossed over the brown, muddy Klang and walked
along the side of the Magistrates' Court, an enormous faux-Moghul
building designed by British architects imported from India and built
by Tamil labour. Clerks and lawyers, male and female, improbably
dressed in dark suits, wearing ties or scarves, hurried beneath the
grand colonnades. Next door was the Supreme Court, grandiose as
well, and opposite that a wide green rectangular lawn with mock-
Tudor pavilions on the far side. On its southern edge, in the shadow
of an enormous flagpole, was a small brown building calling itself the
National Museum of History.

I walked down a narrow path running along the edge of the lawn
towards the river. Coming towards me was a tall skinny black man
wearing a shirt, trousers, sandals. He stopped, smiled, asked me where
I was from and how I liked KL. I said I liked it fine.

Oh, you should have been here when the British ruled, he said. *Those were
the days.*

We sat down to talk; he carried a small cushion because the seats
were hard and his bottom thin. He had no teeth, caved-in cheeks, and
when he spoke his very red tongue protruded from his mouth, top
side up, like a plum. His name was Gerald John Baptiste and he was,
he said, a Christian—probably a Portuguese Christian at that, though
I didn't ask. He showed me his plastic identity card, with a gap where
the word *Muslim* would have been written if he was one.

Three percent of the population, he said. *We get a hard time.*

This was not his only grief. As a homeless man he faced endless
persecution from the police, who like to keep the Colonial District
free of vagrants. They pick them up in their cars, take them far away

and let them out in another part of town, which means they then have to walk back to where they stay. The pristine oblong of grass between us and the law courts was in fact a cricket ground where John Major once played, but its primary designation was Merdaka or Freedom Square. Here Malay independence was proclaimed in August 1957.

Gerald pulled a selection of tourist brochures from his bag, a pen from his pocket, put on the glasses hung around his neck and gave me a detailed, informative and very clear account of the local attractions—where the best markets were for electronic goods, and so forth—all the time annotating the map in a firm, fine hand. His ambition was to be a tourist guide but there was no way the government would let one such as him do that, even though he went to church every day; of the other religions, he liked the Hindus best because when there was a wedding the homeless could go to the temple and share the feast. He was not a sad or an angry man; resigned, perhaps, but cheerful along with it. After all, he said, he had a two-million-dollar bed, pointing to the immense flagpole at the end of Freedom Square.

That's where I sleep, he said.

Can I give you some money? I asked him.

Oh, yes, he said, *I am very hungry.*

His eyes flashed when he saw the colour of the notes in my wallet. Then we shook hands and said goodbye.

My first impression of Melaka was of bad drains and crows. The drains were open channels with slab concrete covers which in various places were missing or broken, allowing the happy rats living within to skip and play; the crows were small, with bluish heads and a speckled brown saddle across the back of the neck. They were everywhere, recalling the crows that are said to have accompanied the incorruptible body of St Iago on his journey from the eastern Mediterranean shore to Iberia, and which still appear on the coat of arms of one of Melaka's sister cities, Lisbon.

The Travellers Lodge was in Taman Melaka Raya, the new town built on reclaimed land on the south bank of the river, before the hill

where the Portuguese enclave was. From its back veranda you could
see the masts of a replica Portuguese merchant ship and, to the north,
the ruin of A Famosa, the fort Afonso de Albuquerque constructed on
the site of the great mosque after he took Malacca by siege and battle
in 1511. I could not help myself; I had to go there straight away.

It was a ten-minute walk to the base of the green hill where the last
remains of A Famosa stand: the Porto de Santiago, the St James Gate,
the only one of the several entrances to have survived. The rest of the
fort has gone too, demolished in the 1820s by the British, who were
afraid that the Dutch, whom they were in the process of supplanting,
would use it against them. It's just a rectangular tower with a small
hexagonal turret to one side now, about ten metres square; you walk in
one gate, through a wide, dog-legged passage, and out the other.

Above each gate is a relief of a soldier and a priest, with a cartouche
bearing the image of a ship between them. The priest holds a palm;
the soldier bears a shield. Round about are figured various artefacts:
pistols, rifles, jars, swords, daggers and other things I could not make
out. The Dutch had messed with the original, replacing the Portuguese coat of arms on the soldier's shield with the monogram of the
Dutch East India Company. Below was a face with grim staring eyes
and obdurate mouth, and a date, now obscured, inscribed either side.

There was something terrible about this gate, as if the rough
granite stones quarried on an island offshore had been mortared
together with human blood and entrails, not burnt coral. I did not
want to approach it, let alone walk through, although in the end I did.
Later I found out there is a local tradition that says whoever dares pass
the gate risks disappearing off the face of the earth. I kept thinking
of a fragment from one of W. B. Yeats' poems: *a bloody, arrogant power.*
Nearly 500 years later, and despite the many tourists round about
and the importunate souvenir sellers within, you could still feel the
implacable will, the savage imperative, the doomed grandeur of the
Portuguese enterprise.

They arrived first at Malacca in 1509, in a fleet of five ships
commanded by Diego Lopez de Sequeira. The locals initially established friendly relations with these, the first Europeans they had
seen—they called them white Bengalis; and a series of elaborate

meetings took place. It seemed that trade, as opposed to war, might be possible between the Malacca Sultanate, then about 100 years old, and the Portuguese. But something—a *misunderstanding*, according to the official history—took place and a battle ensued. Sequeira, who was playing chess on board ship with the Sultan's brother when the trouble began, departed, leaving his factor and a trade embassy of twenty men ashore as prisoners.

The nature of this misunderstanding was not clear to me at this stage, but there is no doubt about Albuquerque's intentions when he arrived two years later. He had come to free the prisoners, and decided that the only way to do so was by conquest; although it took him some months and several attempts, with the help of treacherous elements within Malacca's varied trading community he prevailed, burning most of the city in the process. Before the final battle, a Chinese junk modified into a siege platform was set drifting towards the bridge that commanded both river banks; the Portuguese landed, secured the bridge, fortified it, regrouped and fought their way hand to hand through the streets until they took the palace. Albuquerque allowed his men to sack the city, but insisted it be done in an orderly manner; and the property of those individuals who had aided the Portuguese was protected.

The treasure was described by Albuquerque as *the richest on earth that I have ever seen*; it included 60 tons of gold booty, gilded furniture and the Sultan's throne. Ingots and coinage valued at over 15 million crowns came from the palace alone. An equal amount of gold was pillaged from the loyal merchants of Malacca, most of whom were murdered or fled the city. More than 200 chests of diamonds, emeralds, rubies, sapphires and other precious stones were included in the spoils. Among these treasures were two bronze lion sculptures, a gift from the Emperor of China to the Sultan of Malacca, which had stood guard over the palace doors; these were taken by Albuquerque as his own, to be placed on his tomb. The bulk of this booty was loaded into Albuquerque's flagship, the *Flor de la Mar*, or Flower of the Sea, to be taken back to Lisbon. It was a replica of this ship whose masts I could see down by the river; it sank in a storm off Aceh at the northern tip of Sumatra, and that fabled treasure (but not the lions) was lost forever.

Past the Porto de Santiago, a path leads upwards through the foundations of ruined walls towards the old church on the crest. This church, built in 1521 of that same obdurate granite with its equivocal mortaring, and later consecrated as a cathedral, after 1660 became a Dutch Protestant church; later still, when the English had the place in the nineteenth century, they demolished the steeple and built a tower out front which was used as a lighthouse. Now it is roofless, crumbling, weed infested, braced within by enormous steel girders to prevent the sides collapsing, but retaining the same desolate grandeur as the St James Gate. Inside, leaning against the walls, are a series of massive stone slabs taken from the graves of Portuguese, Dutch and English buried roundabout. The inscriptions on most of these slabs were so worn as to be indecipherable; but one, at least, was a Japanese Christian missionary recruited by the Jesuit St Francis Xavier; his slab, like several of the older ones, had a crude skull and crossbones carved in the centre, with script above and below.

In the centre of the crypt floor was a deep rectangular recess with a wire grill on top. I peered inside: as in a wishing well, there were coins scattered over the dusty floor below, in amongst rogue ferns and other detritus. Here the corpse of Xavier was interred for nine months after his death off China and before a ship was found to take him to Goa, where his allegedly uncorrupted body, minus one arm, still lies. There's a recent (1952) statue of the saint in white marble out the front of St Pauls, thin, intense, bent forward over the town in the image of a fanatic with, strangely, one hand broken off: serendipity, I wondered, or an example of attempted verisimilitude by a faithful vandal? I felt an obscure debt to Francis Xavier, because it was the inclusion of his portrait in Eredia's *Description of Malaca* that helped preserve it for all those hundreds of years in the repository at Goa. I went back inside, past the busker with a guitar singing a Tom Jones song, and dropped a coin into the crypt, wishing the same fate for da Nova's book that had been Eredia's.

Next morning I bought a copy of the *New Straits Times* to read over a breakfast of pork and noodles at the Chinese restaurant down the street. There was a development in the story of the murder of the Taiwanese woman: a twenty-four-year-old Singaporean man, a compulsive and unlucky gambler who lived in the same condo, was missing. Police wished to question him urgently. Meanwhile the daughter, lying in the hospital just across the way from the back of the Travellers Lodge, was improving. But the incident had shaken business confidence, the paper said, and investors in Taiwan were shy of making any further commitments to a place where such violent and lawless acts were possible. This seemed a bizarre twist to the tale, and made me smile.

After breakfast, I went across to the next street where, on the ground floor of the Budget Hotel, there was an internet cafe. I had no particular expectations; I thought there might be news from home. What there was, was an email from Henry Klang. I opened it with shaking hands.

Dear Edmond, it read. *I am receiving your news of visit to Melaka with surprise. Perhaps it is being possible for us to meet. I am working office hours but stopping for lunch at one o'clock. Please reply letting me know if convenient. Yours truly, H. Klang.*

There was no phone number or address appended. I looked at the time line—the email had actually been sent the day before. If I'd thought to check last evening, we might have been able to meet today; whereas, if Henry was working, it might not be so easy to set something up for tomorrow, Saturday. Still, it was good news. I replied immediately, thanking him for his prompt answer and saying I was in Melaka until next week and available to meet at any time, any place, at his convenience, whatever ... and sat back to wait. It was too much to hope that he was at his screen and would reply instantly but I had to be sure.

Minutes passed. Nothing happened. According to the range of dusty clocks on the wall, time had stopped in New York too. I disconnected, paid and left.

It was about eleven on a hot and sticky morning. I decided to cross the river to Chinatown to try to find the fabled street of antique shops over there. I was mindful of a friend whose first overseas travel, more than twenty years ago, had been to Melaka, which he selected by sticking a pin into a map. He had stayed in a Chinese hotel on the north bank of the river, where he met a magician who could make prophetic words appear as if written on the inside of his forearm, and had been directed to an island offshore where, if you slept, you dreamed your own future.

I crossed the bridge over the brown river and walked in a cacophony of traffic down the street opposite. It was called Blacksmith's Street; there were, among the souvenir shops, food stalls, motorcycle garages, dark and smoky little rooms where Chinese men, stripped to the waist, laboured over forges. The next street up was Goldsmith's Street but I did not see anyone working the precious metal. Further along was a Chinese temple built just a few doors from a mosque with a beautiful white conical tower that had a slight lean to it. Both of these were apparently open to the public but, as always, I felt a certain reserve about going into places of worship as a mere sightseer. Opposite the mosque, however, was a shop of the kind I was looking for.

It was small, dark, cluttered, selling a variety of carved wooden statues along with an equally large range of cast bronze, copper and iron work. The wooden goods were animist images of humans and animals, or mythological beings that were both human and animal; the metal ware was mostly, though not exclusively, Buddhist. Up the back on the right were shelves and shelves of tiny Buddhas in the four traditional poses, sitting, reclining, standing, walking, mixed up with images of Shiva, Ganesh, Kali and others from the Hindu pantheon.

The owner was a grave, thoughtful, cultivated man about my own age. He took some pieces of early Qing Dynasty Chinese porcelain from a dusty pile to show me. They were white, hand painted with great delicacy of colour—lemon yellows, limpid greens, startling reds.

He held a small plate up and flicked it with his thumb so I could hear the clear ringing tone it made.

Three hundred years old, he said.

Beautiful as they were, they were not to my taste and anyway outside my price range. It was the Buddhas I was interested in … but there were so many I began feeling overwhelmed. I told the owner I needed time to think and would return.

Where is the street of antique shops? I asked him.

He told me, but added a caveat:

Most of them are not selling genuine antiques. Rich people from Singapore or somewhere else open shops here and fill them up with cheap modern goods that they pretend are old. Nobody realises …

Where do your things come from?

Melaka, he said simply. *Everything comes from here.*

Everything?

Not all of my things are old, he said. *But I do not buy outside the local area. And I do not pretend.*

I believed him. Already he had several times indicated items that were modern or made of inferior metal.

Thank you, I said. *I will be back.*

Most of the antique shops were as he described. There seemed to be a vogue for vast heavy pieces of furniture in dark wood for which you needed prior Customs clearance to ship out of the country; garish paintings of horses, dragons and maidens; gold ornaments which probably were not gold at all. But halfway along the street I came to a place where two dour young Indian men were manhandling an old carved wooden chest into their shop. I waited until they cleared the door, then went inside. The shop stretched on and on, like a tunnel into the past; here the immense and various bric-a-brac of the entrepot had been gathered and conserved. There were clocks, lampshades, chandeliers; typewriters, gramophones, bicycles; old Chinese teacups with the names of forgotten soft drinks printed upon them; brass belt buckles with clasps figured from the denizens of the eastern horoscope; Japanese money, Victorian furniture, bentwood chairs, spears, wide shelves cluttered with enormous broken Chinese funerary ornaments.

Partway down was a rack displaying an extraordinary assemblage of ceramic tiles, both Dutch and Portuguese, salvaged from demolished houses. At the very back of the shop was a high dusty room where tiles yet to be restored were piled in great heaps, illuminated here and there by shafts of sunlight falling through cracks in the roof. You could sense the river flowing just beyond the warehouse doors through which these items had been loaded. What to buy out of this vast assemblage of the past? I did not know. The dour young Indians didn't care; they were examining yet another find, a copper tub out of some washing device of unknown provenance. It did not seem necessary to say I would return. I passed on, looking for somewhere to lunch.

The oldest buildings in this, the old part of town, were of Dutch or Dutch-Chinese design. Unlike the Portuguese, who tended to live within the enclave defined by their fort, the Dutch had settled in numbers in the city itself. Their houses took account both of their own traditions and the exigencies of the tropical climate: a narrow street frontage with small windows opening into one or two low rooms which, in turn, gave onto a kind of atrium, high, square, open to the sky; living and cooking areas, roofed but also open to the atrium, were placed behind, with the bedrooms upstairs. The Chinese took aspects of this design and adapted it to their own purposes, and it was in one of these, fitted out as a restaurant-cum-art gallery, that I ate.

The tables were lined up under a roofed area alongside the sunken courtyard in the atrium. Dutch tiles, just like those I had seen in the second-hand shop, decorated a fountain whose font was a large openmouthed goldfish; real fish swam in the pond below. There was a crumbling plaster frieze around the top of the room, with painted reliefs of elephants, herons, palms. A circular metal staircase led up to the sleeping quarters above, and in the living area within, women sat and sewed, or fiddled with the radio, or simply talked.

The cuisine was one peculiar to Melaka called *Nyonya*, or alternatively, *Peranakan*, a blend of Chinese and Malay cooking emphasising sour sauces like tamarind tempered with creamy coconut milk. Here at Jonkers Melaka they offered a set meal: Nyonya chicken rice; roast chicken (a somewhat overdone drumstick); chilli prawns; black pepper lamb (delicious); cucumber pineapple *acar* (pickled, with red chilli); *tiow mu* (pea greens with chilli and spices); a clear and delicate cabbage soup; followed by a *local dessert* which turned out to be boiled wheat in coconut milk with a little sugar added. This banquet was served in tiny portions, each one, with the possible exception of the chicken, delectable.

Just as I was finishing it began to rain, first as great heavy fat drops falling out of a seemingly clear blue sky; then, as the thunderclouds drifted across, in sheets within the great high room. The courtyard at my feet filled with water that drained away only just fast enough to prevent an overflow; the women within laughed and joked; I smoked my clove cigarette and finished my beer in perfect dryness apart from a few splashes on my bare legs. It was a peculiarly satisfying feeling.

Afterwards, in the dregs of the storm, I walked back to the south side of the river, pausing to buy a slice of yellow watermelon off a cheerful street vendor with a great hole in one side of his face where an eye had been, and eating it on the bridge while a metre-long lizard swam lazily along the bank. I had not met any magician or seen the future but it did seem there was still some enchantment abroad in old Malacca.

At the Budget Hotel there was another email from Henry Klang. He said he could meet me at one o'clock Saturday in the gardens of the replica of the Sultan's Palace, by the fountain where the names of the half dozen or so fifteenth-century rulers of the Sultanate were recorded. Would I please confirm? I confirmed.

I was ten minutes early, walking down a wide path leading away from the massive wooden building that was the Istana Ke Sultanan, the replica palace. Malay palaces of that era were distinguished by the number of peaked roofs they had: this one was three storeys high and boasted seven peaks. It was, naturally, a museum.

The gardens were formal, laid out geometrically, with the fountain that had the Sultans' names upon it in the centre. It was not spouting and the pool was dry, the sun hot, so I kept going until I found a shady seat by a wall at the back of the park with a view down the path I had come up. Behind me was a convent school bearing the name of Francis Xavier. No one around. I watched some fat brown ants running across the concrete. A rustling in the long grass growing by the convent wall turned out to be another cat with, like almost every cat I saw, a mutilated tail.

Ten minutes after the hour I saw a slight dark figure coming down the stairs into the gardens. I stood up and walked towards the fountain; we met right there, stopped, looked at each other.

Henry? I asked. *I'm Martin.*

Call me Carlo, please, he replied. *Henry is just my pen name.*

Pleased to meet you.

We shook hands, formally. He was a small man, wearing glasses, a neatly pressed blue shirt, dark trousers with a knife-edge crease, black shoes—the standard dress of a certain class of Malaysian: those who work in offices. He did not look like a classic Malay, though: his eyes, dark but with strange blue lights in them, were deep set, his cheekbones high and gaunt, his face bony, and there was a curl in his hair. He was looking expectantly at me. I realised I did not know what to do or say next.

There's a shady seat back there, I ventured, waving my hand to where I had just been sitting. *Or we could go somewhere.*

No, he replied. *Let us sit. I do not have long.*

As we walked back to the seat, he told me he was a clerk at Perbadanan Muzium Melaka, the Melaka Museums Corporation, in the ticketing section, dealing with the design, printing, issuance of tickets and, at the other end, with receipts and accounts and tallying of those sold. I'd been to enough museums to know a bit about this: at every one you paid a small amount of money and were given in return an elaborate ticket, issued in duplicate, to carry with you.

It is very boring, he said. *But what can I do? Since the eclipsing of my reputation ...*

What happened? I asked.

He sighed. He looked worried.

First you must be telling me what you are wanting.

We had reached the seat by now. I took out my clove cigarettes and offered him one. We lit up and sat down.

I'm very grateful to you for sending me your abstract of da Nova's book, I began, *but I have some questions about it.*

He sighed again.

That is where all my troubles are beginning, he said. *I too am grateful to you for putting it in your book. There is no other way now.*

But don't you have the manuscript? I asked.

No, he said. *It is gone. All I have I am giving to you.*

How come?

He began a tale of woe. He was a trained librarian. Da Nova's manuscript had come to his notice while he was working at the National Archives in Kuala Lumpur. He had copied it, illicitly I gather, intending to make and publish a translation; he hoped that the Malaysian Branch of the Royal Asiatic Society, which had published the reprint of Eredia's book, would take it on. But this, it turned out, was *politically unacceptable*. His superiors at the archive had learned of the plan; he had been censured for making an unauthorised copy, dismissed from his position and, under the circumstances, the MBRAS felt bound to refuse any further dealings with him.

How do you mean, politically unacceptable? I asked. *And where is the copy you made?*

Confiscated, he said. *The police took it. You do not understand how things are here. I am Malay, but I am Portuguese as well. Like Eredia. And I am not Muslim. No one will credit my story. No one believes in a Portuguese discovery; no good can come from the Portuguese. Portuguese are villains. Look at that stupid story they tell about Sequeira.*

What story? The misunderstanding?

Yes, the misunderstanding. Do you know what it really was?

No, what?

It was a betrayal. He was betrayed, just like me. And then blamed for it.

How so?

The Gujarati merchants were feeling their trade was being threatened. They were turning the Sultan against the Portuguese.

OK. So. How were you betrayed?

They said my manuscript was a fake. It is no longer in the archive. I do not know what they have done with it. Maybe they are destroying it.

This seemed a little extreme, but I could not doubt his sincerity. He was leaning forward, sucking on his *kretek*, tense and unhappy.

But why? I asked. *Surely, if it is genuine, it's a major historical discovery?*

He turned to me, a wounded look in his eyes.

You are disbelieving me also? he said.

No, no, I said. *Of course not. I mean …*

But what did I mean? His story was unconvincing, however much he believed it himself. It didn't seem likely that a reputable body like the MBRAS would turn down something of this order unless they thought its provenance dubious. Nor the National Archives either. It was certainly true that the national discourse, as represented in the museums, cast the Portuguese as historical villains but that hadn't prevented Eredia, who thought of himself as Portuguese, from being published, celebrated and even quoted here and there in museum captions. I remembered what Cheah Boon Kheng wrote: *Mr Klang has at times suffered from an illness, one of whose manifestations is a fervent belief in speculations which are clearly delusory …*

I believe you, I said, though I wasn't sure that I did. *I would just like some kind of documentary proof.*

And that I am not being able to give you, he replied, hopelessly. *You see? This is where I am ending up.*

He seemed on the verge of tears. It was an impasse. I tried a different tack.

So, Carlo … why Henry Klang?

He smiled, the first time he had done so. There was something delightful, both impish and sly, in his look.

Henry is from Henry the Navigator. Klang is from Klang. It means tin. So I am Tin Henry.

It was funny. I laughed out loud. He looked pleased, nodding his head.

Yes. A good name.

Have you ever read Fernando Pessoa? I asked. *The Portuguese poet? He of the heteronyms?*

He shook his head.

Frank Person, he said. *That is also a good name. But I am not reading modern writers. I read only old books. Historical.*

I did not ask how he knew Pessoa was a modern.

So you are believing me? he said, almost shyly.

Well, I said. *Eredia sent someone to Luca Antara, I'm sure of that. You say it was your ancestor, António da Nova. You can't prove it, but it's a good story. I'd still like to put it in my book.*

He was shaking his head again. I felt a sudden qualm. Was he going to refuse permission after all?

Not my ancestor, he was saying. *Not by blood. Spiritual ancestor maybe.*

OK, I said. *Spiritual ancestor, then.*

Yes.

He pulled out his own cigarettes, the milder version, in the white packet, of the *kretek.* We lit up again. I remembered seeing a book in the mall that morning: *1421: The Year the Chinese Discovered the World* (London, 2002), by Gavin Menzies. Had he read it?

He became impassioned.

A stupid book, he said. *Full of lies. The Chinese did not discover the world.*

Zheng He or one of his admirals might have reached Darwin, though, I said. *There was that statue they found under the banyan tree.*

So what? he said angrily. *Who cares? When they are getting there, there was no there there. What is Luca Antara? A desert. Nothing to buy or sell, nothing to trade, just sea slugs. It turned out to be nowhere, a silly dream. And look at those Australians now. Racists, xenophobes, criminals, drunks. They do not know what their life is for.*

I decided to ignore the slurs.

Have you been to Australia?

Only in imagination. Again that sly look.

But you have celebrated its discovery ...

He smiled a second time. A rueful smile, acknowledging my point and, perhaps, his own foolishness.

Ah, but it was being a great adventure, don't you think?

Yes, I do.

My discovery is better than the Chinese one.

I didn't know what to say. It sounded like an admission that his version was, after all, a fiction. He ground his cigarette out under his immaculate shoe.

Anyway, he said, *I am moving on.*

Is your lunch hour over already? I asked.

No, I am meaning I have new subject to study.

Really? What's that?

Have you heard of Waq Waqs?

Again that transfiguring smile. Pure delight.

Yes, I said, *I have.*

Wonderful story, he said. *I am writing this one next. I go back to my Malay side now.*

The Waq Waqs! It is indeed a wonderful story: people of this name from somewhere in South East Asia, perhaps Sumatra, perhaps Malaya itself, perhaps even Cambodia, sailed to the east coast of Africa early in the Common Era and established colonies there. Return voyages were made across the Indian Ocean; and the Waq Waqs are thought to be the ancestors of some of the indigenous peoples of Madagascar who, like the Malays, the Indonesians and all of the Pacific peoples, speak an Austronesian language. We talked happily about the Waq Waqs for some time.

Suddenly an electrical bell rang stridently in the convent behind us. Henry started, shocked out of his reverent enthusiasm for these legendary people. He looked at his watch.

I must go back to work. Good luck with your book. You will be sending me a copy?

Of course. If it gets published. But I don't have your address. Or your surname for that matter ...

Email me, I will send it to you.

But you don't reply ... I began, then thought better of it. *Look, that was fascinating. Shall we meet again? Could we have lunch together? Tomorrow? I have many questions ...*

He looked fey, evasive.

I am looking after my mother. She is not well. Otherwise I would ask you to my home. Another sly look. *I live in Portuguese Settlement. Jalan Eredia. Have you been there?*

Not yet. I would like to.

You should.

He was definitely going now.

What about lunch on Monday? Do you know Jonkers Melaka?

Yes, he said doubtfully. *Perhaps.*

Same time? I said.

Maybe.

Alright, see you then.

As we shook hands again, he said with a sudden return of his paranoia that it would not be a good idea for us to be seen together. I watched his slight figure walk away through the formal gardens without a backward glance. It seemed unlikely I would see him again.

This encounter with the mercurial Mr Klang, or Carlo, or whoever he was, had a curious and unsettling effect on me. Everything started to look provisional, even fictive. Or had I been spending too much time in museums? The Sultan's Palace was a replica but the gardens I walked slowly back through were real, weren't they? They did not seem so; there were raised walkways, bridges, lookouts, all on a Lilliputian scale, and no one around at all. I felt like I'd gone through the looking glass and was not at all sure of the way back. I needed to see something actual, tangible. I decided to go down to the sea.

The way led past the St James Gate and through another garden, ragged and unkempt. It, too, was a kind of museum, this time of technology. There were trains, trucks, an aeroplane, various military vehicles. Beyond, you crossed a busy highway and entered an area that was part commercial, part residential. Enormous square buildings, whole blocks big, with shop frontages alongside roller doors and dark entrances to rubbish-choked stairwells. Some of the shops were upmarket boutiques with display windows in which European-style mannequins modelled fashions from some other decade. Others sold highly priced furniture and statues like those in the antique shops across the river. Still others retailed electrical goods—stereos, TVs, computers. Another highway, raised on concrete pillars, bisected this area, leading north across the river.

Beyond the commercial district the town simply stopped. There was a single empty street, on the other side of which a line of rubble and fill, overgrown with grass, marked the littoral. I climbed up onto a rock and sat down, looking out over the sea. These were the fabled Straits of Malacca: a white haze through which, distantly, the ghosts of ships passed. Something like seventy percent of the oil consumed in China and Japan comes through here, along with myriad other goods. It is also the most pirate-infested stretch of water in the world. Closer in, the sandy shore was strewn with garbage and sea wrack. You couldn't call it a beach: it had the makeshift, unnatural look of the man made. A stray dog came to investigate: a tan-coloured bitch with enormous dugs swaying below. We looked at each other, companionably uncompanionable. She wandered off again.

To the south I could see an enormous steel pier enclosed in wire mesh, stretching outwards. It led to a vast condominium. Beyond that, seeming to float like mirages above the white sea, were other condos built on offshore islands. Behind me traffic roared up and over the concrete bridge spanning the river mouth. The river itself looked more like a drain than the conduit of fabulous events. Even so, there were said to be half a dozen or more treasure ships sunken off here, the wrecks of which had never been located. My sense of unreality increased. I felt as if I had woken into a science fiction story by J. G. Ballard: derelict condos, polluted seas, rusty abandoned piers, a drift of mutant crystalline debris in the gutters of the deserted street. I decided to investigate the pier.

It was flanked on one side by a go-cart track, on the other a mall. The go-cart track, a wide square of marked-up concrete, was empty and unused, but I could hear music ahead. It got louder as I approached. Another Tom Jones song? No, it was ... Jim Reeves. Singing 'He'll Have To Go'. There was a pair of massive speakers set up outside a souvenir shop tucked under the entrance to the pier. The system was high quality, turned up to the max, but there was something odd about the recording: it finished abruptly halfway through the song, to be succeeded by another male vocalist singing a version of the song made famous by Patsy Cline: 'I Fall To Pieces'. This too didn't finish; it segued into the Everly Brothers doing 'All I Have To Do Is Dream'.

I was trying to get onto the pier, climbing a long ramp to where the steel mesh began, but before I was halfway up I could see that it was padlocked shut. I went back down and checked out the shop. There was a cage out front with two large iguanas in it, immobile, primeval, terminally bored. In the corner of their enclosure was a plastic container for some kind of biscuit, and a few pieces of mango lay scattered on the floor. They were for sale. I stared into their lidless eyes while Gene Pitney sang '24 Hours to Tulsa'.

I stumbled away into the mall, trying to find an exit on the other side, and eventually made it back to the Travellers Lodge. I was exhausted. I had a shower, turned on the air conditioning and lay down on the bed. As I was dropping off to sleep I heard in the distance a brass band playing 'O When the Saints' … or at least I think I did.

Next day I caught a cab out to the Portuguese Settlement about twenty minutes south of where I was staying. We turned off the main drag, bumped down a narrow paved road lined with walled bungalows, and through an ornate archway into a wide concreted space with an outdoor stage, like a sound shell, in the middle of it. To one side was a soccer ground and, beyond, the white sea of the straits. The cab driver was dubious. He said the Settlement only really got going at night when people came here to eat, drink and make merry; in the day time it was dead. He wouldn't leave me until he'd made sure there was a restaurant open where I could have lunch.

First, though, I walked down to the shore. I was back in the J. G. Ballard experience, only this time the pier was a ramshackle wooden affair tumbling waterwards. The vast condos floated offshore on their illusory islands, as before. The beach was strewn with rubbish; a cat with a mutilated tail gnawed some indescribable bone. There were fishing boats with eyes painted on their bows moored in the bay, others working out to sea. A small outrigger with a blue sail crossed in front of me. The air smelled of fish. Again, I could hear music—country music.

The restaurant was in an enclosed square where there was another sound stage. It was the only thing open, apart from the pay toilets and the museum; and it was from the museum that the music came. Country, but not exactly; the melancholy of *fado* was mixed into it, and the words seemed to be Portuguese. I wandered over to check it out. It was a local recording of a local singer named Noel Felix.

The museum was basically a collection of photographs of the Portuguese community in full traditional dress on festive occasions, mostly from the early 1950s. The Settlement wasn't that old; it had been set up by the British in 1927 as a home for the scattered, displaced and disadvantaged Eurasian community. Land was reserved, houses were built and leased; later financial help was given so that people could purchase their own places. The dilapidated pier dated from that time too; it had been built by the local residents, most of whom earned their living by fishing.

Many people have remarked upon the extraordinary persistence of Portuguese traits in those parts of the world they colonised, if that's the right word. Although the Dutch established themselves far more visibly in Malacca, and most of the surviving old buildings, both public and private, are Dutch, there is no Dutch-Malay community; whereas the Portuguese, who lived almost exclusively within the confines of the fort, are still here, with their dances, their music, their language, their *saudade*, their fantastic dreams. One of the reasons was political: the common soldiers and sailors were actively encouraged to take wives among native populations, as were the men of the army of Alexander the Great two millennia before. Later many Portuguese *casados*—artisans, merchants or farmers—followed the flag and settled in Malacca, also marrying locally. Their children were usually raised as Catholic and religion is of course a great cementer of tradition; but you can't help suspecting there is some more intrinsic, and more mysterious, reason for this phenomenon.

I sat at a table outside on a terrace where I could see the sea. The only other people at the restaurant were a Japanese couple eating prawns with great concentration. An old man was tending to a small boy of about three, who regarded me with a mixture of awe and amusement. I ordered a bottle of beer and asked the old man what was good today; he recommended fried rice and *ikan bilis*, with Portuguese soup as an entrée. While I was eating, Noel Felix's CD yodelled to a close and the one from yesterday started up; perhaps they were the only two in town. A pair of muscular young guys manhandled fold-up tables out of a room across the square, preparing for the night's festivities. Various other patrons drifted in to eat: an ageing, grumpy Frenchman in a dirty white suit, and his immaculate and unhappy-looking younger girlfriend; two young Indians who scowled at my beer, smoked Marlboros and drank lemonade; a Chinese couple with three pudgy kids; the extended family of the old man and little boy, a cheerful dozen or so of all ages and sexes speaking animated *Papia Kristang*, Portuguese creole. I finished my beer, paid and left.

The street outside the gate, running parallel to the beach, was Jalan Eredia. I stopped at the crossroads, wondering in which house Henry, or Carlo, was tending to his sick mother. It was tempting to try to look for it, but clearly impossible: the street stretched away in both directions until lost in the shimmering heat haze. I walked on down Jalan Albuquerque towards the main road, passing Jalan Sequeira, Jalan Coutinho, Jalan Castro, as if walking out of legend into the world of fact again. What had I learned, what found? It wasn't clear.

On Monday morning the *New Straits Times* reported the arrest over the weekend of the twenty-four-year-old Singaporean gambler. He had been found in his hotel room in Johor and detained without incident. Police alleged he was under the influence of some kind of hypnotic drug. The jewels of the woman he killed were recovered at the same time. He had known her, they were 'friends', hence his easy access to the apartment in the condo. The daughter, still in hospital, was recovering. There was no further news about the investment scare the case had caused in Taiwan.

After breakfasting on roast duck and noodles in the usual place I set off to find the Dutch cemetery. It was on the other side of the hill from the St James Gate, tucked away behind the Stadhuys, built in 1660 as the Dutch, and then the British, town hall, and now, inevitably, a museum. A flowering tree, some kind of frangipani, spread graciously over the small collection of mouldering tombstones, scenting the air and letting fall small white and yellow flowers into the long grass. Most of the graves were in fact of English men and women who had died in the early to mid-nineteenth century, including two Captain Kidds: a David and a John. The few Dutch graves were much older and could be identified by the same skull and crossbones motif I had seen in the church. The coincidence of Kidds and skulls gave a piratical ambience to the graveyard, which was otherwise quiet, peaceful, melancholy, deserted as such places often are. I thought of the folk tradition, still alive in Melaka, that shrouded white figures are sometimes to be seen hovering over these massive stone slabs in the evenings, as if the dead were unwilling either to be here or gone; and felt much the same way myself.

My last museum was the replica of the *Flor de la Mar*, whose hold is full of paintings of the Portuguese siege of Malacca and display cases featuring elaborate and very beautiful models of the various boats and ships which have used the great port in times past: Arab, Indian, Chinese, Malay, Sumatran, Portuguese, Dutch, British. The paintings were naive but appealing; they gave, like those in the Sultan's Palace, a *Boy's Own* version of events that was vivid, geographically and historically accurate, and somehow charming in its artlessness. It was like looking at the separated pages of a classic comic. I also appreciated the grim humour in placing this Malay-centric tale in the bowels of a replica of the doomed ship that had carried the Sultan's treasure away.

Afterwards I crossed the river again and searched the narrow, traffic-clogged streets for the mosque with the white, circular, leaning tower, wondering if the house where da Nova grew up, the one he writes about so sweetly in his book, had stood somewhere nearby. But that mosque was not old enough—not, surely, 400 years old? Or was the house behind a different mosque, elsewhere in the warren of streets in the old part of the town? Why had I not asked Henry about it? I would have to do so when we met for lunch. Meanwhile, the map I had in my head clearly did not correspond to the actual layout of the streets and I wandered around distractedly for some time before suddenly, unexpectedly, happening upon the leaning tower. It was as if it had reconstituted itself out of my desire to find it.

Once again I did not go in. I stood looking at the white, enclosed courtyard, the shoes by the arched doorway, the cool, dark space within where worshippers prayed; then turned and crossed the street to the shop where I chose a small, delicate, standing Buddha from that great array. Down the street of antiques I dropped into the Indian second-hand shop and bought two cylindrical Chinese teacups with stag's heads printed on the side: one, red, advertising soda water, the other, yellow, sarsaparilla.

It was nearly one o'clock. I went to the restaurant where I had asked Henry to meet me but Henry did not come. After eating alone I made my way back across the river for the last time; later in the afternoon I caught the bus back to Kuala Lumpur. My Melaka experience was over, but I had one more thing to do in the city.

The offices of the Malaysia Branch of the Royal Asiatic Society were upstairs in an unprepossessing double-storey block of shops and businesses in the largely residential suburb of Brickfields. A dry cleaner's; a garage; a warehouse for plastic furniture. I walked up the narrow dark stairs and pushed the door open. They were not expecting me. This was the only chance I had to come here, and I'd feared that if I rang ahead I might not be given an appointment. The door led into a stock room where boxes of books were stacked on metal shelves. It was cool after the sticky heat outside. The dry smell of paper. Nobody around. I called out but no one answered. The office was around the corner, overlooking the street. There were two men inside, one at a desk, the other at a computer. I knocked and entered. They were civil but clearly disconcerted. I began my explanation ... I had bought a copy of Eredia's book by mail order from them and I wanted to see what else they had for sale. My particular interest was in the Portuguese history of Malacca. And I was inquiring about an alleged manuscript by one António da Nova that they might have heard of.

Both men looked blank. I wasn't even sure if they knew what I had said. Perhaps they had poor, or no, English? The older man, at the desk, a Muslim by his dress, shook his head.

You see, we have a meeting this morning ... he began.

A woman entered, obviously just arrived at work. She took over. I made my explanation again, omitting mention of da Nova. She said something in Malay to the younger man and he left the room, returning a few moments later with a copy of Eredia's book.

I already have this, I said. *Are there more in the series?*

She led me to a shelf in the corner where they kept single copies of their books. Next to it were bound volumes of their *Journal*, stretching back into the nineteenth century. She was gracious and kind; I could buy any of the books and I could look at any of the *Journals*; anything I was particularly interested in she would photocopy; there were also some individual *Journal* copies for sale; but she couldn't attend to me personally right now because there was an important meeting scheduled. If I had rung first ... In truth, I had already seen a list of reprints and knew there was nothing there I wanted. I made a show of looking through them and then moved on to the *Journals*. They were fascinating. Most fascinating of all was a fragment a scholar in the 1930s had found in the archives at Goa and translated. It was about Sequeira's 1509 visit to Malacca. A list of the names of his ships, the names of their captains, number of crew, dates, manifests ... and, below that, an account of the 'misunderstanding'.

The Sultan had prepared a grand banquet for his visitors, to be held ashore. It was a trap: he planned to massacre them and take their ships. A Javanese woman who had a lover among Sequeira's crew learned of the plot and swam out to the ships to warn them. This was the event that interrupted the game of chess. It was, just as Henry Klang had said, a betrayal—though whether or not it was instigated by Gujarati merchants was unclear. I felt that thrill of discovery all researchers yearn for and sometimes get.

I was marking the page preparatory to having it photocopied when another man entered: an Englishman of about sixty years with a ruddy complexion, wearing khaki shorts and a khaki shirt. He barked at me.

What have we here?

It was the exact tone an impatient headmaster might use on

a refractory schoolboy. For the third time I made my explanation, sounding lamer than ever.

Humph, he said. *The Portuguese, eh? We like to encourage independent scholars, of course, but today we have a rather important meeting scheduled.*

I'm quite happy looking through your Journals, I said. *If that's alright?*

Humph, he said again. *I suppose, for the moment ...*

There is one thing I'd like to ask you, however.

What's that?

The manuscript of António da Nova. About 1610. He was a colleague of Eredia's. He may have sailed to Australia. Do you know of it?

His face darkened, his eyes swelled. I thought he was going to have a fit, put me on detention, schedule a caning. But he did none of these.

Never heard of him, he said, and abruptly turned away to speak in British-accented Malay to his underlings.

I went back to the shelf; not very long afterwards another man entered, grander even than the Headmaster. He was a Malay; ancient, courteous, abstracted, in a magnificent robe: this was Datuk Haji Burhanuddin bin Ahmad Tajudin, the Honorary Secretary of the MBRAS with whom I had first corresponded about Eredia. The Headmaster, who had not asked my name, introduced him to me but not me to him.

An independent scholar, he said. *Interested in the Portuguese.*

We shook hands. The Datuk looked past me into some depthless abyss of time.

So pleased to meet you, he said.

His arrival changed everything. The woman would no longer meet my eyes. The men neither. The meeting was convened in the next room; it was a job interview attended by the Honorary Secretary, the Headmaster, the younger clerk and an extremely nervous applicant, a man in his fifties. I could hear them murmuring through the glass panel next to where I sat flicking through the bound *Journals*. I made my selections and approached the woman again. She shook her head.

I am so sorry, she said. *We do not have the facilities.*

Well, can I purchase individual copies?

We do not have any of those you want.

I could see in her eyes a kind of pleading. She wanted me to accept that under the circumstances she could do nothing. She wanted me to go. There was nothing else I could do. I thanked her and the older clerk and went, nodding vaguely to the four men in the interview room, who gave no sign that they had even seen me. I took with me an application form that the woman had given me. For just 30 ringgit a year I could become a member of the MBRAS and receive a discount on all purchases as well as free copies of the *Journal*. I have it still; I never filled it out.

That night at the Coliseum I tried, without much success, to get drunk. Not that I felt bad; but it was my last night and I needed to sleep. During my earlier stay there I had failed to realise that the clothes shop opposite the hotel had an in-house PA and its own DJ, who played vile music at a coruscating volume through outside speakers directed at the street, interspersed with his own faux-Jamaican patter designed to encourage shoppers to buy. This began at around eleven in the morning and continued well into the evening, and made my room—number four, the same I had previously—more or less uninhabitable. I had lain there in the afternoon trying to read Somerset Maugham's wonderful book about the Spanish Golden Age, *Don Fernando*, until the music drove me out into the streets again.

Gauguin was back in his seat by the door, smiling sardonically into his ashtray. A small group of regulars were drinking next to me: Doctor Mike, an incredibly thin Indian who was an anaesthetist at a local hospital; a fine-featured, deeply unhappy man who looked like Peter Sellers; Chris, one of the desk clerks, who had the night before spent quite some time trying to enlist me into a Perth-based scheme for multi-level marketing, aka direct marketing, aka pyramid selling; and a dark, burly man with a perpetual scowl who never spoke.

We are selling dreams, futures ... Chris had said. And this: *There are three types of people: those who make things happen; those who watch what happens; and those who wonder what happened.*

I'm the second kind, I'd replied. And so I am. I gave up the unequal struggle with the insipid beer and wildly overpriced Drambuie and, leaving Peter Sellers looking with increasing melancholy from his watch to his drink to the clock on the wall, went up to try to sleep in the demented disco my room had become.

On the bus to and from Melaka I had seen big green signs indicating *The Palace of the Golden Horses*; now, on the daylight train to the airport, I saw the place itself: a vast, outré building in cream and gold with a dizzying array of turrets, ten storeys high, as improbable as a 3D Escher construction. The entrance, with its white steps up to a great colonnade, was flanked by two golden horses. What was it? A hotel? A condo? Or apartment building? In its grandeur and folly it mirrored the enormous terrace housing estates scattered through the equally large coconut palm plantations, many of which were unfinished, uninhabited or already derelict. Were these the result of a tiger economy terminally afflicted with bird flu?

In a bookshop at the airport, I was lucky enough to find a copy of Alfred Russel Wallace's classic *The Malay Archipelago* (Periplus, 2000). I'd had a virtual copy on my computer for a year or two, but virtual books are hard to read and harder to carry around with you and, anyway, mine lacked the illustrations that this paperback facsimile had.

There were long lines of people waiting at Customs, and the officials were dilatory and slow. Or were they being overly officious? The Malaysian government had just declared a two-week amnesty for an alleged two million overstayers, many of whom were Indonesians; perhaps the impecunious young men without baggage whose documentation and bona fides were being meticulously interrogated at the head of the queue were illegals. In the event I had to run along the moving footpaths to the gate to my Garuda flight, hearing my name in ghost-speak over the tannoy as I arrived breathlessly at the plane.

At Denpasar airport I negotiated a cab ride to Ubud for what seemed a fantastic amount of money—150 000 rupiah plus a tip of 20 000 for the driver named, like so many young Balinese men, Wayan.

In fact this was a total of about $AU25 for an hour and a half ride. Darkness fell as we drove out of town; little street-side stalls lit by fairy lights and attended by children sold fizzy drinks, skewers of chicken and tiny packets of rice in woven palm-leaf receptacles; further on, the road was lined with a multitude of carved stone images, large, medium sized, small and tiny, of all the many Hindu deities.

Is there a god in every one? I asked Wayan.

He smiled. *Yes, every one.*

The losman I had chosen to stay in was down a laneway too tight for a car to drive; Wayan left his taxi on the street and carried my bag in. The compound we entered was an oasis: hibiscus and palm and other flowering plants; the sound of water falling; a big fish swimming lazily in an illuminated tank; discreet lights burning in the house where the extended family—five generations—lived. One of the young men came out and showed me to the room nearest the entrance: a double bed, a mirrored desk to write at, a basin by the bathroom door and both shower and bath within. It was perfect. All I wanted to do for the next few days was relax before my journey east; I couldn't have imagined a better place to do it. After Wayan left, I showered then sat outside on the little terrace that went with the room, smoking a *kretek* and listening to the frogs creaking in the ponds.

It was in Ubud that I received an email from a friend telling me about the discovery of the remains of prehistoric people on the island of Flores. I already knew that ancient stone tools, about 800 000 years old, had first been found at Liang Buah (Ice Cave) by Dutch missionary and amateur archaeologist Theodor Verhoeven in 1957. They were associated with the remains of the stegadont, a pygmy elephant, and appeared to suggest that both humans and elephants had managed to cross the Wallace Line—*between Bali and Lombok … the most important biogeographical demarcation line in the world.* No one doubts the elephants could have swum—herds of elephants have been recorded swimming for forty-eight hours at a stretch across African lakes—but the humans must have had boats. The significance of this is that the complex task of boat building is considered by archaeologists as one of the likely signs of the possession of language. Since Verhoeven's find, similar deposits had been uncovered on Timor and Roti, but until now no one had discovered incontrovertible human remains.

The dating of the bones suggested this new species of human must have co-existed with modern peoples; but the most controversial aspect of the find was their size: they were tiny, not much more than a metre tall. And then there were the folk tales recorded, disbelievingly, by Dutch travellers in the seventeenth century: locals on Flores asserted there were little people living in caves in the hills, for whom they left offerings of food. Actual evidence for the co-existence in modern times of two species of human is unprecedented, if you ignore tales of the Yeti, the Bigfoot, the Alma and so forth. Little people, then, on Flores, hunting little elephants; hunting or being hunted by komodo dragons; and living in some kind of relationship with the Manggarai, the Ngada and other tribal peoples.

If I had been debating the wisdom of trying to get as far east as I could in the time available (and I had), this news acted as a decider: it suddenly seemed imperative to go to Flores and perhaps even Sumba, as I had planned all along to do. I spent some time with travel agents and my *Rough Guide*, working out an itinerary. It was bitterly disappointing to learn that, though I could probably get as far as Waingapu on Sumba, there was no flight which could get me back to Denpasar in time to make my connection to Darwin. I could, however, fly back from a place called Labuanbajo on Flores. I booked my air ticket and set out for Wallacea, which the Indonesians call Nusa Tenggara.

As I was waiting at the head of the alley in Ubud for the shuttle bus, five big white birds waddled around the corner—a gander, two geese, two goslings—walking with that mixture of inordinate pride and foolishness peculiar to geese. They stopped next to me and drank with alacrity from a puddle of brown water left after the night's rain, then continued on up the driveway to the Medical Centre opposite.

At Padang Bai I bought a through ticket, by ferry and bus and ferry and bus and ferry, to Labuanbajo. A boat was waiting to go, but the guy in the agency said I should take the next one because it was cleaner, faster, more comfortable. I took his advice, had a salad for lunch, checked my emails at the internet cafe next door; and in the meantime saw the old ferry leave and the new one docking. When I went outside for a better look I had what seemed at the time an epiphany: the part I could read of the ferry's partially obscured name was ... *Nusantara*. It belonged, in fact, to an archipelago-wide ferry line called Nusantara, but it was so close to Nuca Antara, and Eredia's redaction, Luca Antara, it seemed like a sign. But what did it mean?

When I embarked, I found a spot near the port bows where I could watch the sea ahead and the land disappearing behind yet still be in shade. It was just after noon on a killingly hot day. I was soon joined by a formidable-looking Hungarian-Russian woman, Bella, who had, she said, mislaid her boyfriend. I minded her bags while she went to look for him. He was an Armenian with more than a passing resemblance to Alexi Sayle: vast, hairy, sweating and quite distressed. He sat on his bag and puffed; I offered him some water but he shook his head. The boat blew its horn and pulled slowly out of Padang Bai; as the cooling south-easterly sea breeze began to blow, Alexi started looking a little better. He took a quart bottle of Karloff vodka from his backpack, broke the seal, uncapped it, took a long, long swig, then handed it over to me. We were on our way.

Bella was a sun-worshipper; she discarded her top and, wearing only a bikini bra and shorts, leaned back on the railing, eyes closed, facing the west. Alexi, whom she had anointed all over, even on the crown of his head, with sunblock, sweated in the shade, swigging from the vodka bottle. All the young men who had crowded around us gazed with mingled disbelief, opprobrium and furtive admiration at Bella's big body and Alexi's insouciant drinking; they were mostly Muslims going home to celebrate the Eid ul-Fitr, the three-day feast of fast-breaking which concludes the holy month of Ramadan. I fell into conversation with one of them, a man called Amil who lived and worked in a shop in Surabaya but was going to spend the rest of the month with his family in Bima on Sumbawa.

What does Nusantara mean? I asked him.

All the islands, he said. *The whole archipelago,* pronouncing the word Archie Pelago, like the name of a character in a book. *They go between all the little islands.*

Nus, it turns out, can mean *small islands*; *antara* is properly *between*; the ferry line Nusantara does indeed go between all, or nearly all, the little islands. So what then had Eredia been seeking? The very islands he lived among? Or, perhaps, more psychologically, his own island self, that lost part of his heritage which belonged with the Bugis? Nowhere in his writings, apart from the brief autobiography, does Eredia refer to his mixed heritage. The question required further research.

It was a fine but hazy day, but you could still see Lombok from Bali, Bali from Lombok. As the massive cone of Gunung Agung faded to a pastel silhouette against the bluer sky behind, the even more massive cone of cloud-shrouded Gunung Rinjani firmed in dark outline ahead. There was a slight swell once we cleared the reefs but it was calm enough, I thought, to steer a primitive raft or paddle a small canoe all the way. I saw flying fish with the full spectrum flashing from their gossamer-pink wings; two sharks basking; black frigate birds with vivid white underbellies high above as we neared land.

This, the south-west coast of Lombok, is hilly, dry, barren, rugged, with vivid green strips of coconut palms growing along the shore, sheltering huts made of woven fronds. We entered a long wide south-tending bay, then turned 360 degrees about a small sandy point to enter the port of Lembar, where double outrigger canoes, encased in rigging like spider-web, were moored. A man in a much smaller outrigger with a blue triangular sail crossed in front of us as the ferry slowed. A riffle of wind lifted the straw hat from his head and blew it into the water; he reefed his sail, picked up his paddle and went patiently about to retrieve it.

Lembar is tiny. There were a couple of coastal steamers at one of the wharves, a ferry at another, several *prahu* at a third. A small collection of bedraggled buildings and, on the dry brown hills behind, the vivid white tower of the mosque. There was a larger mosque under construction further along the ridge. We stopped a little way out from the wharf and marked time, waiting, it seemed, for the other ferry to leave. Sampans came out from the shore, bringing hawkers who clambered with their wares through a low metal door into the vehicle deck below. Bella, Alexi and I, tired of waiting, decided to catch a lift ashore in one of these narrow boats with tiny, tinny outboard motors. We edged past the buses and trucks on the vehicle deck, through the low door and, precariously balanced with our luggage in hand, stepped aboard.

Once ashore we were mobbed by more young men wanting to carry our things, sell us tickets, take us to town, whatever. The only way to get them to back off was to assert that you already had a ticket, but it was dangerous to show the actual piece of paper, because someone would immediately try to take it off you, allegedly to read what it said but in fact to capture your journey, as it were. But there was no malice aboard. Once you showed your ticket, and proved able to hang on to it, everyone immediately became highly solicitous, making sure you were joined to the operator scheduled to take you on.

We three, with a Dutch couple, crowded into a mini-bus and set off through the narrow, dusty streets of Lembar, dodging teams of small tan cattle harnessed together with rope, the two-wheeled brightly painted *cidomo* or pony carts, goats, skinny chooks, and the people passing to and fro in their sarongs, the women with bundles of food or containers of water on their heads, the men smoking and spitting. Once outside town we drove through fields of corn and rice, their green fertility seeming improbable in front of the brown, blasted hills. The smiling, handsome driver's assistant ascertained where we were all going: the name Labuanbajo, not for the last time, evoked an exclamation of joy. The others were all headed for Senggigi, the coastal resort north of Mataram and leaping-off point for the snorkelling paradise of the Gili Islands. I had been planning to stay in the Hotel Zahir at the old port, Ampenan, but the guy in the ticket office at Padang Bai advised against it.

Ampenan's old, he said.

I'm interested in old places, I said.

There is old interesting and old bad, he replied. *Ampenan is old bad.*

As we entered the flat, wide, busy town of Mataram I was still considering asking to be dropped at the Zahir but I never got the chance. The mini-bus pulled up outside a place called Widja Wisata.

The smiling man, who'd been telling us, with an odd mixture of embarrassment and pride, how the Islam of Lombok is *soft* not *hard*, smiled directly at me.

You staying here, he said, pointing to the hotel across the road. *Someone pick you up Monday, take you to bus.*

I did what I was told. It just seemed easier.

As it turned out, I'd bought more than a bus and ferry ticket: about an hour after I arrived at the Widja Wisata I was sitting on the cool first-floor balcony outside my room, smoking a *kretek* and staring into the dark green leaves of a mango tree, when a guy named Ryan turned up. He was skinny, with big teeth and a big nose, wearing a baseball cap, nondescript t-shirt and shorts.

I am your guide, he said.

Guide?

Yes.

He sat down and began to go over my travel arrangements. The bus would not be leaving at 8 am Monday as I'd been told; it would go at 2.30 in the afternoon. He would make sure I was there on time and, in the interim, I would have to surrender my ticket to him so he could write out a new one. I was leery about handing it over but he reassured me. He didn't have time to do it right now, but would return at eight that evening, at which point we could also discuss what we would do tomorrow.

You can trust me, he said.

And in fact I did: there was something open, honest and real about him. The seriousness with which he took his role was appealing. I found out later he had been a guide for at least ten years.

Okay, I said. *See you then.*

But I didn't. After eating at a restaurant next door I lay down to rest, leaving the door of my room slightly ajar and keeping an ear out for Ryan. He came, making no sound, and left without disturbing me. He came again next morning but by then I had already gone out. I was not to see him again until noon.

There were two things I wanted to do in Mataram. One was to see the old port at Ampenan, where da Nova is alleged to have sailed for Luca Antara; the other was to look for traces of the Wektu Telu. It was relatively easy to get to Ampenan; I just walked down the road until I reached a major cross-street, turned left and began walking westwards. The streets of Mataram are wide and leafy, pleasant to stroll along, but it was way too hot to walk the whole eight kilometres; soon enough, I hailed a cab that took me the rest of the way.

We crossed a river and entered Ampenan: narrow, traffic-clogged streets, old tumbledown buildings, dirt, dust, noise. There were pony carts everywhere, accentuating the feeling of a medieval town. The driver threaded his cab through the business district and out the other side. A crumbling arch spanned the entrance to a parking lot, beyond which was the sea. He offered to wait for me but I said no. He seemed worried.

Be careful, he said before driving away.

I walked over towards some makeshift stalls selling food and drink. A couple of young guys sitting in the shade near the largest of these hailed me; one of them introduced himself as Feven. We swapped cigarettes and chatted. What was I doing?

Just going for a walk along the beach, I said.

Be careful, said Feven.

The black volcanic-sand beach was narrow and long, stretching south to the river mouth, north towards Senggigi. There was a rusty pier straggling out into the blue water, and a sea wall to walk along. Back of that, on the other side of a concrete road, was a line of shanties. People everywhere: fishing, strolling, just sitting. It seemed an improbable place for a port, as Alfred Wallace, who landed here, also thought: *The beach … is very steep and there is at all times a heavy surf upon it … many serious accidents have occurred.* He'd been relieved when he had all his boxes, and himself, safely ashore, and afterwards quoted a local saying with pride: *Our sea is always hungry and eats up everything it can catch.* But there was no surf today and no wind either. It was hot and still. I climbed down over tumbled boulders onto the sand and started walking south. I was looking for boats.

They were pulled up onto a high sandy shelf at the river mouth, well away from the shore, but none of them was large enough to attempt an ocean voyage. They were fishing boats, single hulled, some with the ubiquitous double outrigger, some without. I couldn't see where you could even moor a bigger boat. Wallace says his one anchored about a quarter of a mile offshore and, presumably, they landed from a smaller craft. He also wrote: *Sometimes this surf increases suddenly during perfect calms, to as great a force as when a gale of wind is blowing, beating to pieces all boats that may not have been hauled sufficiently high upon the beach, and carrying away incautious natives.* It was all very confusing.

Nor was it clear to me how old Ampenan is. It was certainly the port the Dutch used on this, the western coast of the island, but they were not here in 1610; at that time Lombok was a Sasak kingdom, part Muslim, part animist—this was before the Balinese conquest later in the century—and the Portuguese do not seem ever to have come here in any numbers. I wondered, then and now, if Henry Klang had made a mistake: perhaps he mistook Mataron, in eastern Java, for Mataram, the main city of Lombok? Eredia himself says the voyage his servant made to Luca Antara left from the Bay of Fishermen, which I have been unable to locate, but which could have been on the south-eastern shores of Java. It was, thus far, the strongest indication I had that Henry had made up his enigmatic text, but it wasn't by any means definitive.

I retraced my steps up the beach. Feven and his mate were sitting in the same spot. He offered to get me a coffee from the nearby stall: sweet, black, strong *coffee Lombok*, with a hint of some spice I could not identify. What was I doing now? At the Widja Wisata the proprietor had written down three names on the back of a card: Lingsar, Narmada, Suranadi. One of these, but I did not know which one, was the *unique temple* where Hindu, Wektu Telu Muslim and animist all came to worship, as well as Chinese of different persuasions. I asked Feven if he knew which it was. It was a mistake.

An hour later, I was still sitting in his tiny room in one of the shanties as he tried to work out a way of taking me to a destination I was not sure he knew. His room was heartbreaking: all it contained was a shelf with empty liquor bottles on it and a stereo that he could not get to work. We sat on the concrete floor under a large line drawing of a naked woman charcoaled onto the wall. This floor was also where he slept at night; he had no bed. His auntie, his beautiful, very pregnant sister, his friend, numerous small children came to stare or to offer advice in Sasak. The plan seemed to be to obtain a motorcycle from somewhere and go on that. I could tell that everyone except Feven himself doubted he could do it, but he was imploringly determined. It was extremely difficult to leave, and the only way I could do so was by giving him the name and address of my hotel and agreeing to meet him there at one o'clock. I did not think he would come.

I said goodbye at last and stumbled out into the heat, leaving the car park and walking back towards the business district, feeling conspicuous and distinctly unsafe; the reiterated, alarming *Be careful* resounded in my head. Only now did I realise I did not actually know where my hotel was; all I had was the card with the address on it.

Two men leaned out a second-storey window and called to me:

Where going?

I'm looking for a taxi, I called back.

No taxi, one of them said, pointing up the street. *Maybe that way. Be careful.*

A pony cart clopped slowly towards me. I hailed it. The dark young man at the reins looked terrified. He shook his head and clopped on. I walked a bit further and hailed another; this time it stopped, turned, let me on and swayed towards the town. The driver spoke no English. When I said *Mataram,* he blanched. It might as well have been Jakarta to him. My other problem was, the only money I had was a 50 000-rupiah note: about eight dollars, but far too big a denomination for a pony-cart driver to change. I started scanning the shops for one in which I could buy something; we were in the busy part of Ampenan now, going along chaotic, traffic-snarled streets towards the bridge. At last, improbably, I spotted a bookshop. I got the driver to stop and wait while I went inside.

A notebook, I said urgently, as if I needed to write something important down right away. *Quick.*

A bemused, immaculately dressed young man sold me a tiny green notebook for a few thousand rupiah and gave me change. I rushed back outside and paid the pony-cart driver. Just then a Bemo—a van fitted out with benches in the back—pulled up. I hauled myself inside and showed them the card from the hotel. It turned out they didn't know where it was either, and dropped me off in some unknown part of town; but I didn't care. I caught another taxi back to the Widja Wisata, feeling both relieved and foolish after my probably unnecessary panic.

Ryan arrived minutes after I did; and minutes after that, and an hour early, Feven and his friend. They'd hired two motorcycles.

Acting like a complete heel, I introduced Ryan to them.

This is my guide, I said.

Feven's face changed. He was a sweet young man, only nineteen, and he was certainly trying to help; like so many of the unemployed young men around, he also needed to find himself work. To him, guiding me to the unique temple could have been the beginning of a new career. I could not tell which was stronger, my shame or his disappointment. He and his friend went to sit and wait in the communal room off the balcony while I explained the situation to Ryan.

Can you handle it? I asked.

I will, he said.

He went next door and spoke, quite sternly, to Feven and his friend in Sasak, then came back to report to me.

They already paid the deposit for the bikes, he said.

How much?

Twenty thousand.

I pulled the money from my pocket and gave it to him. He went back out to give it to them. There was more talk in Sasak, not as animated as before. Then they walked away down the stairs with their heads bowed, their shoulders slumped: another disappointment to add to all the others. Another dream gone west. But Ryan was upbeat. He shrugged and smiled.

It happens, he said. *Now … this afternoon …*

Ryan's full name was Bahrain, like the country; some Americans he guided had given him the diminutive. He was an engaging man, but mysterious and sometimes distracted. Calls to his mobile, which he kept in his bag, furrowed his brow as he scrappled through his things to retrieve it. They were usually from his boss, relaying instructions. He was always leaving, saying he would be back at a specified time. Eventually I understood that, as a good Muslim, he was required to pray five times a day. At one point he apologised for spitting in my presence: during Ramadan, believers are not permitted to swallow even their saliva in daylight hours. But, like so many other Sasaks I met, he described himself as a soft not a hard Muslim.

When he returned at 2.30 that Sunday afternoon he said we would visit a village where traditional weaving was practised before going to the temples. I rode pillion on his motorbike out through Chakra, the western district of the sprawling city, and on into the countryside. At Pelangi, in a dusty compound, on a rectangular, roofed wooden platform, a woman of sixty years or so was sitting cross-legged inside her loom, like an ox harnessed to a plough, weaving *ikat*. *Ikat* means to tie or to bind, and refers to the process of tie-dyeing the spun threads of cotton before they are woven into cloth; it is at this point that decisions about the colours and the motifs of the finished article are made: an act of extraordinarily complex conceptualisation which is then realised in the actual weaving. The women also prepare the dyes from local plants and minerals: predominantly earth browns and yellows, indigo blues, crimson reds, purples, greens, blacks and whites. This woman, Bahrain said, could sit and weave for twelve hours at a stretch.

Don't you get sore? I asked.

She laughed. *A woman not marry if she not weave,* she said.

But you are long past the marrying age.

Yes, and I weaving since I little girl.

Next door was the shop. Shelves and shelves of the beautiful cloth in all the traditional forms: shawls, sarongs, tubes, blankets, winding cloths for the dead. This was, I realised, a situation in which it would be extremely bad manners not to buy something. Fortunately, I wanted to do just that. I was in fact travelling with a piece of cloth given me many years before, to sleep under, unaware that this was its traditional use; similar cloths were folded up on the ends of the beds in most of the places I stayed. They are coarse and rough when new but over time achieve a silky softness, while the motifs gently fade, approximating the hallucinatory blurring of perception in some states of intoxication. Bahrain and the shopman, Eddie, dressed me as a Sasak prince and stood me before a mirror, incongruous and dripping with the heat; then the bargaining began. I rode away later delighted with the red, black and yellow *selimut*, or blanket, I bought for about $25. Bahrain was happy too: his commission was a shoulder bag for his eldest daughter.

Lingsar, the *unique temple*, was a few kilometres to the north of Narmada, the summer palace of the Balinese kings who ruled here from the mid-seventeenth century. We left the bike at the gate and walked down a long crumbling path, then turned off towards the walled temple complex. It was necessary to hire a piece of yellow cloth to wear before entering, to show respect. The man who gave them to us was also selling hard-boiled eggs. The complex, built in 1714, and rebuilt since, is the most sacred spot on Lombok and includes both Balinese Hindu and Wektu Telu places of worship. A ceremony was in progress in the Hindu temple; robed, garlanded and perfumed men and women at their devotions. We did not go in.

The Wektu Telu temple to the south was inscrutable, at least to me. There was a terraced garden with flowering plants that, Bahrain said, it was forbidden to pick from; and below that a freestanding rectangular pool where eels, sacred to Vishnu, lived. That was what the boiled eggs were for: you could draw the eels out of their hiding places by offering to feed them. Next to the eel pond was another enclosure with an altar where white and yellow cloths hung and many small mirrors flashed, catching the late-afternoon light; these were tokens from Chinese business people seeking good luck. The smooth stones wrapped in cloth also hanging from the altar were animist offerings. I felt, as always, a kind of transgressor, an unbeliever trespassing spaces sacred to those who do believe. We returned our yellow sashes and left.

Most accounts of Wektu Telu say it began in the town of Bayan on the north coast of Lombok where a community of about 30 000 worshippers still live. It is clearly the kind of syncretic belief that has the effect of conserving local culture against outside influences: in Wektu Telu areas traditional dance, music, art and craft survive in more authentic form than elsewhere. But how did it arise?

Islam was brought to South East Asia first by Arab, then Gujarati traders; most sources say this process began in the thirteenth century, but it may well have been earlier: Sindbad, after all, sailed to Timor as well as to China. Muslims did not proselytise; their religion took root essentially because traders awaiting the homeward monsoon married local women, raised their children to follow Islam and, later, built mosques where they could worship and brought in imams to instruct them. It is likely that these imams were Sufi.

No one knows either when the synthesis with Balinese Hinduism took place. Common sense suggests after the mid-seventeenth century Balinese conquest of western Lombok; but, on the other hand, the Balinese have been Hindu for a very long time, and Bali and Lombok are very close to one another. The animism of the native Sasaks certainly underpins Wektu Telu in much the same way that the animism of the Balinese informs their particular version of Hinduism. Could this have been the commonality that has allowed a unique synthesis to occur?

Da Nova is described walking out to the north along a white sandy path. North of Ampenan is Senggigi, where white coral sand does replace the black volcanic sand of Ampenan; and north is where the Wektu Telu still are, though a lot further north than Senggigi. Is it likely there were Wektu Telu communities in that part of Lombok in 1610? I simply don't know, but the possibility does exist. Maybe Henry was right, after all, about Ampenan being the port of departure for the voyage? Maybe its very obscurity made it a safe place to leave from? Where was the Bay of Fishermen? No one I asked knew this name, but everybody allowed that, in the evenings, the great double outrigger canoes of Ampenan set out into the Lombok Strait to fish, as they still do from innumerable other ports in Nusa Tenggara.

That night I went to Bahrain's place for a Sasak feast. He lived in a small house in a compound with his wife and two daughters; across the way lived his father and his step-mother; his wife's mother was close by; brothers and sisters and cousins too. His wife was big, beautiful, smiling; she spread a cloth on the bare floor beneath the large TV showing an Indonesian soap opera and brought in the food: rice; *kelor*, or hot soup with vegetables; a salad of beans, bean sprouts, cucumber and water convolvulus, a kind of cress you saw growing in all the rivers, served with *pelecing*, a sauce made of chilli, fish paste, tomato; village chicken dipped in chilli sauce; a kind of tabouli wrapped in banana leaf; boiled eggs; an egg salad; prawn crackers; and a sweet white cordial to wash it down. The food was hot—after all, the name Lombok does mean chilli—but not disagreeably so. Bahrain and I were served a whole chicken each but they aren't like our chickens: skinny, high-stepping, bright coloured, they are far more closely related to the original chook, the jungle fowl, and have scarcely any meat on their bones at all. They were, as was all the chicken I ate, overdone, but toothsome anyway, as was the rest of the feast with the exception of the *pelecing*, which was too fishy for me.

Bahrain ate hungrily, scooping up the rice in his right hand like a man who had not eaten all day; my inexpert attempts to do the same made his wife giggle, and eventually she brought me a fork. She also found the look on my face when I tried the *pelecing* hilarious. Their daughter, shy, sweet, about eight years old, was radiant with her new bag. Afterwards the remnant of the feast was gathered up and carefully put away, then the fruit was brought in: raw mango, paw paw and banana grown right outside where we were eating. Bahrain's father, a venerable, toothless man without any English, joined us. He had planted the trees from which this excellent fruit came, and nurtured them all his life. I complimented him so far as I was able. He was gracious and somehow benevolent. He and Bahrain and I smoked *kreteks* together while the women and children sat outside where it was cooler and talked murmurously, laughing often. Bahrain's dad finished his cigarette, said goodnight and left. When he had gone, Bahrain told me that it was a great compliment to me that he had joined us, as it was a great pleasure to him that his father had liked me.

Afterwards he took me back to the hotel on his motorcycle and introduced me to some of his friends. We sat on plastic chairs outside under a mango tree, watching the traffic, vehicular and pedestrian, pass in the busy street. One of Bahrain's mates, a dark and handsome cruise-boat sailor called, improbably, Danny Boy, asked me:

Would you like to buy some beer?

Well, yes ...

Three quart bottles of Bintang, the local ale, and one of lemonade for the only strict Muslim amongst us, were fetched. We drank, smoked and chatted in the warm night air. Bahrain had, upon entering his house, said somewhat earnestly to me, perhaps by way of apology for the sparseness of his dwelling:

I am an ordinary man.

Ordinary, in this sense, I thought, meant something more than just average: he was, I told him now, a good man too.

Yes, he said, after thinking about it for a moment. *Thank you.*

One of Bahrain's calls from his boss had been about another Westerner who would be accompanying me on my journey east.

Where's he from? I asked nervously. I wasn't keen to share my ride with one of the lugubrious Scandinavians or Germans who were almost the only other tourists I'd seen on Lombok.

I don't know, said Bahrain. *Maybe American.*

At the bus terminal I was joined by my travelling companion: Soichi Yasuhara, a chubby Japanese man from Tokyo. He was benign, self-contained, amusing, and, as our time together elongated like some infinitely elastic band, I came to like him more and more. Soi (= Soy), as he wanted to be called, had a rare and inestimable quality in a fellow traveller: he was always available but never intrusive.

As we set off at last, stopping here and there in Mataram to load up with bundles of newspapers, sacks of carrots and much else besides, then drove across Lombok past fields of rice, corn, tobacco, water peanuts, water chestnuts, pineapples, bamboo plantations and brick and tile manufactories, he pulled a small flask of rum from his shoulder bag and began, with relish, to drink it, recapping the bottle and replacing it in his bag after each sip and sigh of satisfaction. I had some snacks: Iraqi dates, sweets made of jackfruit and rambutan paste, and peanuts, which we shared companionably.

He was a part-time tutor at a university, marking the essays students submitted preparatory to admission (or not) to the halls of higher learning. A dull job, he said, but casual and moderately well paid.

What's your real interest? I asked.

I am interested in psychiatry from a sociological point of view, he said in his heavily accented but painfully correct English. He paused, his mouth working towards articulating the next bit. *I have mental illness myself.*

Oh, I said. It never seems right to ask exactly what kind of mental illness someone has.

When I am in Japan, I cannot sleep without … um … medication. But when I travel, I can sleep. So. Maybe Japanese society make me crazy.

He laughed his bubbly high-pitched laugh and we passed on to other things. Later, when we knew each other better, he confessed that he was in fact a schizophrenic and only ever felt normal during the displacements and alienations of overseas travel. Well, there was nothing wrong with his sleeping on this trip. We shared the two back seats on the bus; mine, by the window, was jammed in a half-reclined position, but Soi's was completely broken so that he was able, once night fell, to recline it flat as a bed. He slept like a baby through most of that phantasmagorical night while I gazed wakeful out the window.

But first we had to get to Sumbawa. The land crossing to Labuan Lombok (Port Lombok) took less time than the wait at the terminal for the bus to leave. There, as the yellow sun set over the volcanic land and the big double outriggers set out under the massive purple cone of Gunung Rinjani for the night's fishing, the bus negotiated the wharf into the bowels of the ferry with relative alacrity and we, leaving our baggage aboard, squeezed along the side of a stinking truck full of live chickens and went up to the passenger deck. It was a quick and uneventful trip; I swapped Iraqi dates for rambutans with a man carrying a branch of them torn off a tree, but we had no common language and could not converse. Along with the fruit, he had two cages, one containing a cock, the other a hen, which he was taking back to his village. He was tall, handsome, smiling, with beautiful teeth like a Sumbawanese film star, if ever there could be such a thing. Soi seized with hilarity and delight upon the label of the politic Iraqi date package. He was going to take it back to show his friends in Tokyo.

Darkness fell as we crossed the Alas Strait to Poto Tano. There was nothing there. We re-boarded the bus, bumped ashore and set off into the night. Music began to play loudly through the speaker above our heads. It was 'Food for Thought', the first track on *Signing Off*, UB40's 1980 debut album. For some reason I had always thought the Ivory Madonna dying in the dust while waiting for manna to come from the west was Margaret Thatcher but now realised it's actually Mary Mother of Christ. The album played through in its entirety twice, leaving me with another lyric repeating in my head, the chorus of the song *One in Ten*. That lament for those forgotten by history and bureaucracy, who are always there but remain both unseen and unknown, seemed peculiarly appropriate to the desolate scenario unfolding out the window.

The first town we passed through was called Alas. It was the night of 1 November in that part of the world, the night before the US election. Everyone was awake; all the lights were on—greeny-blue low-wattage bulbs which give hardly any illumination. Every house had a TV set on too, brighter than the lights in the room, showing soap operas, dreamy laid-back music videos, advertisements for things the people watching would never be able to buy, interspersed with Muslim hymns, sermons, prayers and rants.

The people were awake because it was Ramadan and they had spent the day fasting, and were now spending the night eating and talking. All the young men with nowhere to go and nothing to do sat outside watching the traffic, playing guitars or chess, talking and not talking, waiting. For what? Alas, like every other town we passed through on that strange hot night under the gibbous yellow moon, was a town of hovels with, every now and then, a resplendent mosque in which the light was bright white, a tiled, clean, well-lighted place where white-robed men and women sat and talked or sang or prayed. The hovels explained the mosques or the mosques explained the hovels, I couldn't decide which, but in Indonesia it is the case that a mosque will be made available if there are ten believers who want one, and some towns, the larger ones, really do seem to have a mosque for every ten hovels.

But not Alas. Alas was just a small town, a few hovels, one mosque, and still that crowd of young men with or without guitars sitting outside on the stoops in the hot night, waiting. Small children dressed in rags ran after the bus as we passed down the dusty main street, yelling out in shrill high voices, dropping behind as we turned the corner and changed down and headed further east, where the road ran out of town and along a low shore with palms and the shadows of islands further out, behind which the swollen yellow moon rose higher in the brown sky.

We made only one stop, but I don't know where it was. The bus pulled into a car park and we all got out and went to the toilet and then to a restaurant where a meal of hot, delicious chicken soup, rice, vegetables and the inevitable chilli was served gratis, courtesy of the bus company. I looked at the paper napkins folded into triangles in a glass on the table: on Bali, these same napkins unfolded into the familiar four square shape; on Lombok, they were half as big, only two squares; here, on Sumbawa, they were halved again and the single square folded once along the diagonal: an apt index, I thought, of the increasing poverty of both land and people. And yet, every now and then, and especially further east, we passed huge warehouses, or rather granaries, where rice was stored. This grain is not, however, for the people to eat. Indonesia exports rice, and these granaries, owned by state corporations, gather the local produce for sale overseas.

I began to fall into a hole. I couldn't sleep, I couldn't read; there was nothing much to be seen out the window, and nothing, either, going on in my head ... apart from the inane repetition of the UB40 lyrics. I felt like I had become an eye, just an eye, which saw but did not comprehend what it saw. I doubted what I was doing: where was I going? Why was I going there? How would I get back? Would I get back at all? There seemed no answers, not even possible answers, to these questions. There is an expression for how I was feeling, though I did not know it then: *setengah mati*—half dead. This term refers specifically to the effect long Indonesian bus and ferry journeys has on travellers.

Around 4.30 am we reached Bima, once the most important port in Nusa Tenggara and the magnificent seat of Bugis kings. It was just another dusty, rubbish-strewn bus station where we were ordered off the *Surabaya Indah*, our transport all the way from Mataram, and told that another bus would come to take us on to Sape. The sky was lightening to a translucent indigo; the moon was setting. The food-stall owners were packing away their trellises before another day's fasting as the inexpressibly melancholy call of the muezzin began to sound from a mosque nearby. There was some local disturbance. All the young men ran to their motorcycles, leapt on and roared off to see what it was. Soi and I smoked our *kreteks* and waited, anxious that the next bus would not come in time to deliver us to the *fast boat* which was, we had been assured, leaving Sape at 8 am and would, after stopping at Komodo, reach Flores in the early afternoon.

I don't know what time we did leave Bima. Six-thirty perhaps. The bus was half the size and twice as uncomfortable as the *Surabaya Indah*, which is saying something; but the journey was only a couple of hours. The narrow road wound up in switchbacks to the summit of a brown, jagged range, and then ran along the ridge, with precipitous falls on the other side to green river deltas where rice, corn and tobacco grew, and goats and cattle grazed. Once I saw a pig. So early, but the people were already out in the fields working. We passed through hilltop villages with houses made of the traditional woven palm and bamboo in which the only signs of modernity were the ubiquitous motorcycles; then, with saucers of blue sea showing between the umber hills, began the abrupt descent into Sape.

It was Tuesday in Sape, market day, the narrow main street like an Arab *souk*. Goats and dogs wandered among the food laid out for sale. Pony carts jingled their bells. Very few of the people wore Western dress, certainly not the older ones; but, as elsewhere, in amongst the chaos and the dirt, the robed men, and the women in sarongs with their heads and sometimes their faces covered, immaculate, beautiful young girls in tight blue jeans or tight skirts and pink or yellow embroidered tops passed.

The port was a kilometre or two beyond the town, a concrete rectangle the size of several football fields, lined by buildings on two sides with a pier in one corner; here lines of trucks waited in the sun. Soi and I looked anxiously for the fast boat but there was none. Had it gone already? Or not yet arrived? The lines of trucks suggested some

kind of ferry was coming, but we had to be sure. At the back of the
wharf area were a few shanties: shops, restaurants, depots. The bus let
us off outside one of these, the Warang Pusaka Indah, and we were
given to understand this was where we could wait for the ferry. The
tall, world-weary proprietor of the restaurant-cum-depot pointed to
the clock on the wall, which showed that the time was a little after
eight in the morning.

Five-fifteen, he said.

I could not comprehend what he had said.

In fifteen minutes? I asked.

He shook his head sadly.

No. Five-fifteen in afternoon. You wait here.

Soi and I looked at each other in disbelief. We had been travelling
for more than sixteen hours already; now we were facing another
sixteen before we reached our destination. It seemed … impossible.
We looked around for help. Another man had joined us, neat, well
made, dressed in a shirt and trousers, solid shoes. He'd smiled at me
on the bus from Bima but we hadn't spoken.

He says five-fifteen, I said faintly.

Joseph smiled and shook his head. It was news to him too, but not
unexpected. He spoke to the proprietor in Bahasa Indonesian, then
translated the reply. The ferry was just now leaving Labuanbajo, eight
hours away. That's what it always did, except on Friday, when it didn't
come at all, since on that day it made a run to Waingapu on Sumba.
There was no fast boat—there had been once, but it was unlicensed,
unsafe and withdrawn from service years before. Nor was there a
stop-off on Komodo, which is where Soi thought he was going, and
had paid to go. The journey to Labuanbajo would not begin until
this evening. We would get there in the early hours of the following
morning. There was absolutely nothing we could do. He smiled again
and sat down.

We wait, he said.

So that's what we did.

⛧

Joseph was returning to his village near Ruteng on Flores for the first time in five years. He had just completed training as a school-teacher and was hoping to find work on his home island. There was something about him that reminded me of the hero of a social realist novel: determined, committed, idealistic, sane. He told me people on Flores, who are mostly Christian, were watching the situation in East Timor closely. There was a nascent movement towards independence for Nusa Tenggara Timur, the islands of the eastern tribal area. Flores, West Timor, Roti, Alor and some of the smaller groups could secede and make a state of their own, just as the East Timorese had done. But things were not so good in East Timor. Crime, disease, poverty were all on the increase. It did not help that the Australian government was behaving like a greedy playground bully with respect to the oil and gas reserves under the Timor Sea.

Jakarta would resist you every step of the way, I said.

Yes, he replied, *but that is not a reason for not trying.*

I could not help thinking of what, in an earlier age, would have been called the *revolutionary potential* of these islands: if all the idle young men could be mobilised to a cause, what could they not accomplish? On the other hand, the police and the army, who were never far away, would undoubtedly respond to any kind of civil disturbance with ruthless violence, as they currently were in both West Papua and Aceh. I mentioned this to Joseph and he nodded, serious and sad.

I know.

He was not overly earnest, however. We soon started up a routine about praying for divine intervention in our stalled travel plans. And for further connections to be made. It was funny then, perhaps more than it seems now; and it passed the time. After a while he said he was going to the gatehouse to see if he could phone ahead to tell his people he was delayed. That left Soi and me in amongst the constant drift of people in and out of the restaurant. We ordered coffee. The proprietor brought a plate of long green mangoes and began to sharpen a wicked-looking knife. Soi was brooding. He was annoyed at being rooked: he had paid a large amount of money for a boat and a destination that did not exist. He started to stress, becoming vehement, which had the effect of making him splutter his words. The locals watched him, smiling to themselves. They thought he was unusual, which he was; and although they politely hid their amusement from him, I think he knew. On the other hand, he was probably used to it.

When Joseph came back, he said the phone wasn't working now but might later. We decided to ring the bus company ourselves, to complain about Soi's treatment. We walked in blinding sunlight across the concrete to the *wartel* at the gate but the phones were still not functional. There seemed nothing to do but walk back. Still, having made an attempt at redress, Soi seemed mollified. He took a book from his bag and went to sit outside to read. It was a work on social psychiatry written by an Australian woman he had met in Melbourne, who was about to visit Tokyo for a conference Soi would be attending on his return home.

I wrote the words *Luca Antara* on a piece of paper and showed it to Joseph. What did they mean? He frowned, thinking hard. *Antara* he knew—it meant *between*; but not *Luca*. We discussed all the possible permutations: Nuca, Nusa, Nusantara. Suddenly his face cleared.

I think I know, he said.

What?

The day after tomorrow, he said. *In the future, you know? The day between is tomorrow. It means the day after the day between.*

I didn't fully understand his explanation but the translation pleased me. Luca Antara, whether in Eredia's book, da Nova's, Henry Klang's or my own, was certainly prospective, a destination, part mythic, towards which to work and dream.

Meanwhile, there was this day to get through. I thought of visiting the market in town but the prospect of walking two kilometres there and back in the incandescent heat was daunting: Sape seemed as far away as Switzerland. I put off eating lunch as long as I could but gave in to hunger about 11.30. Afterwards, the proprietor, giving me a few filthy, tattered notes from the locked drawer under the counter as change, said I could go through into the back where the women and children were and sleep on the floor if I wanted to. I would have loved to sleep, but knew I would not be able to. A little later he went in there and lay down himself. I took Wallace out of my bag and started to read.

The Malay Archipelago is a curious book, constructed geographi-

cally, not, as you might expect of a travel book, chronologically.
Wallace spent eight years criss-crossing the archipelago, making over
sixty separate journeys, most of them by boat, and covering some
14 000 imperial miles; but when he came to write up his notebooks he related his adventures region by region, starting with
Malacca in the west and ending in New Guinea in the east. As if in
fealty to this eccentric construction, I did not read the book from
beginning to end but approached it as serendipitously as it was written.
Regrettably, the only major islands he did not visit were those where
I was travelling: he was on Lombok for a while but never went to
Sumbawa or Flores. Or Sumba, for that matter. He did visit Timor
and he did send his assistant, Charles Allen, to Flores and Sumbawa,
but there is no first-hand account of these two latter islands.
This is a shame, not so much for any lacunae in the natural history—
Allen supplied him with those details—but because Wallace was an
incomparable observer of peoples as well as creatures, and a wise
and witty raconteur of his encounters. Never mind; I was stranded in
Sape, but in my mind I travelled happily through the Moluccas to the
north.

The day wound on. A goat wandered along, climbing onto a sack
of some kind of foodstuff left in front of the restaurant and pissing
a copious stream of urine over the contents, looking derisively at
us through yellow-devil eyes before wandering on. There was a cat
fight: two scraggy toms with mutilated tails squalling and hissing in
the corner until the proprietor flushed them outside with a broom.
Young men passed to and fro on their motorbikes, sometimes with
one of those immaculate girls riding pillion. Joseph had met someone
who was into direct marketing and they had begun a long, involved
conversation about it. Soi was dozing. I walked over to the edge of the
wharf to look at the boats moored before low brown islands in the
blue sea, then walked back again.

It's hard to remember now how we got over the hump of the torpid
afternoon, but there was a point at perhaps three or three-thirty when
the atmosphere changed. People stirred, stretched; the shower next
door, which you could hire for a few thousand rupiah, all of a sudden

got busy; the drivers sleeping under their trucks or in the depot next door started to get up and check their ropes and loads.

Then someone cried out:

The ferry!

Sure enough, there it was, a smudge of smoke drifting towards us on the horizon. I looked across at Joseph.

Hallelujah! I said.

Hallelujah! he replied.

But the voyage was a nightmare. If I had been feeling *setengah mati*, half dead, before, I was now three-quarters or seven-eighths the way there. The ferry was older, slower, dirtier, more dilapidated and more crowded than the one we had sailed from Lombok to Sumbawa, which was itself in worse condition than the one from Bali. I was exhausted but still could not sleep; and, although I know my native anxiety and paranoia increase exponentially with prolonged sleeplessness, the knowledge did not help allay these feelings. The television blared, showing bizarre and violent soap operas interspersed with ranting mullahs and soft-porn music videos featuring pouting, stilted blonde starlets and greasy leering male singers dripping gold chains.

There are no rubbish bins on Indonesian ferries; everything, mostly food or plastic, just goes over the side or onto the floor which, because so many smoke, rapidly turns into an ashtray-cum-compost heap. Tiny delicate women lay down in the filth with their naked children to sleep. The young man who had the kiosk and foam-mattress concession strutted among us, radiating his arrogance and contempt for those who could not afford the 6000 rupiah for a squab. For 10 000 rupiah you could upgrade to first class, a room towards the bow with long, high-backed foam seats covered in torn black vinyl, but it was already full. Soi had found a spot on the raised wooden sleeping platform towards the stern and was stretched out dozing. Joseph was deep in conversation with the Direct Marketer. I sat on a hard grey bucket seat, sharing cigarettes and snacks with the guy sitting in front of me who was going to Ende; became involved in a series of desultory conversa-

tions with young men wanting to practise their English; or hung over
the rail watching the dark sea travel past, the yellow moon rise to the
north, the Pleiades, Taurus and Orion, stars of the southern heavens,
climbing slowly up the sky ahead. I thought of da Nova, with the prow
of his *prahu* pointed in the direction of Antares, the red eye of the
bull. I thought about Luca Antara, the day after tomorrow, the fabled
or perhaps delusory destination for besotted voyagers like myself.

The world seemed doomed, humanity like vermin crawling on a
rubbish heap, assailed by the poison of the television and suffocating
in our own waste. The dignity, grace and forbearance with which most
Indonesians endure the poverty and attendant squalor which is their lot
somehow only made the situation worse; and the strutting arrogance
of the authorities, be they police, army, ferry crew or the man with
the mattress concession, truly sinister. Such officials are viewed by the
people with a mixture of fear, pity and dislike; they ignore and avoid
them if possible, but are never allowed to forget where the power lies
and what it can do if provoked.

It is no wonder, I thought, that Islam which, unlike Christianity, offers
its community a real, if intermittent, respite from the terrible condi-
tions in which they live, is so entrenched here; the social conscience of
Islam works in a direct and practical manner to alleviate, if not change,
the way things are. As that dark voyage continued into the night, on
the other side of the world the American people were voting George
W. Bush and his criminal cohort back into office in almost complete
ignorance of how things are for most people on most of the earth.
The situation seemed impossible, without remedy, an endgame. And
perhaps it is.

All journeys end. Some interminable time later the man from Ende
touched my arm and pointed ahead, where a tiny glitter of lights shone
out of the gloom.

Labuanbajo, he said, a name I never heard spoken without joy.

I went to the rail. The shadowy, gun-metal grey, lithe shapes of
dolphins traced white foam trajectories through the black water at

our bow. Cut-out silhouettes of islands, darker than the sky behind, passed astern. The half-dead of our company began to stir, wake their children, find their things. I felt someone at my elbow and turned to see Soi, blear-eyed but happy as he lit yet another *kretek*.

Labuanbajo, I said, just to hear how the word sounded on my own lips. It sounded good.

The *Rough Guide* said we would be met *by touts and boats waiting to take you to losmen* but we disembarked unsolicited into the warm, somnolent air. Soi wanted to go to a place called the Wisata but I liked the sound of the Gardena Bungalows better. Neither of us knew where either place was, so we simply walked up the street until we met someone: a tall, dark young man in a ragged t-shirt, shorts and thongs. He pointed vaguely up the hill, then asked for money. I gave him one of the soft, greasy 1000-rupiah notes from Sape.

We climbed a steep, curving stone staircase to a roofed, open restaurant area. The soft, sweet scent of a flower, perhaps a gardenia, drifted over us, indescribably beautiful. There was a note on a desk under one light burning. It said there were four rooms available and, if we wanted one, we should go to the staff cottage. A map on the wall behind gave directions. We stumbled around in the dark for a while before we found it. A young woman in a blue and white hibiscus-pattern dress, deliciously sleepy, came out and gave us each a key. It was scarcely believable that she could show such graciousness on being woken at three in the morning. She went back to her bed and Soi and I to our respective bungalows.

They were made of woven fibre over a wooden frame, square, high ceilinged, airy, bare of all furniture but a double bed, with ensuite bathroom. I showered, washing off the filth of nearly forty-eight hours' sleepless travel, then fell onto the bed. As I closed my eyes I saw, as in a dream, a field of grasses and flowering plants where small dinosaurs grazed, sitting up on their two hind legs like kangaroos before the low blue cones of distant volcanoes. Was this the day after tomorrow or the far past I had come to? It didn't matter; I'd arrived.

✳

What is it gives a place its special magic? Probably a combination of the seen and the unseen. Sitting in the restaurant next morning, waiting for my omelette and fruit salad, listening to the girls laughing and talking in Portuguese creole, I looked out over the wide blue bay to a complex skyline of low brown islands and the perfect cones of old volcanoes. Before the sea rose and drowned this harbour perhaps 7000 or 8000 years ago, it might in truth have been the grassy, flowery plain of my eidetic vision before sleep; and if the raptors, or whatever they were, must have disappeared many thousands of years before that, there were still relict populations of dinosaur-like creatures here: two of the islands offshore were Rinca and Komodo where the fabled dragons live.

Our angel from the night before was called Celeste; her friends were Maria and Helena; they waitressed, cleaned, gardened, picked mangoes from the trees, did the guests' laundry, received the numerous deliveries of fruit and produce that locals (including, one morning, two children bearing a silver fish longer than either of them was tall) carried up the steps, all with the same lightness of spirit of their morning conversation. Maria, a trim, dark girl with glossy black hair, almond eyes and a wide mouth, giggled and blushed every time I looked at her; Helena was calmer, more circumspect; Celeste did everything with an unconscious grace that was lovely to watch. She brought my coffee, smiled shyly and went about her tasks. Soi joined me, having showered, he said, twice before going to bed and again on rising, trying to scrub away the greasy meniscus clinging to his skin from the journey.

The first thing I did was find the Merapati office so I could confirm and pay for my travel out the following Saturday: flights to and from the eastern islands are uncertain. If there aren't enough passengers the plane might not go; if there are too many someone might be left behind. Afterwards I walked down the hill to the single main street crowded with shops and businesses, and wandered back towards the Gardena. Along the way I happened upon a craft shop: it was tiny, dark, apparently unattended and full of a fascinating array of locally manufactured goods, mostly, but not exclusively, made of cow horn and wood. Amongst the statuary were some small cast-metal figures of dinosaurs—a triceratops, a tyrannosaurus, a stegosaurus. In the cabinet where the precious things were kept I saw a smooth black stone sitting alone on a shelf next to a small round metal container once used for holding the lime that is an indispensable accompaniment to betel-nut chewing. I saw instantly how the stone would fit in the container and knew I had to have both. When, later, I bargained, and paid too much for them, the owner of the shop could barely control her amusement that someone would even consider paying 50 000 rupiah for an ordinary stone, even as she insisted it was actually a rare and incomparable jewel.

Labuanbajo was like that: there was laughter under everything, a light-hearted acknowledgement that life, while absurd and sometimes tragic, was also, and perhaps consequently, hilarious as well; and that you might as well live it in the most nimble and elegant manner you could. I'd already more or less decided, out of sheer physical exhaustion, against attempting further travel; it would be far better just to idle my way through the next few days, eating the superb meals in the Gardena's open-air restaurant, reading Wallace, drinking beers in the late afternoon with Soi or anyone else who happened along; sleeping; and, perhaps, visiting one or two of the local attractions. There were two possibilities that interested me: Mirror Rock, just fifteen minutes away by motorcycle in the dry hills behind the town; and Rinca, which you could go to on a day trip by boat to see the dragons.

I went to Batu Cermin the next day on the back of a boy called Alexander's motorbike. At the entrance to the park, he delivered me into the hands of a guide, Sebastian. We walked through the dry, thorny scrub towards a tumbled, tree-covered limestone outcrop rising directly out of the plain. At the base of a high cliff Sebastian pointed upwards: clinging to a dark, shapeless extrusion on the rock wall about fifteen metres above us were hundreds, perhaps thousands of black bees making a deep humming sound. We went on into a wide overhang, then climbed down a ladder and squeezed through a narrow rocky aperture into a cave.

It was vast and gloomy, with stray gleams of light falling from far above. Sebastian played his torch around: there were stalactites and stalagmites shaped like stupas or pagodas or jackfruit; the roots of banyan trees snaking down the walls and along the floors like electrical cables; the faint ammoniac smell of bats. Theodor Verhoeven had excavated here as well, finding, Sebastian said, a human skeleton which is now in the museum at Maumere, a large town in the east of the island.

Was it a small person? I asked.

Yes.

Where?

Just there, he said, pointing with his torch. *Behind that rock.*

At that moment, I felt a strange dizziness, like vertigo, come over me. I swayed on my feet, seeking with one hand a rock wall for support. The deep humming of the bees from far above sounded loudly in my ears; or was it my own blood roaring? I stumbled after Sebastian and looked at the dusty floor where the body had been dug up. Had this person fallen to their death in the cave or had they lain down here, old, sick or wounded, to die? How long ago? The only clue I have is the word *Neolithic*; and there is nothing in the written sources about a skeleton in Maumere Museum.

Further on, Sebastian showed me the fossilised body of a turtle, complete in all details, upside down in a low section of the cave roof; and some antediluvian fish, perhaps a flounder or a sole, in a depression in a wall. There were tiny bats poking their foxy heads between their wings to peer at us; swallows nesting in mud-made nests on high shelves; and Mirror Rock itself, a deep crack in the outcrop into which the noonday sun briefly shines, lighting up the limestone so that you can see the shapes of hidden things reflected there. But this was afternoon, so we saw nothing.

On the way out, Sebastian pointed to a small tree growing in the floor of an open, ravine-like cave. It was about three metres high. He said he remembered seeing it as a boy, twenty years ago, when it was half the height it was now—so slow-growing he had outstripped it in his own lifetime. We wandered back through the strange, blasted landscape where komodos are also sometimes found; those that are, are captured and sent to one of the islands offshore, to boost the declining populations there and also to remove a dangerous predator.

The boat to Rinca (= Rin-cha) was leaving at 6 am the next day. Papa Subu, a skinny old man in t-shirt and shorts, no shoes, met me on the restaurant steps and we walked down to the steel gates onto the wharves. They were locked. He was thin enough to slip through the gap between the gatepost and the wall but I, to his amusement, was too big and had to climb over. His nameless boat was long and narrow, and he sailed it all by himself, letting go the moorings, starting the diesel engine, then expertly negotiating a way past the many other craft moored in the roadstead. It was a slow ride, and I was the only passenger. Papa Subu steered from the cabin towards the stern most of the time but, for some reason I could not comprehend—there was no wind to speak of—kept leaving the wheel to clamber over the cabin roof or into the bows to rig or lower sails made of stout blue woven plastic. When he did this the boat tended to port, so that there were times when we seemed about to run aground on one of the low, green, mangrove-haunted shores. At the last minute he would scurry back past me with a small duck of his head and a hand-wave of reassurance, to put us back on course.

It was fascinating to learn that all the brown islands, and the brown mainland shores, which from the town seemed uninhabited, were in fact the sites of small fishing villages, with pole houses built out into the sea. Some of these were derelict, abandoned; one, of only half a dozen crumbling houses had, at the end of the strand, under a spreading tamarind tree, a crumbling circular mosque constructed like the houses of woven pandanus and coconut-palm leaves. Most of these half-marine villages, with an only notional connection to the arid land behind, belong to the *orang laut*, the sea gypsies, who are also sometimes known as *bajau*; the name Labuanbajo is in fact derived from these people and so properly means Port of the Sea Gypsies: another index to its romantic ambience.

Approaching Rinca, upon which there are no villages, the otherwise deserted shores were home to monkeys fishing for crabs among the rocks with their long prehensile tails. At the landing, a few long, thin boats were moored, with woven shelters constructed along them; fish, gutted and laid open in butterfly shapes, dried on the roofs of these cabins; and a dozen or so people, young, old, men, women, children, squatted in the shade of the gatehouse on the wharf: *orang laut* who had not, as so many now have, abandoned their house-boats for a dwelling ashore. They were whip thin, with worn, sun-wrinkled faces, dark skinny limbs, and a wild, old look in their eyes which seemed to gaze utterly beyond anything in the modern world. *Orang laut* are born, live out their days and die on their boats, but they are always buried ashore. Papa Subu instantly melded into their group while I, with three French people just landed from another boat, walked inland to the tourist offices.

The buildings were raised on poles, and in the dusty shade beneath lay the grey-black, primeval shapes of *ora* and *komodo*: *ora*, the young dragons, were the size of large goannas; the adults were the size of crocodiles. They seemed somnolent, benign, but it was still disquieting to see the casual proximity of predator and prey. My guide was a gloomy man called Bernardo. He took a long stick, forked at one end, and we set off down a path edged with boulders of white quartz like so many human skulls into the desolate wastes of Rinca.

Every so often, above and among the dusty tamarinds, the prickly pear, the scrub, rose the stout, robust trunks of lontar palms, their leaves incredibly green against the brown land. The fronds rattled like corrugated iron if you brushed against them; when the hot wind blew across them they made a sighing like a distant sea. Megapodes scratched in the dust or chased each other through the scrub; unknown birds, sounding like pigeons, called from the trees, but Bernardo said there were no pigeons on the island, although there were cockatoos; monkeys chattered and gibbered at us; we saw deer, buffalo, wild pig: an extraordinary richness of wildlife considering how barren the island seemed.

Just above a dry watercourse Bernardo stopped, touched my arm and pointed. In the discarded fronds under a small group of lontars, like a great grey log with legs, an enormous komodo lay sleeping. We went up to within a couple of metres of it; it opened one lazy eye, then closed it again.

Is it safe? I hissed to Bernardo.

He shrugged. *He's sleeping. And I have my stick,* he said. *Besides, they have eaten already … look.*

Between rough boulders tumbled in the river bed below lay the whitening bones of a buffalo, with dark patches where pieces of dried flesh still adhered.

One week ago, said Bernardo, *there were twenty komodo down there, feeding.*

We went on, following the course of the river until we reached a mud-hole where a lugubrious-looking buffalo, surrounded by flies, stood up to its haunches in the ooze. Another komodo almost caught Bernardo by surprise. Smaller than the one we had seen sleeping, it made its ponderous way down to the mud-hole, crawled across to the other bank and lay there like another, muddier log. Its yellow, forked tongue flicked in and out, testing the air, reminding me that some ascribe the legend of fire-breathing dragons to a perhaps fantastical view of this same tongue.

Oddly enough the komodo contributed, albeit unwittingly, to the making of one of the great films of our era. In 1926 the American explorer W. Douglas Burden, along with Henry Fairfield Osborn, President of the American Museum of Natural History, and a camera crew they picked up in Singapore, sailed to Komodo Island on a steamer called the *SS Dog* in an attempt to capture a pair of dragons and take them back to New York. After some fairly hair-raising adventures with snakes and buffaloes, as well as komodos, he succeeded in doing just that. Returning to the States, Burden told the strange story of his trip to Merian C. Cooper, a film producer. Cooper changed the objective from a giant lizard to a giant ape, added a beautiful heroine, Fay Wray, and made the 1933 classic *King Kong.* The ape was animated by the great special-effects pioneer Willis O'Brien, who had spent much of his career up to then doing the same thing with dinosaurs in pictures like the movie version of Arthur Conan Doyle's *The Lost World.*

The French, who had caught up with us at the mud-hole, soldiered on with their guide into the uplands. Bernardo said:

Do you want to go into the savannah? Or back the way we came?

It was quite clear what he wanted to do.

What's up there? I asked, looking dubiously at the brown hills.

Nothing. Just the panorama. Very hot.

I'm not sure.

Up to you, he said, hopefully.

Let's just go back.

He brightened up then, becoming more communicative. And, when he learned that I had come alone with Papa Subu, looked almost happy. A friend, he said, was ill. Could Emanuel ride back to Labuanbajo with me?

Of course.

Emanuel was not ill at all, but his eighty-two-year-old grandfather had died the night before in his village on the mainland and he wanted to go back for the funeral. He bought some dried fish from the *orang laut* at the boat landing; Papa Subu appeared from somewhere and off we sailed. Flying fish skidded across our bows; big silver barracuda jumped; in a shoal of smaller fry, tuna leapt bodily from the water as a pod of dolphins joined in the feeding frenzy. Radiant white discs floated above the blue water ahead; the tide had dropped and these were banks of coral sand along which, as we neared, the dark immemorial forms of humans browsed, along with the herons, for molluscs.

A swim was part of the deal. Papa Subu cut the motor and let the boat slide gently ashore on the white sandy beach of a small islet. The French were hanging up their clothes in a small grove of trees as I went ashore, undressed into my swimmers, crossed the jagged coral beach and dived into the pellucid waters of the Flores Sea. It was warm, like a bath; but I did not stay in long, because Emanuel had a bus to catch and a fair way to go. When I returned to the boat, Papa Subu was kneeling down in the wheelhouse, wearing an incongruous orange woolly hat, facing towards Mecca and praying. Now and again, as we chugged back to the port, Emanuel turned the fish he had bought, which was on the wheelhouse roof, to face the sun. An elegant white *prahu*, an inter-island trading vessel, glided past, leaving for Bali and carrying, Emanuel said, *all kinds of things*. It was still early afternoon when I got back to the Gardena. I had *gado gado* for lunch, then went to lie down: the sun had given me a filthy headache.

When Soi joined me for dinner that night he was looking pink but happy; he had spent the day snorkelling and got a bit too much sun as well. I resumed my haphazard attempt to construct a biography of him. His father was a retired businessman who now simply read the newspapers and watched television; his mother, the President of the Japanese Woman Inventors Society, travelled the country gathering up and publicising new inventions; he was an only child, unmarried, forty-two years old. Older women liked him, he explained, but he liked younger women; within three years he hoped to marry because he wanted children. Another of his plans was to set up as a travel agent, taking mentally ill, intellectually and physically disabled people on group tours. Meanwhile, the social construction of madness remained his obsession. When in the flower of his schizophrenia he sometimes saw, as in a vision, the end of this world, attended by conflicting choirs singing in the next one.

Do you know it's a delusion while it's happening? I asked.

No, I mistake it for real, he said. *So, my problem. Not the world's.*

We were still laughing as a young man crossed the restaurant floor.

The White House is a Bush House, he said ruefully. The news had taken three days to reach us here, beyond the reach of the internet and most daily newspapers. It seemed somehow inevitable and thus of little moment. As if in response, the call to prayer began to sound croakily from one of the town's two mosques, whose tape-recorder was in need of a good service. The other, more distant mosque, with a much better sound system, began, as always, a couple of minutes later. Young men, spotlessly dressed, came down the dark stairs in answer to the call as they did every evening.

The owner of the restaurant, another Joseph, was leaving for the day. I went over to tell him I would be going in the morning. We had been friends since I'd pointed to a red and white Indonesian flag flying over the school next door and asked if that was the Flores flag. He, like the other Joseph, wanted independence for Nusa Tenggara Timur but knew it would be difficult to achieve.

What time? he asked.

I told him.

I will be here at nine o'clock, he said. *See you then.*

Picking his way past the souvenir sellers who came up each afternoon to sit on the steps with their carved wooden komodos and strings of white, pink and black cultured pearls, he went. The sun had set; the great double outriggers with their unmuffled diesel motors were chugging into the orange sky. The geckos were out, making their reedy cry, *geeeck-oooh,* which when I first heard it in Mataram I heard as *fuck-off* and thought came from what I called the Fuck-Off Bird. I told Soi this; he laughed his wheezy laugh and we began talking about the great Japanese writer Haruki Murakami, author of the *Wind-Up Bird Chronicle* and other fine books. Soi was flying back to Tokyo the same day I was flying to Sydney, but he—bravely—was returning to Bali by ferry and bus. As the darkness thickened, he said goodnight and went up to bed, leaving his towel and bag slung across the back of a chair. When I returned them to him later, he was sitting out on his balcony, feet on the railing, head thrown back, eyes closed, in a deep reverie. I put them quietly down and left. I didn't see him again.

As I was coming down the steps of the Gardena with my luggage next morning, Maria smiled and waved prettily from amongst the hibiscus.

Byeeee … she called, even though we had never really said hello.

A four-wheel-drive full of riotous young men gave me a lift to the airport. They told dirty jokes to each other in Bahasa Indonesian and laughed uproariously. In the terminal, laying my book aside, I saw lines of print strobing through the air. Something wasn't right. When the flight was called I found I could stand and walk only with the greatest difficulty. My balance had gone awry. It was like the moment of vertigo in the cave, only this time it didn't pass. I made it onto the plane and sat down near the back. There didn't seem to be anything else wrong: no pain, no upset stomach, no sore throat. Just this weird wooziness. Turning my head made the whole world dip and sway. Turning it back had the same effect. I had to stare rigidly ahead.

There was an official party of some kind catching the same twice-weekly flight to Denpasar. One of them sat down in the seat next to mine and we struck up a conversation. Adam had trained as an anthropologist, partly at Macquarie University in Sydney. Now he studied 'conflict in Indonesia'.

That's a big subject, I said.

He smiled. His group were on their way to a conference in the city of Ujung Pandung, or Makassar, on Sulawesi, in parts of which island there is ongoing, and vicious, violence between Christians and Muslims. While we were on the subject, I asked him about the possibility of independence for Nusa Tenggara Timur. He smiled again.

The people of Flores cannot even agree on a provincial capital, he said gently. *I think it will be a long time before we are able to deal with the larger issues ourselves.*

We talked politics for a while, canvassing the situation of indigenous people in that part of the world I come from. My condition, whatever it was—probably an inner-ear infection—made me excessively emotional. When Adam asked about the situation of the Aborigines, I felt a rush of hot involuntary tears in my eyes and had to turn my head away to look out the window, where the blurred brown hills of Sumbawa were passing by; perhaps the tiny seaside town I could see below was Alas.

Adam was from Ruteng, the nearest town to Liang Bua where the remains of *Homo floresiensis* were found. What did he think about that? He shrugged and said the find was perhaps not so unusual when you consider that the Manggarai people who live in villages near the site are renowned for their tiny stature.

How big? I asked.

He held his hand out into the aisle of the plane, a metre and a bit from the floor. There was a sense in his conversation of not exactly scepticism but rather a kind of amusement that the whole world was talking of something that he and others had known about for a while. I asked him if he'd heard that the Dutch in the seventeenth century gathered reports of little people living on Flores, which they dismissed as folk tales. He smiled. The Dutch, he explained, did not really colonise Flores until the early twentieth century.

These stories persist, however. In the *Sydney Morning Herald* of 6 December 2004 it was reported that one of the small people, a pretty woman with long pendulous breasts, had been seen as recently as three weeks before in the Ngada tribal area, adjoining the Manggarai to the east. The alleged sighting was on the slopes of the volcano Gunung Ebulobo near the village of Boawae, where there is a long history, or tradition, of interaction with people locals call *Ebu Gogo*, which means *grandmother who eats everything.* They are described as being about a metre high, hairy, with long arms and pot bellies, and are said to be voracious, even stealing babies to eat. This sounds rather more like folklore than fact, but who knows? New species of animal are still being found in parts of Asia. Why not humans? The archaeologists who excavated Liang Bua doubt there are such living fossils on Flores; but there is a cave on Gunung Ebulobo that they hope to excavate, if they can persuade the local Nage-Keo to perform the appropriate rituals and allow them onto the mountain.

When we disemplaned at Denpasar, Adam invited me to join his group, who had hours to wait before their plane to Makassar, as I did before mine to Darwin. I thanked him but declined; I was feeling too strange.

The next two nights and days are a blur through which I staggered like one of those mad cows you used to see on television. It was like being falling-down drunk, with a visual effect reminiscent of LSD. I remember staring into the palms that grew around Frogs Hollow, the place I stayed in Darwin, unable to focus my eyes for more than a millisecond, as the jagged green fronds twisted and swarmed.

I was crossing the road Monday afternoon to the Medical Centre, hearing the sound of Cold Chisel's 'Cheap Wine and a Three Day Growth' blaring out from a nearby bar, when an Aboriginal man seeking cigarette butts around the trunk of a palm tree hailed me.

How are you, bro?

Not too good, I said. *I'm dizzy and disoriented and I can't walk straight.*

Me too, he said, falling into lurching step beside me. *Where you going?*

The doctor.

I'll come with you.

We went together into the pastel-painted air-conditioned haven of the Medical Centre. As I gave my details to one receptionist, I could hear him explaining his predicament to another. He'd been a boxer in his youth, was punch-drunk, couldn't work any more. More to the point, so far as he was concerned, he'd once badly hurt one of his opponents, a man named Michael, and this bothered him. He started becoming quite emotional. The receptionist, a middle-aged woman, was gentle, kind, but firm, shunting him out of the Centre and down the road to some other, more appropriate institution.

The doctor was genial, derisive, fascinated: genial because that's the kind of guy he was, derisive that I had been to Flores without taking anti-malaria pills, fascinated because he thought he might have discovered a new tropical disease.

I'm not letting you out of here until I know what you've got, he said.

Half an hour later, he regretfully admitted defeat and let me go. I staggered back out into the street.

Yet the consultation was not entirely wasted: although I was still unsteady, that night I was able to walk with my film producer down to the wharf at Port Darwin for a dinner of fish and chips, which we washed down with lemonade while the great silvery shapes of fish rose towards the arc lights clouding the aqua ocean to gulp down morsels thrown them by diners; next morning I felt much better. I didn't exactly leap into action but I did manage to get myself on to a bus and out to the Museum and Art Gallery of the Northern Territory in Fannie Bay. It was here, in the magnificent annex of the Maritime Museum out the back, that I found da Nova's boat.

I had been looking for a Bugis *prahu* everywhere I went, without much idea of exactly what I was seeking: Wallace gives an accurate description of one, but no drawing, and anyway written sources, however precise, are not the best way of identifying sea craft. I gazed hungrily at each boat I saw in all of the many harbours I visited—Melaka, Padang Bai, Lembar, Labuan Lombok, Poto Tano, Sape, Labuanbajo and on the voyage to and from Rinca—without ever experiencing the shock of recognition I hoped for. Now, here, in the most unlikely spot—or perhaps not—was the *Hati Marege*.

The *Heart of Arnhem Land*, to give its name in English, was made by Konjo boat builders at Tanah Beru in the Bonto Bahari district of south-east Sulawesi for the Australian Bicentennial celebrations in 1988 and sailed from Makassar to Darwin by a crew of thirteen—one more than the traditional twelve, but the exact number on da Nova's voyage. The boat builders made it without a plan and without nails; they worked from a picture on the one hand, and their own tradition on the other. The *prahu* is a bit more than fourteen metres long, with a beam of just over four metres. More than half a dozen different kinds of wood were used in her construction. She has twelve ribs and a navel, for there is an explicit analogy between a boat and the human body; two rudders, one either side of the stern; two rectangular sails woven from the leaves of the karoro palm; a bamboo tripod mast; rigging made of rattan, coir, hemp and the ijok palm; and a wooden anchor weighted with a stone. On the deck I could see, in front of the mast, the firebox galley for cooking and the bilge pump made of bamboo. The cabin, aft, was thatched with coconut palm leaves and lined with bamboo laths; this would have been where da Nova slept and wrote.

The *Hati Marege* is a replica of a mid-nineteenth-century *prahu*, not an early seventeenth-century one; but the *prahu*-building tradition is highly conservative, as is shown by the fact that the Konjo boat builders could accurately craft in a style at least 150 years old. Da Nova might well have sailed in a boat like this, although his had a mainmast made from a single piece of timber, not a triangular bamboo one. I thought back to Wallace's description of how it was to be on one of these *queer old-world vessels,* which he took from Makassar to Aru:

I have never, either before or since, made a twenty days' voyage so pleasantly, or … with so little discomfort. This I attribute chiefly to having my own cabin on deck, and entirely to myself … and to the absence of all those marine-store smells of paint, pitch, tallow and new cordage … Something is also to be put down to freedom from all restraint of dress, hours of meals etc. and to the civility and obliging disposition of the Captain … The crew were all civil and good-tempered, and with very little discipline everything went on smoothly, and the vessel was kept very clean and in pretty good order … I was delighted with the trip, and inclined to rate the luxuries of the semi-barbarous prahu *as surpassing those of the most magnificent screw-steamer, that highest product of our civilization.*

There were other craft in the high, purpose-built shed: fishing boats from Java; canoes from Fiji, the Solomon Islands and New Guinea; a pearling lugger from Broome; a vessel in which Vietnamese boat people had sailed; most heartbreaking were two small native craft, one from Roti, off Timor, the other from central Flores. The first of these had, in 1991, during a shark-fin boom, sailed into the Arafura Sea hoping to make a valuable catch; the other had set out for Bathurst Island with a cargo of corn to sell to the Tiwi. Both had entered Australia's exclusion zone and been confiscated by the Coast Guard, their crews repatriated and the boats—that is, their livelihood—turned into museum pieces. Amongst the other replicas was a *lipa lipa,* a houseboat of the *orang laut.* It had been built by an old craftsman somewhere up in the Sulu Sea, where the sea gypsies are thought to have originated. In form exactly like the plain ones I had seen at Rinca, it was elaborately and beautifully carved with relief work down both flanks.

I went back outside and down to the beach at Fannie Bay: orange-brown sand, the flat sea banded from pale aqua to deep blue, the almost transparent shapes of distant headlands and islands. Was this where the Degredado's shack had been? To the west, where the beach ended at a place now called Doctor's Gully, an image of the Chinese ocean goddess Tien Hou, rescuer of drowning sailors, was found buried in the roots of a banyan tree. Perhaps it had been left by the great fifteenth-century Ming dynasty voyager Zheng He, perhaps by a later visitor; but banyans are not native to Australia and they are also called by some the World Tree, joining heaven, earth and the underworld. I thought of the old Chinese man da Nova saw going that way nightly to worship: I could almost see him myself, shuffling along the dusty path as the sun went down in the western sea.

Distant echoes: Fannie Bay was also where, in 1953, the artist Ian Fairweather set out for Asia, which he loved, on a raft he built himself. He drifted all the way to Timor, arriving sunburned, starving, delirious, more dead than alive, only to be arrested by the Indonesian authorities and deported to his native Scotland. A distorted mirror, perhaps, of the Australian government's decision in 1906 to ban the Macassar *prahu*s from taking trepang from these shores.

I saw the dawn as a line of spectral green light in the east as we flew towards Sydney. A few hours later I was taxi-ing through the grey streets with an Egyptian at the wheel. The trip was over; I was back where I started from. What had I learned? I thought of Eredia's peculiar decision to spell the fabled land he sought with an initial L, when all the indications are that it should have been an N. Was he in some unconscious manner alluding to his Lusitanian birthright, in the same way that one translation of the name, *the islands between*, somehow indicated that other side of his soul, his Bugis heritage? Could it have been an involuntary recall of Camoens' epic, the *Lusiads*, first published, to no great acclaim, in Lisbon in 1572?

The legendary founder of Lisbon is Lusus, the companion or, in some versions the son, of the wine god Bacchus; Lusus is the origin of Lusitania, the old name for Portugal; but some say Ulysses was the first Greek to touch those shores. Was Eredia himself some kind of Odysseus figure, trying to find a way back to an Ithaca of the mind? Or is there an echo here of Marco Polo's fabled land of Lucach, sometimes written Lochac which, through a bizarre series of misreadings and typographical accidents, gave us our word *Beach*? Then there was that other translation, not *the islands between* or *between the islands* but *the day after tomorrow*. It reminded me for some reason of a billboard I saw several examples of in Mataram: *The Past Is Gone*. No one I asked could explain the context of this undeniable statement, but it was as undeniable that the residues of the past are all around us, all the time.

We were coming up King Street from St Peters into Newtown, passing the Railway Station on one side, the mouth of Australia Street on the other. I had come full circle. This was the exact place where I had begun my journey a month before, lunching with a friend at the Courthouse Hotel before catching a cab to the airport. I remembered the gnarled old drinkers in the dusty light of the public bar; the blinding sun outside where we sat under frangipani trees drinking Wolf Blass Yellow Label; the untroubled ambience of the sparse weekday crowd: Sydney at its most louche and easy-going.

My friend and I had recently read the same book, *Eden in the East: the Drowned Continent of South East Asia* (London, 1999) by Stephen Oppenheimer, an English paediatrician who has done a great deal of specialised research into the differing strains of malaria in various parts of Asia. We discussed the thesis of the book: that a great, and early—perhaps the earliest of all—civilisation had flourished in Sundaland, that is, South East Asia as it was before rising seas at the end of the last Ice Age drowned much of the land. Refugees from this flood had fled inland, into the hills, or taken to their boats, like the *orang laut* and the precursors of the Polynesians, one of whose words for island, *Nuku*, recalls the Malay word *Nuca*.

It may be that folk memory of that ancient cataclysm is the origin of all the many tales, from Ptolemy to Marco Polo to Quieroz, of a rich and fabulous Great South Land. Through myth and story, Oppenheimer traces aspects of this civilisation west as far as the Indus Valley and the Fertile Crescent explaining, for those who can entertain such a radical proposition, why wisdom always came from the East. Da Nova's vision of the city under the sea on the voyage to Kaju Djawa leaps into focus: this tsunami-drowned world must have been what in his delirium he saw, if Henry Klang did not see it for him. This, too, was Luca Antara.

After lunch we wandered back through the almost deserted streets to my friend's place so I could call a cab. The sound of children playing in the nearby Australia Street Infants School drifted on the air; the old sandstock blocks of the terrace houses turned gold, drinking the sun; bottle brushes were flowering, dusting a faded crimson on the pavements. We passed by a curious, storeyed building, dated 1909, whose doors were open, showing a wide hallway with a first-floor balcony running right around it. A man of Middle Eastern appearance, as they say, with a folder of papers under his arm was just entering this somehow antique-looking place. I asked my friend what it was: some kind of institute, perhaps educational, perhaps religious? No, it was the communal home of half a dozen families belonging to an obscure orthodox Jewish sect.

The mysterious other face of Sydney, which I first glimpsed in Antiquarian Books so many years before, then lost driving cabs and have known only intermittently since, floated before my eyes; I do not think I will lose it again. Every world city, howsoever modern, carries traces of the first city; and if the first city truly was in sunken Sundaland, then Sydney is heir to that lost city too; and who knows what other travellers might not have set out from there with a wild surmise for these shores? Looking perhaps for Luca Antara; perhaps just for the day after tomorrow.

Notes on Sources

Part One *Castaway*

Artwork:

'Portrait of Jean Baptiste Cabri' from: *Voyages and Travels in Various Parts of the World During the Years 1803, 1804, 1805, 1806, 1807*; G. H. Langsdorff; London: Henry Colburn, 1813.

English translation of Pessoa's vast, fragmentary, epical oeuvre continues. Of the selections of poetry in English, I prefer *Poems of Fernando Pessoa*, edited and translated by Edwin Honig and Susan Brown (New York: Ecco Press, 1986). For the occasional writings I used Richard Zenith's *The Selected Prose of Fernando Pessoa* (New York: Grove Press, 2001). There are a number of versions of *The Book of Disquiet*, each with a different selection of texts; my favourite is that edited by Maria José de Lancastre and translated by Margaret Jull Costa (London: Serpent's Tail, 1991).

It's hard to imagine a better book on the hoax than *The Ern Malley Affair* by Michael Heyward (St Lucia: University of Queensland Press, 1993). *Damaged Men: The Precarious Lives of James McAuley and Harold Stewart* is a fascinating dual biography of the perpetrators by Michael Ackland (Sydney: Allen & Unwin, 2001). Issue #17 of *Jacket* magazine: http://jacketmagazine.com/index.html is devoted to Ern, who also has his own website: http://www.ernmalley.com. The complete text of Malley's *The Darkening Ecliptic* appears in both *The Ern Malley Affair* and *Jacket 17*.

QVB: The Queen Victoria Building 1898–1986 by John Shaw, with contemporary photos by David Moore (Sydney: Wellington Lane Press, 1987), tells the story in great detail and with many remarkable photos, including some of parts of Victorian Sydney now lost forever. I know of no comparable book about the Hordern Building, whose history, like its timbers, is scattered or gone.

The tale of Jean Cabri has been told from a number of sources, including: *True and Historical Summary of the Stay of Joseph Kabris (sic), native of Bordeaux, in the Mendoza Islands, Pacific Ocean*, translated by Jennifer Terrell and published in the *Journal of Pacific History*, Vol. 17, Nos 3–4, July–October 1982; *Voyages and Travels in Various Parts of the World During the Years 1803, 1804, 1805, 1806, 1807,* by G.H. von Langsdorff (London: Henry Colburn, 1813); *The Marquesan Journal of Edward Robarts 1797–1824*, edited by Greg Dening (Canberra: Australian National University Press, 1974); and Dening's *Islands and Beaches: Discourse on a Silent Land: Marquesas 1774–1880* (Honolulu: University Press of Hawaii, 1980). Mr Dening's bibliography to this latter work lists, among other sources for Cabri's story, two examples of Aimé Leroy's early journalism.

The place to begin the arcane study of Marquesan tattoo is *Tattooing in the Marquesas* by Willowdean Chatterson Handy, Bulletin 1 of the Bernice P. Bishop in Honolulu (1922). Alfred Gell's *Wrapping in Images: Tattooing in Polynesia* (Oxford: Clarendon Press, 1996) attempts an overview which, while intriguing, seems to have been arrived at more by library study and theoretical speculation than experience in or on the skin. *Marquesan Sexual Behaviour: An Anthropological Study of Polynesian Practices* by Robert C. Suggs (London: Constable & Co., 1966) discusses the *pekio* complex in some detail and is otherwise full of accounts of startling practices both from the contact period and the period of Suggs' fieldwork in the 1950s.

The fate of M. Flan's library and the progress of the balloon *Ville d'Orleans* are recounted in Alistair Horne's *The Fall of Paris: The Siege and the Commune 1870–71* (Aldershot: MacMillan/The Reprint Society, 1967). The best translation I know of Isidore Ducasse's oeuvre is *Maldoror; & the complete works of the Compte de Lautréamont* by Alexis Lykiard (Cambridge: Exact Change, 1994). Last time I inquired after *The Diary of Aimé Leroy*, an unpublished manuscript in the Archives d'Outre-Mer de France in Paris, I was told that it was 'lost' (*perdu*).

Part Two *Salvation*

Artwork:

'The Ship Batavia' from: *Ongeluckige Voyagie van't Schip Batavia*, Amsterdam, 1647.

Sources for the story of the three *pastorinhos* are various but include the online *Catholic Encyclopedia*, in which there is to be found voluminous material, descriptive and interpretative, on the visions and prophecies. *The Year of the Death of Ricardo Reis* by José Saramago was first published in Lisbon in 1984; I quote from the Giovanni Pontiero translation (San Diego: Harcourt Brace Javonovich, 1991).

The Kenneth Slessor quotes are from his *Selected Poems* (Sydney: Angus & Roberston 1987); the James McAuley lines from *Poetry, Essays and Personal Commentary*, edited by Leonie Kramer (St Lucia: University of Queensland Press,1988). *The New Oxford Book of Australian Verse* edited by Les A. Murray (Sydney: Oxford, 1986) includes both the Douglas and Harold Stewart lines quoted in the text.

There are now quite a few books about the wreck of the *Batavia* and the ensuing mayhem on Houtman's Abrolhos, most recently by Mike Dash (*Batavia's Graveyard: The True Story of the Mad Heretic Who Led History's Bloodiest Mutiny*, London: Weidenfeld & Nicolson, 2002) and Simon Leys (*The Wreck of the Batavia and Prosper,* London: Black Inc., 2005). My primary sources are two of the earlier ones: *Islands of Angry Ghosts* (London: Hodder & Stoughton, 1966) by Hugh Edwards, a newspaperman and amateur diver who explored the wreck and the islands after the remains of the ship were re-discovered in 1963; and *Voyage to Disaster: The Life of Francisco Pelsaert* by Henrietta Drake-Brockman (Sydney: Angus & Robertson, 1982). Ms Drake-Brockman, whose research led to the identification of the site of the wreck, is also the author of a novel about the *Batavia, The Wicked and the Fair* (Sydney: Angus & Robertson, 1957). I have too a copy of an English translation of a Dutch account, *Disastrous Voyage of the Vessel Batavia to the East Indies*, apparently based upon Pelsaert's own *Ongeluckige Voyagie van't Schip Batavia* which appeared in Amsterdam in 1647. This translation, by Willem Siebenhaar, was printed in *The Western Mail* of Christmas 1897; a more recent version of Pelsaert's account, *The Voyage of the Batavia*, translated by Martin Terry, was published by Hordern House for the Australian National Maritime Museum in 1994.

Information about Johannes Torrentius (1589–1644) is drawn from online sources, particularly those provided by the Rijksmuseum in Amsterdam, which has his one remaining painting and also a recently identified, mildly salacious print of a couple making love.

The most entertaining account of the weird fluorescence of Gnostic sects in Alexandria early in the first millennium of the Common Era is Gustave Flaubert's *The Temptation of St Anthony* (translated by Kitty Mrosovsky; London: Penguin, 1983). More sober reports appear in the *Catholic Encyclopedia*. It was the misfortune of early heretics to have the fullest statement of their beliefs made by those who suppressed them. The main sources among the writings of the church fathers for Carpocrate's ideas are Iranaeus, *Against Heresies*, Book i.xxv and Clement, *Stromateis*, Book iii.ii.

Part Three *Voyage*

Artwork:

'A Bradshaw figure at Kalumburu Mission' from: *The Art of the Wandjina: Aboriginal cave paintings in the Kimberley, Western Australia*; I. M. Crawford; Melbourne: OUP, 1968; with the permission of the Western Australian Museum.

The extensive European writings about South East Asia as a real place begin with *The Travels of Marco Polo*; my copy is based on the Marsden and Yule translations, edited with an introduction by Manuel Komroff (New York: W.W. Norton & Co., 1953). The best general historical introduction I found was Richard Hall's *Empires of the Monsoon: a History of the Indian Ocean and its Invaders* (London: HarperCollins, 1998).

How Manoel Godinho de Eredia's *Description of Malaca, Meridional India and Cathay* came to be in Brussels I do not know, but there is, in the State Library of NSW, a copy of the facsimile and translation into French by M. Leon Janssen published there in 1882. The labyrinthine English version, translated from Janssen's Portuguese copy, with notes, by J. V. Mills, first appeared in Kuala Lumpur in 1930 and was reprinted by the Malaysian Branch of the Royal Asiatic Society in 1997.

Eredia's *Description* should be read alongside two other contemporary chronicles: the *Suma Oriental of Tomé Pires* (1513), translated by Armando Cortesao (London: The Hakluyt Society, 1944) and Fernão Mendes Pinto's *Peregrination* (1614), published as *The Grand Peregrination* in Maurice Collis' translation (London: Faber & Faber, 1949).

Behind Kenneth Gordon McIntyre's *The Secret Discovery of Australia: Portuguese Ventures 250 Years before Captain Cook* (Adelaide: Souvenir Press, 1977) stands George Collingridge's 1895 *The Discovery of Australia* (Sydney: Golden Press, 1983) which was, McIntyre says, 'so mauled by the critics ... that it had little impact'.

O. H. K. Spate's collection *Let Me Enjoy: Essays, Partly Geographical* (Canberra: Australian National University Press, 1965) includes his 1958 piece *Terra Australis – Cognita?* which discusses the possibility of an early Portuguese discovery.

Spate's *The Spanish Lake* (Canberra: Australian National University Press, 1979), volume one of his trilogy *The Pacific Since Magellan*, and *The Portuguese Seaborne Empire 1415–1825* by C. R. Boxer (London: Hutchinson & Co., 1969) are each excellent introductions to the activities of the two great Iberian empires in the east.

Noel H. Peters' paper *Eredia Map, 1602* was published in the December 2003 issue of *Cartography*, the journal of the Mapping Sciences Institute of Australia. It is available online here: http://www.users.tpg.com.au/papag/EREDIA2.html

I am not convinced that the alleged unpublished manuscript, *The Voyage of António da Nova* (*c.*1611) in fact exists; if it does, its whereabouts is unknown; the abstract by Henry Klang certainly exists but, by now, perhaps only among the pages of this book.

There is more about sailing by *prahu* through the eastern archipelagoes of Indonesia in Tim Severin's *The Spice Islands Voyage: The Quest for Alfred Wallace, the Man Who Shared Darwin's Discovery of Evolution* (New York: Carroll & Graf, 2000) and in *Ring of Fire* by Lawrence Blair with Lorne Blair (London: Park Street Press, reprint edition, 1 November 1991). The Blairs, English hippie brothers and film makers, made their voyages in the 1970s and 1980s.

Indonesian Spice Islands: The Moluccas, by Kal Muller (Jakarta: Periplus, 1993), includes a wealth of fascinating ethnographic information. Jocelyn Burt's *The Kimberley: Australia's Unique North West* (Perth: University of Western Australia Press, 2004), with its magnificent photographs, was useful for checking detail of da Nova's land travels.

Part Four *Return*

Artwork:
'Detail of the Alves Map, 1602' from the National Library of Australia;
with the permission of the National Library of Australia.

I travelled in Malaysia and through Indonesia with the September 2002
edition of *The Rough Guide to Southeast Asia*. My copy of *The Malay Archipelago*
by Alfred Russel Wallace is a facsimile edition (Hong Kong: Periplus, 2000).
Eden in the East: The Drowned Continent of Southeast Asia by Stephen Oppenheimer (London: Orion, 1998) is both a last and a first reference.

Two excerpts from *Luca Antara* were published in *brief* magazine, issues 29
and 30, by then editor Jack Ross, to whom acknowledgment is due. The
book was written while I held the 2004 Literary Fellowship at the University
of Auckland; my thanks to all those who secured that appointment and in
particular to Michele Leggott, who made it such a pleasure being there.

Luca Antara *is dedicated to the memory of Alan Brunton (1946–2002), whose suggestion it was that I write an historical work aimed at the Australian market for his imprint, Bumper Books. Preliminary discussions in the weeks before Alan's sudden death arrived at 'a book about the Indian Ocean'. His example as a writer of audacity, innovation and rare achievement remains.*

Author photo by Faye Norman

Previous books by the author include:

The Autobiography of my Father (1992)
Chemical Evolution: Drugs and Art Production 1970-80 (1997)
The Resurrection of Philip Clairmont (1999)
Fenua Imi: The Pacific in History and Imaginary (2002)
Chronicle of the Unsung (2004)
Ghost Who Writes (2004)

Further information may be found at:

http://lucaantara.blogspot.com/

IAVA. MAIOR.
Balambuan
Azenon
PRINCIPIVM. I. CLIMA.
MEDIVM.
Angaman
LVCA. TAMBINI.
Angaman